In this remarkable and innovative collection of essays, the authors give renewed value, meaning and, above all, empirical relevance to the practice of speculation. Speculation is rescued from the hands of the speculators!

Andrew Barry, *Professor of Human Geography, University College London*

This beautifully written collection of essays represents an exciting exploration of the contemporary importance of making speculation centre stage. The book is a landmark in the philosophy and methodology of social science. It does not just illuminate the value of process philosophy – it also provides methodological and practical approaches to doing socially significant research. It is a must read for anyone that wants to take the turn to ontology and affect seriously.

Joanna Latimer, *Professor of and Chair in Sociology, Science and Technology, University of York*

Speculative Research is a truly unique collection that offers much needed inspiration for thinking beyond present conditions and the futures they seem to make impossible. It invites us to engage with a generative tradition of speculative thought that has yet to fulfil its radical practical potential. The stimulating contributions to this volume offer remarkable examples of what thinking speculatively can mean in encounters with specific research fields and problems – faithful to the empirical but not bounded by it, an adventurous yet careful inquiry. In composing this volume, Wilkie, Savransky and Rosengarten have achieved both a generous prolongation and innovative experimentation with speculative thought.

Maria Puig de la Bellacasa, *Associate Professor of Science, Technology and Organisation, University of Leicester*

Speculative Research is a remarkably prescient book that opens up new vistas of experimental thought and practice for contemporary social and cultural research. In reclaiming the question of the speculative from its more recent and notorious variants, this collection crystallizes how the possibilities of more-than-human futures can be engaged with empirical and conceptual assiduousness without relinquishing the challenges and risks of what is to come and what is possible to the logics of the probable. As the editors and contributors insist, developing a speculative sensitivity involves the care for and acceptance of knowledge practices that are part of the cultivation of new futures.

Antoine Hennion, *Professor and Director of Research, Centre de Sociologie de l'Innovation, Mines ParisTech, Paris*

Redeeming speculation against its negative connotations, this exciting book exhibits the multiple potentials of speculative social research. Engaging in a struggle against the deadening effects of probability and inevitability, it opens up for thinking and making alternative futures, inducing readers to come along for the ride.

Casper Bruun Jensen, *Associate Professor, Department of Anthropology, Osaka University*

Speculative Research

Is another future possible? So called 'late modernity' is marked by the escalating rise in and proliferation of uncertainties and unforeseen events brought about by the interplay between and patterning of social–natural, techno–scientific and political–economic developments. The future has indeed become problematic. The question of how heterogeneous actors engage futures, what intellectual and practical strategies they put into play and what the implications of such strategies are, have become key concerns of recent social and cultural research addressing a diverse range of fields of practice and experience. Exploring questions of speculation, possibilities and futures in contemporary societies, *Speculative Research* responds to the pressing need to not only critically account for the role of calculative logics and rationalities in managing societal futures, but to develop alternative approaches and sensibilities that take futures seriously as possibilities and that demand new habits and practices of attention, invention and experimentation.

Alex Wilkie is a sociologist, a Senior Lecturer in the Department of Design and a Co-Director of the Centre for Invention and Social Process, Goldsmiths, University of London.

Martin Savransky is a Lecturer at the Department of Sociology and Director of the Unit of Play, Goldsmiths, University of London, where he teaches philosophy, social theory and methodology of social science.

Marsha Rosengarten is Professor in Sociology and Co-Director of the Centre for the Study of Invention and Social Process, Department of Sociology, Goldsmiths, University of London.

Culture, Economy and the Social

A new series from CRESC – the ESRC Centre for Research on Socio-cultural Change

Editors: Professor Tony Bennett, Social and Cultural Theory, *University of Western Sydney*; Professor Penny Harvey, Anthropology, *Manchester University*; Professor Kevin Hetherington, Geography, *Open University*

Editorial Advisory Board: Andrew Barry, *University of Oxford*; Michel Callon, *Ecole des Mines de Paris*; Dipesh Chakrabarty, *The University of Chicago*; Mike Crang, *University of Durham*; Tim Dant, *Lancaster University*; Jean-Louis Fabiani, *Ecoles de Hautes Etudes en Sciences Sociales*; Antoine Hennion, *Paris Institute of Technology*; Eric Hirsch, *Brunel University*; John Law, *The Open University*; Randy Martin, *New York University*; Timothy Mitchell, *New York University*; Rolland Munro, *Keele University*; Andrew Pickering, *University of Exeter*; Mary Poovey, *New York University*; Hugh Willmott, *University of Cardiff*; Sharon Zukin, *Brooklyn College City University New York/Graduate School, City University of New York*

The *Culture, Economy and the Social* series is committed to innovative contemporary, comparative and historical work on the relations between social, cultural and economic change. It publishes empirically-based research that is theoretically informed, that critically examines the ways in which social, cultural and economic change is framed and made visible, and that is attentive to perspectives that tend to be ignored or side-lined by grand theorising or epochal accounts of social change. The series addresses the diverse manifestations of contemporary capitalism, and considers the various ways in which the 'social', 'the cultural' and 'the economic' are apprehended as tangible sites of value and practice. It is explicitly comparative, publishing books that work across disciplinary perspectives, cross-culturally, or across different historical periods.

The series is actively engaged in the analysis of the different theoretical traditions that have contributed to the development of the 'cultural turn' with a view to clarifying where these approaches converge and where they diverge on a particular issue. It is equally concerned to explore the new critical agendas emerging from current critiques of the cultural turn: those associated with the descriptive turn for example. Our commitment to interdisciplinarity thus aims at enriching theoretical and methodological discussion, building awareness of the common ground that has emerged in the past decade, and thinking through what is at stake in those approaches that resist integration to a common analytical model.

Series titles include:

Theorizing Cultural Work: Labour, Continuity and Change in the Cultural and Creative Industries
Edited by Mark Banks, Rosalind Gill and Stephanie Taylor

Comedy and Distinction: The Cultural Currency of a 'Good' Sense of Humour
By Sam Friedman

The Provoked Economy: Economic Reality and the Performative Turn
By Fabian Muniesa

Rio de Janeiro: Urban Life through the Eyes of the City
By Beatriz Jaguaribe

The Routledge Companion to Bourdieu's 'Distinction'
Edited by Philippe Coulangeon and Julien Duval

Devising Consumption: Cultural Economies of Insurance, Credit and Spending
By Liz Mcfall

Industry and Work in Contemporary Capitalism: Global Models, Local Lives?
Edited by Victoria Goddard and Susana Narotzky

Lived Economies of Default: Consumer Credit, Debt Collection and the Capture of Affect
By Joe Deville

Cultural Pedagogies and Human Conduct
Edited by Megan Watkins, Greg Noble and Catherine Driscoll

Culture as a Vocation
Sociology of Career Choices in Cultural Management
By Vincent Dubois

Topologies of Power
By John Allen

Distinctions of the Flesh
Social Class and the Embodiment of Inequality
By Dieter Vandebroeck

Infrastructures and Social Complexity
A Companion
Edited by Penny Harvey, Casper Bruun Jensen and Atsuro Morita

Speculative Research
The Lure of Possible Futures
Edited by Alex Wilkie, Martin Savransky and Marsha Rosegarten

Coming soon

Film Criticism as a Cultural Institution
Crisis and Continuity from the 20th to the 21st Century
By Huw Walmsley-Evans

Unbecoming Things: Mutable Objects and the Politics of Waste
By Nicky Gregson and Mike Crang

Speculative Research
The Lure of Possible Futures

Edited by Alex Wilkie,
Martin Savransky and
Marsha Rosengarten

LONDON AND NEW YORK

First published 2017
by Routledge
2 Park Square, Milton Park, Abingdon, Oxon OX14 4RN

and by Routledge
711 Third Avenue, New York, NY 10017

Routledge is an imprint of the Taylor & Francis Group, an informa business

© 2017 selection and editorial matter, Alex Wilkie, Martin Savransky and
Marsha Rosengarten; individual chapters, the contributors

The right of Alex Wilkie, Martin Savransky and Marsha Rosengarten to be
identified as the authors of the editorial material, and of the authors for
their individual chapters, has been asserted in accordance with sections 77
and 78 of the Copyright, Designs and Patents Act 1988.

All rights reserved. No part of this book may be reprinted or reproduced or
utilized in any form or by any electronic, mechanical, or other means, now
known or hereafter invented, including photocopying and recording, or in
any information storage or retrieval system, without permission in writing
from the publishers.

Trademark notice: Product or corporate names may be trademarks or
registered trademarks, and are used only for identification and explanation
without intent to infringe.

British Library Cataloguing in Publication Data
A catalogue record for this book is available from the British Library

Library of Congress Cataloging in Publication Data
A catalog record for this book has been requested

ISBN: 978-1-138-68836-0 (hbk)
ISBN: 978-1-315-54186-0 (ebk)

Typeset in Times New Roman
by Wearset Ltd, Boldon, Tyne and Wear

Contents

List of figures	xii
Notes on contributors	xiii
Acknowledgements	xviii

1	**The lure of possible futures: on speculative research** MARTIN SAVRANSKY, ALEX WILKIE AND MARSHA ROSENGARTEN	1

PART I
Speculative propositions 19

	Introduction: speculative propositions MARTIN SAVRANSKY, MARSHA ROSENGARTEN AND ALEX WILKIE	21
2	**The wager of an unfinished present: notes on speculative pragmatism** MARTIN SAVRANSKY	25
3	**Speculative research, temporality and politics** ROSALYN DIPROSE	39
4	**Situated speculation as a constraint on thought** MICHAEL HALEWOOD	52

x *Contents*

PART II
Speculative lures   65

   Introduction: speculative lures   67
   MARSHA ROSENGARTEN, MARTIN SAVRANSKY AND
   ALEX WILKIE

 5 Pluralities of action, a lure for speculative thought   71
   MARSHA ROSENGARTEN

 6 Doing speculation to curtail speculation   84
   ALEX WILKIE AND MIKE MICHAEL

 7 Retrocasting: speculating about the origins of money   98
   JOE DEVILLE

PART III
Speculative techniques   111

   Introduction: speculative techniques   113
   ALEX WILKIE, MARSHA ROSENGARTEN AND
   MARTIN SAVRANSKY

 8 Sociology's archive: Mass-Observation as a site of
   speculative research   117
   LISA ADKINS

 9 Developing speculative methods to explore speculative
   shipping: mail art, futurity and empiricism   130
   REBECCA COLEMAN

10 Creating idiotic speculators: disaster cosmopolitics in the
   sandbox   145
   MICHAEL GUGGENHEIM, BERND KRÄFTNER AND
   JUDITH KRÖLL

11 2Sweet2Kill: speculative research and contributory action   163
   MICHAEL SCHILLMEIER AND YVONNE LEE SCHULTZ

Contents xi

PART IV
Speculative implications   181

Introduction: speculative implications   183
MARTIN SAVRANSKY, ALEX WILKIE AND
MARSHA ROSENGARTEN

12   **On Isabelle Stengers' 'cosmopolitics': a speculative
adventure**   187
VIKKI BELL

13   **Aesthetic experience, speculative thought and civilized life**   198
MICHAEL L. THOMAS

14   **The lure of the possible: on the function of speculative
propositions**   210
DIDIER DEBAISE

Afterword: thinking with outrageous propositions   218
MONICA GRECO

Index   228

Figures

8.1	Day Survey 216 written by a Mass-Observer in 1937	125
9.1	Selected postcards: front	138
9.2	Postcard: instructions	139
9.3	Postcard: back	140
10.1	The sandbox	148
10.2	A start	149
10.3	Another start	150
10.4	Origins	151
10.5	Dice and ship	152
10.6	Pigs deliberate	153
10.7	A wise elephant	154
10.8	Props	154
10.9	Diagrammatic space	156
10.10	Neighbours	157
10.11	Everything in the sandbox	159
10.12	A cosmic unitary mass	160
10.13	Attractive props	160
11.1	PP/S porcelain PPK, strewn flowers, tea cup and saucer	167
11.2	PP/C-G golden chocolate gun	168
11.3	Schoko kid M (from the series 2sweet2kill)	169
11.4	Schoko kid L (from the series 2sweet2kill)	173
11.5	Schoko kids_2 boys	175
11.6	Schoko kid S	176

Contributors

Lisa Adkins is an Academy of Finland Distinguished (FiDiPro) Professor and the BHP Billiton Chair of Sociology at the University of Newcastle, Australia. Her contributions and interventions in the discipline of Sociology lie in the areas of economic sociology (especially the sociology of labour), social and cultural theory and feminist theory. Her recent research focuses on the restructuring of labour, money and time in post-Fordist capitalism. Publications from this research have appeared in a number of journals including *South Atlantic Quarterly*, *Feminist Review* and *Social Epistemology*. Her next book *The Time of Money* extends this work. Key publications include *The Post-Fordist Sexual Contract: Working and Living in Contingency* (with Maryanne Dever, 2016); *Measure and Value* (with Celia Lury, 2012); *What is the Empirical?* (with Celia Lury, 2009); *Feminism After Bourdieu* (with Bev Skeggs, 2005); *Revisions: Gender and Sexuality in Late Modernity* (2002) and *Gendered Work* (1995). She is joint Editor-in-Chief of the journal *Australian Feminist Studies* (Routledge/Taylor & Francis).

Vikki Bell is Professor of Sociology at Goldsmiths, University of London. She is the author of four monographs, including *Culture and Performance* (Bloomsbury, 2007). Widely published in peer-reviewed journals, she has written extensively on the thought of Michel Foucault and Hannah Arendt, and addressed questions of ethics, aesthetics, subjectivity and politics across the social sciences and theoretical humanities. Recently her work has explored cultural-aesthetic aspects of transitional justice in Argentina, where her research has been funded by the Arts and Humanities Research Council and, currently, by the Economic and Social Research Council. The most recent publication from this project is *The Art of Post-Dictatorship: Ethics & Aesthetics in Transitional Argentina* (Routledge, 2014).

Rebecca Coleman is a Senior Lecturer in the Sociology Department, Goldsmiths, University of London. Her research and teaching focuses on visual and sensory sociology, bodies and materiality, temporality, especially presents and futures, and feminist and cultural theory. She recently led the ESRC Research Seminar Series on Austerity Futures: Imagining and Materialising the Future in an 'Age of Austerity' (2012–2014), and is currently

xiv *Contributors*

working on publications and projects concerned with the significance of temporality in contemporary socio-cultural life. These include: editing a collection on futures; papers on the affectivity of austerity futures, and on the temporality of the surface; and projects with academics, artists and designers to develop interdisciplinary methodologies for researching temporality. Recent publications include, *Deleuze and Research Methodologies* (edited with Jessica Ringrose, 2013, Edinburgh University Press), *Transforming Images: Screens, Affect, Futures* (2012, Routledge) and *The Becoming of Bodies: Girls, Images, Experience* (2009, Manchester University Press).

Joe Deville is a Lecturer at Lancaster University, based jointly in the Department of Organisation, Work and Technology and the Department of Sociology. The primary focus of his work to date has been the encounter between defaulting consumer credit debtor and debt collector, which was the subject of his first book *Lived Economies of Default*, published in the CRESC series in early 2015. Further areas of interest include technologies of disaster preparedness, the material politics of issue formation, comparative and digital methods, behavioural economics and theories of money. He has published single and co-authored articles on these and related issues in the *Journal of Cultural Economy, Consumption Markets and Culture, Cultural Studies* and *Sociological Review*, as well as in two Routledge edited collections. He has also co-edited a Special Issue of *Cultural Studies*, a forthcoming book examining the practical work of social scientific comparison, and a forthcoming book in the CRESC series examining techniques of market attachment. He is an editor at *Journal of Cultural Economy* and a co-founder and editor of both Mattering Press, the recently launched Open Access book publisher, and the online consumer studies research network Charisma.

Didier Debaise is a researcher at the FNRS and teaches contemporary philosophy at the University of Brussels. His main areas of research are contemporary forms of speculative philosophy, theories of the event, and links between American pragmatism and French contemporary philosophy. He is a member of the Whitehead Research Project, the editorial board of the journals *Multitudes* and *Inflexions*. He is the author of a book on Whitehead's philosophy (*Un empirisme spéculative*, 2006), and the editor of volumes on pragmatism (*Vie et expérimentation*, 2007) and on the history of contemporary metaphysics (*Philosophie des possessions*, 2011. He has written numerous articles on Bergson, Tarde, Simondon, Deleuze and Whitehead and he is currently working on a new book entitled *Sujets de la nature*.

Rosalyn Diprose is Emeritus Professor of Philosophy at the University of New South Wales, Sydney. Her books include *Corporeal Generosity: On Giving with Nietzsche, Merleau-Ponty, and Levinas* (SUNY 2002); *The Bodies of Women* (Routledge 1994/2007); and the co-edited collections *Merleau-Ponty: Key Concepts* (with J. Reynolds, Continuum 2008) and *Cartographies: Poststructuralism and the Mapping of Bodies and Spaces* (with R. Ferrell, Allen

Contributors xv

& Unwin 1991). Her current research includes examining issues at the intersection between phenomenology and biopolitical theory, including a book length study of 'Natality and Biopolitics' with Ewa Ziarek.

Monica Greco is a Reader in Sociology at Goldsmiths, University of London and a research fellow of the Alexander von Humboldt Stiftung. She has written extensively on the historical, social and political dimensions of concepts in psychosomatics, on vitalism in relation to health and medicine, and on health as a vector of neoliberal forms of subjectivity and self-governance. She is the author of *Illness As a Work of Thought* (Routledge, 1998) and is currently preparing a monograph for Routledge entitled *Participating Bodies: Medicine and the Problem of Subjectivity*.

Michael Guggenheim is a Reader at the Department of Sociology at Goldsmiths, University of London. He has recently (until 2015) directed an ERC starting grant titled Organising Disaster: Civil Protection and the Population. Together with the other authors, he was a member of the research group Communicating Disaster at the Center for Interdisciplinary Research (ZiF), Bielefeld. He has recently published (2014) the co-edited volume *Disasters and Politics: Materials, Experiments, Preparedness*.

Michael Halewood is a Senior Lecturer at the University of Essex. His research interests lie at the intersection of social theory and philosophy. He is the author of two monographs: *A. N. Whitehead and Social Theory. Tracing a Culture of Thought* (Anthem Press, 2011) and *Rethinking the Social through Durkheim, Weber, Marx and Whitehead* (Anthem Press, 2014). He has also written on Badiou, Butler, Dewey, Deleuze and Irigaray and topics such as: tuning (Equal Temperament) and modernity *(History of Human Sciences)*; the form and value of things *(British Journal of Sociology)*; entropy and death *(Social Science)*; conceptions of the self in those diagnosed with Alzheimer's Disease *(Sociological Review)*. He is an Associate Editor of the *Critical Edition of the Complete Works of Alfred North Whitehead* (Edinburgh University Press).

Bernd Kräftner is an artist and researcher. He has realized numerous transdisciplinary research projects on and at the interfaces of science, society and art. He is a founder of the research group Shared Inc. (Research Centre for Shared Incompetence) and teaches at the University of Applied Arts in Vienna at the Departments of Art and Science and Digital Art.

Judith Kroell is a sociologist and as a member of the research group Shared Inc. (since 1999) she has participated in various projects at the interfaces of science, society and art. She is a lecturer at the Department of Social Studies of Science, University of Vienna and works as a Tomatis Consultant in Vienna.

Mike Michael is a sociologist of science and technology, and Professor of Sociology at the University of Exeter. His research interests include the relation xvi *Contributors*

of everyday life to technoscience, biotechnological and biomedical innovation and culture, and process methodology. Current research projects focus on the interdisciplinary use of sociological and speculative design techniques, the role of aesthetics in technological innovation, and a processual analytics of everyday life. Among his most recent major publications are (with Marsha Rosengarten) the co-authored volume *Innovation and Biomedicine: Ethics, Evidence and Expectation in HIV* (Palgrave, 2013), and *Actor-Network Theory: Trial, Trails and Translations* (Sage, 2016).

Marsha Rosengarten is Professor in Sociology and Co-Director of the Centre for Invention and Social Process, Department of Sociology, Goldsmiths, University of London. She is the author of *HIV Interventions: Biomedicine and the Traffic in Information and Flesh* and co-author with Mike Michael of *Innovation and Biomedicine: Ethics, Evidence and Expectation in HIV.* Recent articles focus on biomedical research within the field of HIV, ebola and tuberculosis drawing from feminist and process-oriented approaches. Her work offers alternative ways of conceiving intervention, bioethics, randomized controlled trials and, hence, the nature of scientific evidence.

Michael Schillmeier is a Professor in the Department of Sociology and Philosophy at the University of Exeter. His work combines process-oriented Sociology, Science and Technology Studies (STS) and Empirical Philosophy. He graduated at the LMU Munich, Germany and received his PhD from Lancaster University. He held a Schumpeter-Fellowship (VolkswagenStiftung) to research 'Innovations in Nano-Medicine' in Germany and the UK (2010–2015). The main focus of this project is to analyse and engage with the emergence of nanomedical knowledge practices, objects and technologies. He is co-editor of *Space & Culture*. Michael's empirical and conceptual work is concerned with the becoming of social relations, actors, practices and concerns whereby the 'non-normal', 'unexpected', 'uncommon' or 'unknown' plays a central part. Linking social sciences, philosophy and art he has widely written on the material dynamics and heterogeneity of societal orderings and change. Research topics include STS, dis/abling practices, care practices, health and illness, human/non-human relations and cosmopolitics.

Yvonne Lee Schultz is a Berlin based artist who gained her diploma at the Academy of Fine Arts, Düsseldorf. She has exhibited internationally in group shows as well as solo exhibitions. In 2012 Yvonne was the winner of the Light Flatters competition, University of Rostock.

Martin Savransky is a Lecturer at the Department of Sociology, Goldsmiths, University of London, where he teaches philosophy, social theory and methodology of social science. He works at the intersection of process philosophy, the philosophy and methodology of the social sciences, and the politics of knowledge. He has published widely on the ethics and politics of social inquiry, postcolonial ontologies and social theory. He is the author of *The Adventure of Relevance: An Ethics of Social Inquiry* (Palgrave Macmillan, 2016).

Contributors xvii

Michael L. Thomas holds a PhD in Social Thought from the University of Chicago. His research combines work in process philosophy, social theory and the arts to address questions of human action, forms of cooperation and the relationship between thought and experience. Michael's current project, undertaken as a research fellow at the Forschungsinstitut für Philosophie Hannover, uses insights from the Pragmatists, College de Sociologie and the Frankfurt School to develop a methodology for interpreting sociological practices as aesthetic phenomena.

Alex Wilkie is a sociologist and a Senior Lecturer at the Department of Design, Goldsmiths, University of London. His research interests combine aspects of social theory, science and technology studies with design research that bear on theoretical, methodological and substantive areas including, but not limited to: aesthetics, design practice and design studios, healthcare and information technologies, human-computer interaction design, inventive and creative practices, user involvement and participation in design, practice-based design research, process theory and speculative thought. Alex is a Director of the Centre for Invention and Social Process (CISP), alongside Michael Guggenheim and Marsha Rosengarten, and convenes the PhD programme in Design at Goldsmiths. He has recently co-edited *Studio Studies: Operations, Topologies and Displacements* with Ignacio Farias (Routledge, 2015) and he is preparing the edited collection *Inventing the Social* with Michael Guggenheim and Noortje Marres (Mattering Press). Alex is also a founding editor of *Demonstrations*, the journal for experiments in social studies of technology.

Acknowledgements

This collection is the outcome of an adventure in thought that began with a workshop entitled 'Speculation and Speculative Research' in May 2014, followed by another 'Thinking Through Possibilities' in May 2015. Both were held under the auspices of the Unit of Play in the Department of Sociology, Goldsmiths, University of London. We are immensely grateful to the contributors to these workshops for the dialogue that took place and especially to those whose work has subsequently contributed to this volume. Along the way we met others whose interest in speculative thought encouraged us and has further contributed to the different ways in which speculation takes form in the collection. We are grateful to all.

Penny Harvey, Professor of Anthropology at Manchester University and an editor of the CRESC series, welcomed the prospect of this volume with great enthusiasm, and we would like to return her considerate and careful support with what we hope is a timely and well-received volume. Alongside Penny, we would like to extend our appreciation to the other CRESC editors as well as the anonymous reviewers of the book's manuscript, who provided diligent and cogent advice. Finally, we would like to thank Alyson Claffey at Taylor & Francis for her support throughout the editing and production process.

1 The lure of possible futures

On speculative research

Martin Savransky, Alex Wilkie and
Marsha Rosengarten

Introduction: beyond the impasse of the present

Is another future possible? It appears that we inhabit a peculiar time, somewhat suspended in its own frantic movement, where the future has never been more present, yet the present keeps prolonging itself, insisting, with its own order of continuity, on a time that does not quite seem to pass. The world is witness to a proliferation of crises of diverse orders and scopes, from the financial crash of 2008 that plunged it into a global economic crisis that still persists and threatens social, political, and economic futures today (Mirowski, 2014), through new and ongoing global health challenges, to the proliferation of environmental disasters and the planetary problem of climate change in an age that some refer to as the 'Anthropocene' (Crutzen & Stroemer, 2000) and others as the Capitalocene (Moore, 2015), to name but some of the most obvious ones. Despite this, the dominant modes of response to the futures that these transformative events generate still largely privilege a 'business-as-usual' approach that reduces futures to matters of anticipation, calculation, management and pre-emption of risks and uncertainties in the present. An approach, in other words, that cannot engage possible futures without simultaneously submitting them to the logics, rationalities, and habits that govern the problematic of the present.

In some respects, there is something anachronistic about the impasse that characterises what we may nevertheless call our 'contemporary' situation (Savransky, 2012). For the sense of an immutable present, whereby knowledge of what has been, and anticipation of what is yet to come, remain connected through a kind of temporality 'in which nothing essentially new could occur', was a central feature of what conceptual historian Reinhardt Koselleck (2004: 58) calls the 'horizon of expectation' of the West before the French revolution. In this understanding, it is the revolution itself, as an inaugural event of European 'modernity', that marks 'the start of a future that had never before existed' (ibid.: 59). One whose most distinctive signature was that of an ever increasing *acceleration* of social, political, economic and natural life that contracted the horizon of expectation and abbreviated time by exposing the present to ever new, and unexpected, historical events. Perhaps it is true, then, that we have never been modern (Latour, 1993)?

2   *M. Savransky* et al.

And yet what is distinct about the current impasse, modern or not, is that what restores linearity to the present is, paradoxically, a pervasive concern across all fields of practice and knowledge with anticipating the future. The immutability of the present, in other words, is no longer a taken-for-granted historical experience, but becomes the achievement of complex, laborious and uncertain human and other-than-human practices aimed at knowing and securing the future. It is in contrast to the dominant modes of futurity involved in what we have associated with the impasse of the present, that *Speculative Research* seeks to make an intervention.

This edited collection constitutes an attempt to offer some conceptual, methodological and practical tools that can contribute to confronting the challenge of articulating a response, however partial, to this suspension of time and, in doing so, may enable social and cultural researchers to be lured by the possibility of futures that are more than a mere extension of the present. Gathering together a range of engagements by social and cultural researchers with questions of speculation, possibilities and futures in contemporary societies, *Speculative Research* responds to the pressing need to not only account for the role of calculative logics and rationalities in managing societal futures, but to develop alternative approaches and sensibilities that take futures seriously as possibilities that demand new habits and practices of attention, invention and experimentation.

Modes of futurity: risk, temporality, speculation

As the poet Paul Valéry (1988: 192) famously put it, the problem with our times is that 'the future, like everything else, is not what it used to be'. 'We have', he said,

> lost our traditional means of thinking and foreseeing: [...] our deepest habits, our laws, our language, our sentiments, our ambitions, have been engendered and sedimented in a time that admitted *longue durées*, that was founded and thought over an immense past, and which pointed to a future measured in generations.

The future has become problematic. Indeed, the question of how heterogeneous actors engage futures, what intellectual and practical strategies they put into play and what the implications of such strategies are, have become crucial scientific, technological and societal concerns (e.g. Adam & Groves, 2007; Brown, Rappert, & Webster, 2000; van Lente 1993). Nevertheless, as Valéry (1988: 195) also noted, our attitude towards the future remains fundamentally inadequate, for 'we enter the future backwards'. In the social sciences, much of the concern with futures testifies to Valéry's diagnosis. Until recently, futures had been largely addressed from the point of view of the ways in which societies deal with their threats and uncertainties. According to sociologists of risk (e.g. Beck, 1992, 2008), for example, risk analysis, calculation and the management of uncertainties have become the defining features of late modernity, where

The lure of possible futures 3

hazards and risks have proliferated as an upshot of modern ideals of progress notably including social and economic processes of industrialisation, urbanisation and globalisation. In this view, and in contrast to the early modern era where threats and dangers posed to societies were largely the outcome of natural causes, human practices and inventions now figure as the primary sources of risk-generation as well as the primary sites of responsibility for their coordination, minimisation and amelioration (Rosa, Renn, & McCright, 2014).

Other theoretical approaches to social futures have challenged both the epistemological and historiographical assumptions that underpin the concept of the 'risk society' (Adam, Beck, & Van Loon, 2000). In addition to socio-cultural (Douglas, 1992) and systems theories of risk (Luhmann, 1993), the critical social constructivism of the 'governmentality' school has approached the question of risk and the calculation of futures not as a logic inherent to an age of proliferating uncertainties, but as a neoliberal rationality of government that displaces its focus of attention from the disciplining of individuals to the management of entire populations. In this view, new modes of neoliberal governance operate through the institution of, and reliance on, an indefinite number of precautionary factors that seek to measure, organise, tame and influence the conduct of the population (Baker & Simon, 2002; Miller & Rose, 2008; O'Malley, 2004). Notwithstanding their theoretical and historiographical differences, such approaches seem to share the sense that 'risk' and 'uncertainty' – but also unacknowledged 'indeterminacy' (Wynne, 1992) – constitute the defining keystones by which contemporary societies conceptualise and negotiate the relationship between present and futures. Risks are said to pervade all aspects of life, from financial and insurance practices (Baker & Simon, 2002, de Goede, 2004), the politics of security and war (Ericson & Doyle, 2004, Larner & Walters, 2004), environmental forecasting, regulation and disaster prevention (Lash, Szerszynski, & Wynne, 2000) and scientific and technological innovation and governance (Flynn & Bellaby, 2007; Kerr & Cunningham-Burley, 2000), to processes of governmental and individual decision-making and regulation regarding health (Petersen & Wilkinson, 2008), education (Brynin, 2013) and everyday life (Tulloch & Lupton, 2003).

The lesson that such accounts yield, however, is more paradoxical than might appear at first sight. As many of their proponents also attest, and as has become particularly salient in Science and Technology Studies (STS) and in the so-called 'Sociology of Expectations' (Brown et al., 2000, van Lente, 1993), techniques of forecasting and risk-management do not operate merely to represent and know the future. Such studies detail how, for instance, the hopes and expectations associated with biotechnology and genetic engineering, the institutional deployment of future forecasting techniques such as Delphi and Foresight (De Laat, 2000), the financial commoditisation of the future and the identification and indemnification of risks and uncertainty associated with modern industrial society, and even the routine material practices of the designers of computational technology (Wilkie, 2010), such as prototyping, become part and parcel of routine scientific, technological and policy practices. Insofar as they inform

4 *M. Savransky* et al.

decision-making processes through authoritative knowledge-claims (Selin, 2008) or through the construction of expectations about futures (Brown & Michael 2003; Michael & Rosengarten 2013; Wilkie & Michael 2009), such practices orient social action in the present. Thus, more than providing reliable knowledge of the future, these practices become *factors* in the constitution of a yet-to-come, a not-yet that, as we have intimated above, too often strives to coincide with the 'already' on which it is based.

Part of the reason for this is that the logics and practices by which futures are reduced to forecasting and risk-management themselves presuppose that futures are ultimately a prolongation of the present. In effect, they are bound to a logic of anticipation whereby future uncertainties and contingencies are calculated, represented and said to be tamed through statistical and modelling techniques that make predictions about likely future scenarios based on knowledge of the present (Adam & Groves 2007). What allows for these probabilistic modes of forecasting is the presupposition that time moves linearly, along a modern arrow of progress, such that the present conditions upon which calculation are drawn will be conserved in the future state which calculative inferences are supposed to provide information about. Crucially, however, as historians and philosophers of science and time have shown (Bergson, 2002; Grosz, 2004; Hacking, 1990; Whitehead, 1967), when engaging with futures, it matters what we take *time* to be. It matters whether we think of time as extending over a metrical arrow of progress, or whether we engage with it, for instance, in the manner of a handkerchief, to be spread, crumpled and torn, forming a topological image of time (Serres & Latour, 1995: 60). Resisting the modern arrow of time matters because it enables us to consider temporality as it is formed through its own patterns of becoming rather than through the imposition of a preformatted geometry. It matters, moreover, because it enables us to pay attention to, and experiment with, the very *processes* of crumpling, folding and 'tearing' time, and not just to their culmination.

This edited collection takes stock of many of the lessons afforded by the aforementioned traditions of social and cultural research on 'futures' and temporality, but it simultaneously departs from them in a fundamental sense. While such studies evince a preoccupation with the temporal patterns and dynamics at play in shaping developments in science and technology, in politics and economics, in education and art, and so on, common to their preoccupations is an approach to futures that regards them as yet another (past) empirical object, to be illuminated through the customary methods and techniques of 'social' and 'cultural' analysis and explanation. S*peculative Research*, by contrast, is *not* primarily about how 'others' imagine, manage, calculate, pre-empt, secure, know or speculate about, the future. Throughout the different chapters that compose this collection, possible futures are never simply 'objects' of knowledge, to be conquered by the conceptual and practical tools and methods of the various disciplines and approaches they espouse. To the extent that these diverse contributions share a common concern, it is the sense that, to paraphrase Marilyn Strathern (1992), *it matters what futures we use to cultivate other futures with*. In other words, it matters how we enter the future, what senses of futurity we bring into play, which modes of relating to the not-yet we enable knowing and thinking practices to nurture. Thus, rather than objects of knowledge or thought to be captured by a backward-walking present, possible futures are here engaged as vectors of risk and creative experimentation. It is futures themselves that, whenever one takes the risk of cultivating them, can escape the impasses of the present, and lure our own practices of thinking, knowing and feeling to unforeseen possibilities. Thus, what each of the chapters in this collection attempts, with the means and challenges of its own situated engagement, is to take the risk of experiencing a mutation of the commitments, sensibilities and constraints that characterise their own research practices – as well as other practices with which they are concerned – as they become *lured* by the possibility of futures that are more than the mere extension of the present.

The politics of the (im)possible: reclaiming speculation

Choosing to characterise this lure as speculative is not, to be sure, without risks of its own. Born of the perplexing and poetic capacities of mirrors (*specula*), both material and conceptual tools – for *speculum* was also the name for medieval encyclopaedias – to provoke modes of knowing and thinking that brought together the visible and the invisible and thereby served as a 'testing ground, providing the clues with which man rises beyond the known to the unknown' (Melchior-Bonnet, 2001: 113), the notion of 'speculation' enjoys a long and complex history in philosophical, theological and artistic imaginations at least since the Middle Ages (see also Hunt, 2011). Nowadays, moreover, such histories are themselves witness to a dramatic explosion, as the term 'speculation' proliferates through our contemporary imagination across an impressive range of registers and fields of practice.

In one notorious sense, for example, 'speculation' might be seen precisely to conjure up many of the 'evils' that have endowed this impasse with a tragic character. For nowhere is speculation currently more present in the media and in popular culture than in its association with the irrational, and irresponsible excesses of contemporary high frequency financial trading practices, market dynamics and stock exchanges (MacKenzie, 2006). Such practices, which seek to bring about and profit from the highly volatile fluctuations of markets and their uncertain futures (Pemmaraju, 2015), are now understood to be acutely implicated in the recent global financial meltdown, as well as in generating ongoing disasters such as algorithmically induced flash crashes (e.g. SECC, 2014). In this sense, speculation seems tied to its modern history as a term of abuse, as that which borders on the suspect practices of those who exploit uncertainty and undertake actions often in the absence of any 'reliable' evidence (Ericson & Doyle, 2004).

High finance, however, is not exceptional in its harnessing and exploitation of logics commonly associated with the speculative. Across fields as diverse as security and insurance, product development and marketing, environmental and

6   *M. Savransky* et al.

health forecasting, as well as policy and governance, the very agencies and organisations that create regimes of 'evidence' are actively and productively incorporating what some would refer to as 'speculative' forms of data analysis. These are applications that, informed by new developments in consultancy and information studies, operate alongside (if not beyond) logics of probabilities by incorporating algorithmic logics. Unlike conventional probability-based forecasting, algorithms rely much less on past historical data and bell curves in order to extrapolate probable futures, and instead operate by making multiple associations and correlations among contingent and mutable events seeking to anticipate 'low probability–high consequence' future events (Amoore & Piotukh, 2015).

The seeming association with such practices makes the choice of the word 'speculation' a dangerous one, to say the least. It poses the danger that a cultivation of speculative thought and practice in social and cultural research be seen as making a contribution, however small, to those who, in the face of 'uncertainty' as a constraint upon their engagements with futures, would turn such uncertainties into profit. But to reject speculation because of its associations with financial and security practices poses a different kind of danger, namely, that of falling into a form of obscurantism that denies the importance of other modes of speculation due to the dangers that the aforementioned practices pose. In our view, thus, it is not a matter here of seeking a morally and politically immaculate position from which to craft a critical stance. Such a strategy would quickly leave us wordless. Rather, it is about reclaiming this discredited word by drawing sensitive, and hopefully productive, contrasts with those practices by which it has been captured, such that a different sense of the speculative may become possible, and a different, more creative and responsible sensibility may be cultivated.

An important contrast to be drawn between these different senses of the speculative, therefore, lies in the fact that, even when these financial and security practices have radically changed the forms of data they operate with, their infrastructures, and the ways in which such data is analysed; even when they have loosened the constraints informing judgements on which actions may be enforced; they still participate in the modern dream of a form of 'objective' knowledge that is precise enough, accurate enough, comprehensive enough and reliable enough to anticipate the future. As social researchers have made apparent, the speculative in speculative finance and security practices is understood as an 'invitation of the intuitive [...] within the calculation of probability that characterises the contemporary authorisation of algorithmic judgments' (Amoore, 2013: 44).

While often referred to as acting on possibilities, algorithms do in fact seem to act upon 'a form of probability that is highly sensitive to rapid change, embraces the subjective [and] allows for discretion of choices on the part of the observer' with the purpose not just of preventing but of *preempting* the becoming of unwanted futures (Amoore, 2013: 45; Uncertain Commons, 2013). Consequently, the notion of 'possibility' that is employed in such practices by and large acquires its meaning as the shadow of probabilities, and thus remains premised upon them. The possible still designates here an image of the future,

The lure of possible futures 7

however uncertain, however volatile, however 'unlikely' from the point of view of a statistical curve, that can be rendered calculable, manageable, knowable and actionable. It is still a possible that, as Henri Bergson (2002) would critically argue, is projected from, and belongs to, the order of what is actual, and thus prolongs the order of the present.

By contrast, the attempt made in *Speculative Research* is to cultivate a sense of the possible that concerns, but does not owe its existence to, the ways in which the actual determines the distribution of what is probable, either statistically or algorithmically. As philosopher Isabelle Stengers (2010: 17) has proposed, this alternative sense of the speculative constitutes nothing other than 'a struggle against probabilities'. And not because of some humanist prejudice against quantification *tout-court*, or because of a metaphysical commitment that would denounce the experience of any regular pattern of order as a mere human illusion. To the contrary, speculation constitutes a struggle against probabilities in the sense that, while it acknowledges and affirms the existence of such patterns, it *also* affirms the existence of what any attempt to determine the probability of a future must set aside, or deem irrelevant – namely, the becoming of novel and unexpected events that, against all odds, transform the very order of the possible, the probable and the plausible (Deleuze, 2007; Savransky, 2016). From this viewpoint, then, rather than partake in the problem-space of the normal, the probable and the plausible, speculative possibilities emerge out of the eruption of what, from the standpoint of the impasse of the present seems, in all likelihood, to be *impossible*.

As we proposed above, whenever futures are at stake, it matters what senses of futurity we bring into play. Throughout the pages that follow, the many futures to be engaged belong to a temporality that is neither calculable, manageable nor foreknown. Rather, the futures to be experimented with are those made perceptible by cultivating a sensibility to a temporality we shall refer to as 'eventful': a time marked not by presuppositions of linearity, or by arrows of progress, but by the unexpected eruptions of the (im)possible, of social, political, economic, philosophical and ecological events that cannot be anticipated and open up possible futures that cannot be managed in advance.

Participating in an eventful temporality forces us to come to resist the temptation of reducing futures to presents, of entering futures backwards, and requires that we come to terms with irreducible futures that come into existence through processes of path dependency (Sewell, 2005), temporally heterogeneous and emergent causalities (Connolly, 2012) and global contingencies (Serres, 1995). In other words, an eventful temporality assumes that 'contingent, unexpected, and inherently unpredictable events can undo or alter the most apparently durable trends of history' (Sewell, 2005: 102), enabling a swerve of possible futures and creative alternatives to be explored and harnessed. In this way, futures are fundamentally underdetermined with respect to present actualities, but inhere in the latter in the form of potentialities to be actualised in practice.

Thus, the 'speculative' in *Speculative Research* does not designate a practice of subjective anticipations of futures, nor is it a substitute for ascribing unwarranted

8 *M. Savransky* et al.

meanings to uncertainties when scientific evidence is lacking. Speculating is not a matter of determining what is, and what is not, possible, as if possibilities could always be ascertained in advance of events, that is, from the impasse of the present. By contrast, speculation is here associated with a sensibility concerned with resisting a future that presents itself as probable or plausible, and to wager instead that, no matter how pervasive the impasse may be, it can never exhaust the unrealised potential of the present. It wagers that, despite its obsession with securing the future, there are futures that the present could never anticipate, and these already inhere in it as (im)possibilities to be actualised (Savransky, 2016). In this way, speculating demands the active taking of risks that enable an exploration of the plurality of the present, one that provides resources for resistance, one out of which unexpected events may erupt, and alternative futures may be created.

Thoughts that are creative of the future: cultivating a speculative sensibility

In contrast to its capture by contemporary financial and security practices, then, the sensibility *Speculative Research* seeks to cultivate is more akin to that nurtured in a field where speculation has enjoyed a much longer and productive history – namely, in literature, and most notably, in the genre of SF (which stands variously for Science Fiction, Speculative Fiction, Sci-Fi, Slipstream Fiction, etc.). SF constitutes in itself an immensely heterogeneous field, within which any single definition of 'speculation' remains perennially under dispute, when not *impossible* (Gunn & Candelaria, 2004). SF includes traditions of fiction writing that, in the words of Margaret Atwood (2011: 6), 'descend from H.G. Wells's *The War of the Worlds*, which treats of an invasion by tentacled, blood-sucking Martians shot to Earth in metal canisters – things that could not possibly happen', as well as others that would 'descend from Jules Verne's books about submarines and balloon travel and such – things that really could happen but just hadn't completely happened when the authors wrote the books'. In this literary world, it is not so much the case that the possibility of a future is ascertained from the point of view of the present, but that reality is always already entangled with the 'not-yet', the 'yet-to-come', the 'what-if', the 'already-here', that is, with a sense of the (im)possible. As Atwood (2011: 5) stresses, 'the future is an unknown: from the moment *now*, an infinite number of roads lead away to "the future", each heading in a different direction'. SF is singularly sensitive to the fact it is *impossible* to know in advance just in *which* direction any of those roads may lead. The task, therefore, is to experiment with them, to see their ground materialise as one travels through them, as one explores their contours, landscapes, and horizons, as one witnesses such impossibilities be realised.

As the long history of SF reveals, creating (im)possibles, making possibles perceptible and experimenting with them, is a collective, transdisciplinary task. In recent years, such a task has also surfaced with considerable force in the fields of architecture and design. Forms of visual and material speculation provide an alternative way of conceptualising and directing the role of aesthetic and technological design practices, urban visions, propositions and outcomes (Dunne & Raby, 2013; Lang & Menking, 2003; Rao, Krishnamurthy, & Kouni, 2015; Wilkie, Michael, & Plummer-Fernandez, 2015; Zegher & Wigley, 2001). In challenging dominant user-centred and functionalist assumptions, and rational planning in the case of the built environment, that have long guided such practices, the speculative emerges here as a different sensibility in devising aesthetic and technical processes, propositions and outcomes. Here, the function of the speculative is not to provide techno-aesthetic solutions to pre-defined problems or to 'domesticate' technical inventions, but rather to mobilise design as a 'catalyst for social dreaming' (Dunne & Raby, 2013: 189), the complex genealogies of which can, in part, be traced to experimental post-war architectural design practices (e.g. Gilman & Riley, 2002).

In contemporary continental philosophy, a small but expanding number of scholars grouped under the label of 'Speculative Realism' have recently gained notoriety in debates around ontology, metaphysics, aesthetics and the philosophy of science (see Bryant, Srnicek, & Harman, 2011). While the members of this group openly disagree with one another on key and fundamental issues, they share a commitment to metaphysical speculation against the modern, Kantian culture of thought that Quentin Meillassoux (2008: 5) has called 'the correlationist circle'. In short, this refers to 'the idea according to which we only ever have access to the correlation between thinking and being, and never to either term considered apart from the other'. In an attempt to break away from the anti-realist circle where 'we cannot say that the world either exists or fails to exist outside human thought' (Harman, 2013: 23), speculation operates here as a line of flight into a realm of metaphysical investigation and invention where it is possible to think the 'in-itself' of entities and objects without the need to posit them always already in relation to knowing subjects.

While sharing a common point of departure with the speculative realists in resisting the bifurcation of the world into subjects and predicates, many of the chapters in this book engage with a sensibly different tradition of speculative thought. A tradition that can be traced back to the work of William James and Henri Bergson (see Debaise, 2009), and was subsequently expanded and systematised in the speculative metaphysics of Alfred North Whitehead, the philosophy of Gilles Deleuze, and more recently, through Stengers' philosophy of science. It is such a genealogy of speculation that the chapters of *Speculative Research* seek to make resonate. Making it resonate, however, is not so much about introducing it to others as it is about finding new and productive ways of appropriating it, connecting it with other traditions with which it had not been associated, and above all, experiencing some of its possible implications by putting some of its concepts, ideas, and proposals, to the test of practical encounters. Thus, while some contributions explore the speculative through sustained theoretical engagements with the works of Whitehead (Debaise, Halewood, Thomas), Stengers (Bell, Schillmeier), William James and John Dewey (Savransky), as well as by

10 *M. Savransky* et al.

making connections to the phenomenological existentialism of Hannah Arendt and Maurice Merleau-Ponty (Diprose); others are conversant with some of these thinkers while seeking to engage with speculation in more practical terrains. In so doing, they also invite further conceptual and philosophical contrasts – by way of discussing the work of William Connolly (Bell), Deleuze (Coleman), Donna Haraway (Halewood), Michel Serres (Rosengarten; Wilkie & Michael), Marilyn Strathern (Deville), and Gabriel Tarde (Schillmeier & Schultz) amongst others – to infiltrate the collective site of experimentation that constitutes the collection as a whole.

More than a uniform 'school' of thought or philosophical tradition, thus, a transversal reading of the chapters of this collection discloses, we hope, a plethora of situated engagements, pregnant with interesting contrasts, diverse textures and undertones. At stake here is not so much a common approach or an unwavering allegiance to certain philosophical influences, but the crafting of what perhaps is a common *gesture* (Debaise & Stengers, 2015). One way of characterising such a gesture is by paying attention to the manner in which the contributors to this collection seek to make speculation relevant not only to abstract thought, but also to the *empirical* challenges of social and cultural research. Unlike much of the work done under the umbrella name of 'Speculative Realism', for instance, the explorations in this edited collection seek to sidestep the Kantian problem of correlation not with the aim of affirming the 'in-itself' of things, which must necessarily keep experience at arms length, but with the aim of cultivating what might be called a 'deep empiricism'. That is to say, an empiricism concerned not only with isolated and discrete facts but also with their relations and forms of togetherness; one for which the world is never finished, once and for all, but always in the making (James, 2011 [1907]). An empiricism for which each experience, both human and other-than-human, simultaneously constitutes a perspective of the world while operating as a novel component *of* a world that transcends it (Whitehead, 1967: 228). In this way, speculative practices themselves become active factors and ingredients in the becoming of the world. They make thought not the *correlate* to fact but 'a factor in the fact of experience [such that] the immediate fact is what it is, partly by reason of the thought involved in it' (Whitehead, 1958: 80). This common gesture, then, might perhaps be best captured by Whitehead's (1958: 82) famous formulation, when he proposed that 'the business of speculation is to make thought creative of the future'.

The process of speculative research: organising the collection

To speculate, then, is to take the risk of developing practices that, by engaging inventively with (im)possibilities latent in the present, can disclose, make available and experiment with possible prospects for the becoming of alternative futures. It is, in Stengers (2015: 19) words, to 'respond to the insistence of a possible that demands to be realised'. In so doing, it seeks to furnish social, cultural and natural histories and practices with new contrasts and propositions that may

The lure of possible futures 11

enable them to resist, and move beyond, the plausible and probable tendencies that besiege the impasse of the present.

This is certainly easier said than done. From the beginning, this collection grew out of a collective, transdisciplinary process of cultivating forms of speculative research, which began with a workshop on 'Speculation and Speculative Research', in May 2014, and another on 'Thinking Through Possibilities' in May 2015, both under the auspices of the Unit of Play in the Department of Sociology, Goldsmiths, University of London. In organising these workshops, we chose to experiment with formats that could allow for a greater space for exchange and experimentation than one would otherwise normally expect to obtain in academic settings. This involved bringing together an international group of scholars and practitioners from a variety of disciplines (including philosophy, social theory, sociology, science and technology studies, and design) and theoretical, methodological and practical backgrounds and concerns.

During the first workshop, we asked each participant to submit, in advance, a paper-in-process that would allow for their own concerns to resonate with the following questions:

> Can social and cultural research become speculative? What do practices of speculation consist of and what modes of speculation are there? What are the implications of allowing for speculation to ingress into the practices of researching social and cultural change? What might speculative research offer to the re-invention of otherwise seemingly intractable 'problems'? How can speculation become a productive mode of thinking, feeling and knowing, and not just a practice of conjecturing and managing uncertainties?

Rather than structuring the event around individual presentations and the typical turns of questions and answers upon reception of the papers, we assembled a programme structured entirely around *responses* and discussions. That is, each one of the participants was assigned with the task of constructively responding to two other papers, such that each paper received, in turn, responses by two other contributors. After each round of responses, the entire group would join in for an expanded discussion on the emergent questions, possibilities, challenges and connections that they saw emerging from the propositions that the papers developed.

The second workshop, by contrast, involved no papers at all. Smaller, more experimental still, this forum gathered a number of participants from the first workshop and some others in an informal setting, to spend an entire day freely discussing the stakes of cultivating a speculative sensibility to the possible, and of thinking of research in terms of possibilities, prompted by the following questions:

> What does it mean to undertake research in terms of possibilities? What do possibilities 'open up' and what do they 'close down'? In what ways are

12   *M. Savransky* et al.

possibilities 'real', and what might it mean for speculation to 'make possibles'? What ethical, political and epistemological questions might possibilities pose to practices of knowledge-making?

Speculative Research is thus the result of a process of thinking collectively through the possibilities, difficulties, opportunities and challenges, the hopes, dreams and fears, of cultivating a speculative sensibility to research. Indeed, the many chapters that compose this collection explore, by way of their own situated engagements, diverse aspects of the process of nurturing speculative research. It is thus by attending to such questions and concerns, to both the requirements and obligations of such a process, that we have decided to organise this collection in four parts.

The first part, titled 'Speculative Propositions', gathers together chapters that, in different ways, open up and explore the stakes of a constructive reappraisal of speculative practices as modes of thought that may animate experimental engagements with (im)possibilities inherent in the creative dynamics of social and cultural change. In so doing, a series of pressing questions come to the fore: how can speculative thinking be pressed into the service of empirical research despite its anti-empirical associations? How can the speculative help to understand the novel interplay and emergence of interests and the transformation of habits of those concerned with the question of how to think, imagine and act for the future? If the speculative is not to be reduced to what is merely groundless, far-fetched or fanciful, then what are the constraints of the speculative and how can these be grasped for the purposes of research? The chapters in this part take these and other questions up in different ways by devising propositions for speculative practices of thought, action and care.

Unlike other future-oriented modes of thought, the aim of speculative practices is not that of evoking an abstract, normative future that could finally be rid of all compromises, of everything that inheres in the present from which a concrete form of experimentation with possibles might seek to depart. Speculative propositions, Whitehead (1978: 256. emphasis added) suggested, are 'tales that perhaps might be told about particular *actualities*'. It matters what those actualities are. The second part, 'Speculative lures', takes up this challenge, and asks what might act as a lure for speculation in actual, empirical situations in the fields of global health, commercial design and in debates about the origins of money. Contesting the need for a framing of research where knowledge is determined in advance and where political, ethical and medical achievements risk becoming insensitive to the rich differences that are afforded by the open practice of inquiry itself, the chapters in this part wonder about how to tell alternative tales about particular actualities, tales that could make available ways of resituating and relating to the empirical. In this way, this part takes up the challenge of intervening speculatively in a situation with the aim of shifting the intensities with which a future may be felt in the fugitive present.

Engaging with speculative thought also entails questions around what comprises and counts as the empirical and the methods, instruments and 'devices'

The lure of possible futures 13

used to relate to it (cf. Adkins & Lury, 2009). The third part, 'Speculative techniques', takes up this challenge. Recently, the social sciences have become preoccupied with the constitutive, 'performative' and 'non-representational' dimensions of research methods as well as the acknowledgement and inclusion of non-human agency (Back and Puwar, 2012; Law, 2004; Lury & Wakeford, 2012; Wilkie et al. 2015). Much of the work and debates in this area have also touched upon questions around interdisciplinarity and the broadening of the techniques through which the 'social' may be grasped as a relational, processual and indeterminate reality. This part explores how, on the one hand, approaches inspired by speculative thought resonate with contemporary methodological debates in social and cultural research. On the other hand, it describes how a shift to the speculative register forces one to come to terms with the constructive nature of a process that resists pre-defined research questions and actively formulates and risks asking alternative questions and devising research techniques anew. The chapters in this part, then, detail how the speculative can inform inventive approaches to the tuning of research techniques through three interdisciplinary empirical cases.

We have said that, in a sense, this collection constitutes the *outcome* of a process of responding collectively, and experimentally, to the insistence of the possible by seeking to cultivate forms of speculative research. Simultaneously, however, our hope is that this collection may also serve as an *opening*, an invitation for other social and cultural researchers to engage their own questions, problems and research situations with a renewed curiosity, and with new challenges that seek to take seriously the (im)possibilities latent in the present. The fourth part, 'Speculative implications', takes up the task of exploring some of the possible consequences that these engagements with speculative research and possible futures may enable for rethinking broader political, ethical and aesthetic questions. What might, after all, be the function and role of speculative propositions, and what are the implications of cultivating a speculative sensibility to the world? Indeed, what might it mean to 'live speculatively'? By returning to some of the philosophical sources that provide inspiration for the development of more practical and empirical forms of speculative research, and engaging with their more general, philosophical implications, the chapters in this part provide a series of meditations on the relation between speculation and the art of life: that is, the political, ethical and aesthetic task to live, to live well, to live better (Whitehead, 1958). As such, the chapters in this part offer important and wide-ranging insights on what may be at stake in cultivating speculative orientations to thought, to research, to the future and to the world.

Finally, the collection ends with an afterword by Monica Greco, who reflects on the collection as a whole, and contributes to the opening it seeks to create by wondering about the double challenge, at once ethical and political, of speculative research. That is, that of developing propositions that take the (im)possible seriously – and may thus risk sounding ludicrous, even outrageous, to those who do not – while simultaneously caring for what Isabelle Stengers (2000: 14) calls 'The Leibnizian Constraint' – the one that demands that philosophy, as well as

14 *M. Savransky et al.*

social and cultural research, 'should not have as its ideal the "reversal of the established sentiments"'. A constraint that ties together:

> truth and becoming and assigns to the statement of what one believes to be true the responsibility not to hinder becoming: not to collide with established sentiments, so as to try to open them to what their established identity let them to refuse, combat, misunderstand.
>
> (Ibid.)

It is under the sign of such a constraint, then, that we hope *Speculative Research* may itself constitute a proposition to our readers. A proposition whose only chance of inducing a becoming of the established patterns of thinking, knowing and feeling that affect our practices must be not that of a general denunciation of what it addresses, but that of a risky attempt to attract their interests – to become capable of luring them to the adventures that possible futures open up.

References

Adam, B., Beck, U., & Van Loon, J. (2000). *The risk society and beyond: Critical Issues for social theory*. London: Sage.

Adam, B., & Groves, C. (2007). *Future matters: Action, knowledge, ethics*. Leiden & Boston: Brill.

Adkins, L., & Lury, C. (2009). Introduction: What is the empirical? *European Journal of Social Theory, 12*(1), 5–20.

Amoore, L. (2013). *The Politics of possibility: Risk and security beyond probability*. Durham, NC and London: Duke University Press.

Amoore, L., & Piotukh, V. (2015). *Algorithmic life: Calculative devices in the age of big data*. London and New York, NY: Routledge.

Atwood, M. (2011). *In other worlds: SF and the human imagination.* London: Virago.

Back, L., & Puwar, N. (2012). *Live methods.* Oxford: Wiley-Blackwell.

Baker, T., & Simon, J. (2002). *Embracing risk: The changing culture of insurance and responsibility*. Chicago: Chicago University Press.

Beck, U. (1992). *Risk society: Towards a new modernity*. London: Sage

Beck, U. (2008). *World at risk*. Cambridge: Polity Press.

Bergson, H. (2002). *Key writings*. London: Continuum.

Brown, N., & Michael, M. (2003). A sociology of expectations: Retrospecting prospects and prospecting retrospects. *Technology Analysis and Strategic Management, 15*(1), 3–18

Brown, N., Rappert, B., & Webster, A. (2000). *Contested futures: A sociology of prospective techno-science*. Farnham: Ashgate.

Bryant, L., Srnicek, N. & Harman, G. (2011). *The speculative turn*. Melbourne: re.press.

Brynin, M. (2013). Individual choice and risk: The case of higher education. *Sociology, 47*(2), 284–300

Connolly, W. 2012. *A world of becoming.* Durham, NC and London: Duke University Press.

Crutzen, P. J., & Stoermer, E. F. (2000). The 'Anthropocene'. *Global Change Newsletter, 41*, 17–18

The lure of possible futures 15

de Goede, M. (2004). Repoliticizing financial risk. *Economy & Society*, *33*(2), 197–217

Debaise, D. (2009). The emergence of speculative empiricism: Whitehead reading Bergson. In K. Robinson (Ed.), *Deleuze, Whitehead, Bergson: Rhizomatic connections* (77–88). Basingstoke and New York: Palgrave Macmillan.

Debaise, D., & Stengers, I. (2015). *Gestes Spéculatifs*. Paris: Presses du réel.

Deleuze, G. (2007). *Two regimes of madness: Texts and interviews 1975–1995*. New York, NY: Semiotext(e).

De Laat, B. (2000). Scripts for the future: Using innovation studies to design foresight tools. In N. Brown, B. Rappert, & A. Webster (Eds), *Contested futures: A sociology of prospective techno-science* (pp. 175–208). Farnham: Ashgate.

Douglas, M. (1992). *Risk and blame: Essays in cultural theory*. London and New York: Routledge.

Ericson, R., & Doyle, A. (2004). Catastrophe, risk, insurance and terrorism. *Economy & Society*, *33*(2), 135–173

Flynn, R., & Bellaby, P. (2007). *Risk and the public acceptance of new technologies*. London: Palgrave.

Gilman, H., & Riley, T. (2002). *The changing of the avant-garde: visionary architectural drawings from the Howard Gilman collection*. New York, NY: Museum of Modern Art.

Grosz, E. (2004). *The nick of time: Politics, evolution, and the untimely*. Durham and London: Duke University Press.

Gunn, J., & Candelaria, M. (2004). *Speculations on speculation: Theories of science fiction*. Lanham, MD: The Scarecrow Press, Inc.

Hacking, I. (1990). *The taming of chance*. Cambridge: Cambridge University Press.

Harman, G. (2013). The current state of speculative realism. *Speculations: A Journal of Speculative Realism*, *IV*, 22–28.

Hunt, M. (2011). *Shakespeare's speculative art*. Basingstoke; New York, NY: Palgrave Macmillan.

James, W. (2011) [1907]. *Pragmatism and the meaning of truth*. Milton Keynes: Watchmakers.

Kerr, A., & Cunningham-Burley S. (2000). On ambivalence and risk: Reflexive modernity and the new human genetics. *Sociology*, *34*(2), 283–204

Koselleck, R. (2004). *Futures past: On the semantics of historical time*. New York, NY: Columbia University Press.

Lang, P., & Menking, W. (2003). *Superstudio: Life without objects*. Skira Milano.

Larner, W., & Walters, W. (2004). *Global governmentality*. London: Routledge.

Latour, B. (1993). *We have never been modern*. Cambridge, MA: Harvard University Press.

Lash, S.; Szerszynski, B., & Wynne, B. (2000). *Risk, environment & modernity: Towards a new ecology*. London: Sage.

Law, J. (2004). *After method: Mess in social science research*. London and New York, NY: Routledge.

Luhmann, N. (1993). *Risk: a sociological theory*. New York: A. de Gruyter.

Lury, C., & Wakeford, N. (2012). *Inventive methods: The happening of the social*. London and New York NY: Routledge.

MacKenzie, D. (2006). *An engine, not a camera*. Cambridge, MA; London: MIT Press.

Meillassoux, Q. (2008). *After finitude: An essay on the necessity of contingency*. London: Continuum.

Melchior-Bonnet, S. (2001). *The mirror: A history*. New York, NY; London: Routledge.

16   *M. Savransky* et al.

Michael, M., & Rosengarten, M. (2013). *Innovation and biomedicine: Ethics, evidence and expectation in HIV*. London: Palgrave.

Miller, P., & Rose, N. (2008). *Governing the present: Administering economic, social and political life*. Cambridge: Polity Press.

Mirowski, P. (2014). *Never let a serious crisis go to waste: How neoliberalism survived the financial meltdown*. London: Verso.

Moore, J. (2015). *Capitalism in the web of life: Ecology and the accumulation of capital*. London and New York, NY: Verso.

O'Malley, P. (2004). *Risk, uncertainty and government*. London: Routledge–Cavendish.

Pemmaraju, S. (2015). Hedge/hog: Speculative action in financial markets. In V. Rao, P. Krishnamurthy, & C. Kuoni (Eds.), *Speculation, now: Essays and artwork* (pp. 52–59). Durham, NC and London: Duke University Press.

Petersen, A., & Wilkinson, I. (2008). *Health, risk and vulnerability*. Oxon: Routledge.

Rao, V.; Krishnamurthy, P., & Kouni, C. (2015). *Speculation, now: Essays and artwork*. Durham, NC & London: Duke University Press.

Rosa, E., Renn, O., & McCright, A. (2014). *The risk society revisited: Social theory and governance*. Philadelphia, PA: Temple University Press.

Savransky, M. (2012). An ecology of times: Modern knowledge, non-modern temporalities. In C. Lawrence, & N. Churn (Eds), *Movements in time: Revolution, social justice, and times of change*. Newcastle: Cambridge Scholars Publishing, 264–271

Savransky, M. (2016). *The adventure of relevance: An ethics of social inquiry*. Basingstoke and New York: Palgrave Macmillan.

Securities, U.S., and Exchange Commission (SECC). (2014). *Equity market structure literature review: Part II: High frequency trading. Staff of the Division of Trading and Markets*.

Selin, C. (2008). The sociology of the future: Tracing stories of technology and time. *Sociology Compass, 2*(6), 1878–1895

Serres, M. (1995). *The natural contract*. Ann Arbor: University of Michigan Press.

Serres, M., & Latour, B. (1995). *Conversations on science, culture, and time*. Ann Arbor: University of Michigan Press.

Sewell, W. (2005). *Logics of history: Social theory and social transformation*. Chicago: The University of Chicago Press.

Stengers, I. (2000). *The invention of modern science*. Minneapolis, MN: University of Minnesota Press.

Stengers, I. (2010). *Cosmopolitics I*. Minneapolis, MN: Minnesota University Press.

Stengers, I. (2015). L'insistence du possible. In D. Debaise, & I. Stengers (Eds), *Gestes Spéculatifs* (pp. 5–22). Paris: Les Presses du Réel.

Strathern, M. (1992). *Reproducing the future: Anthropology, kinship, and the new reproductive technologies*. Manchester: Manchester University Press.

Tulloch, J., & Lupton, D. (2003). *Risk & Everyday Life*. London: Sage.

Uncertain Commons. (2013). *Speculate this!*. Durham, NC and London: Duke University Press.

Valéry, P. (1988). *Regards sur le monde actuel et autres essais*. Paris: Folio Gallimard.

van Lente, H. (1993). Promising technology: The dynamics of expectations in technological developments (PhD thesis, University of Twente).

Whitehead, A. N. (1958). *The function of reason*. Boston: Beacon Press.

Whitehead, A. N. (1967). *Adventures of ideas*. New York: Free Press.

Whitehead, A. N. (1978). *Process and reality: An essay in cosmology*. New York: Free Press.

Wilkie, A. (2010). User assemblages in design: An ethnographic study (PhD thesis, Goldsmiths, University of London).

Wilkie, A., & Michael, M. (2009). Expectation and mobilisation: Enacting future users. *Science Technology Human Values*, *34*(4), 502–522.

Wilkie, A., Michael, M., & Plummer-Fernandez, M. (2015). Speculative method and Twitter: Bots, energy and three conceptual characters. *The Sociological Review*, *63*(1), 79–101.

Wynne, B. (1992). Uncertainty and environmental learning: Reconceiving science and policy in the preventive paradigm. *Global environmental change*, *2*(2), 111–127.

Zegher, M. C. D., & Wigley, M. (2001). *The Activist drawing: Retracing situationist architectures from Constant's New Babylon to beyond*. Cambridge, MA; London: MIT Press.

Part I
Speculative propositions

Introduction

Speculative propositions

*Martin Savransky, Marsha Rosengarten, and
Alex Wilkie*

'Spéculer Tue'

On a warm, sunny afternoon in July, during a research stay in Paris in the
summer of 2013, one of us decided to leave the office and walk alongside the
beautiful canal Saint-Martin, which connects the north-east of the city with
the Place de la République. Filled with people of all ages sitting and chatting by
the canal as well as at the many cafés, bars, and restaurants that set tables on
both sides of its silent waters, it was in every way an idyllic, almost atemporal,
Parisian scene. With one exception – hanging from a window frame on one of
the buildings overlooking the canal, there loomed a home-made banner with
an inscription, hand-written on what looked like an old cloth, that read:
SPÉCULER TUE ('Speculation kills'). Recalling the cognitive-based rhetoric
of health warnings on cigarette packaging, this banner was raising a different
kind of alarm. It constituted a stark reminder of the present we have inherited.
Since the financial crash of 2008, speculation has become something of a radio-
active term, with a striking capacity to turn whatever becomes associated with
it into an object of denunciation, of concern, even of fear. Profoundly dishon-
oured by the ruinous consequences that high-tech, global, late modern capitalism has once again enforced upon the people from whom it feeds, speculation
inhabits the contemporary imagination as a recurrent warning and threat to the
future.

Thus, to propose to venture into modes of thought and research under the sign
of 'speculation' is to run the risk of becoming suspect of a fraudulent alliance,
when not the object of an immediate disqualification. Indeed, while certainly
intensified by recent events, the dangerous connotations of the term recalled by
the banner recur time and time again, from Émile Zola's (1900 [1891]) novel
Money, centred around the disastrous 'fever of speculation' of the late
nineteenth-century Parisian *bourse*, to definitions provided by modern dictionaries, where speculation finds definition only in terms of lack, as a shadow of
would-be modern scientific practices that would otherwise rely on 'firm' evidence or foundations. And while in the modern sciences it may sometimes be
conceded that the speculative constitutes a necessary step towards 'progress',
this concession is expressed in the form of a recognition of what can only be a

22 *M. Savransky* et al.

necessary evil – again, recalling Zola (1900 [1891]: 410) – a form of 'human excess, the necessary manure, the dung-heap from which progress grows'.[1]

If, as advanced in the introduction to the collection, it is here a matter of affirming those literary, artistic, and philosophical traditions for which speculation was not to be exclusively associated with what has constituted this ruinous situation, and thus could not be reduced to the confession of human imprudence; if it is about reactivating those marginalised traditions for which modes of speculation that 'made systems and then transcended them, speculations which ventured to the furthest limits of abstraction' signalled also the necessity of transcending the dangerous abstractions of political economy; if what is at stake is the possibility of relaying the sense that, far from a recurrent threat, speculation has also been the very 'salvation of the world' (Whitehead, 1958: 76), then our most immediate task is that of taking the risk of *reclaiming* speculation from the hands of those that have inscribed it in the deadly histories we have inherited.

Reclaiming

'Reclaiming' seems like a very appropriate term to describe the kinds of propositions that the chapters included in this part construct *for* speculation. For as Philipe Pignarre and Isabelle Stengers (2013: 137) remind us, far from the sense of:

> a crusade against the forces of evil, this word [reclaiming] associates irreducibly to cure and to reappropriate, to learn again and to struggle. Not to say 'it is ours' […], not to think ourselves victims, but to become capable once again of inhabiting the devastating zones of experience.

To reclaim, thus, is to address oneself to some of these histories and terms neither to denounce them, nor to echo their destructive forces, but to struggle and learn again how to resist prolonging them. It is to create new, positive associations and concepts for terms that have been discredited, so as to repurpose and re-propose them, to relaunch them again as propositions capable not of poisoning the present but of cultivating a different kind of future.

This first part gathers together chapters that, in different ways, take up the task of reclaiming other senses of speculation, and of devising novel propositions as to what the speculative may enable us to cultivate today, and tomorrow. In this way, they open up and explore the stakes of a positive and constructive reappraisal of speculative practices, attending both to their potential as well as their dangers and limitations. How can the speculative help to understand the novel interplay and emergence of interests and the transformation of habits of those concerned with the question of how to think, imagine, and act for the future? This is a question provocatively addressed by Martin Savransky's chapter, and creatively expanded upon by Rosalyn Diprose in the chapter that follows.

Introduction: speculative propositions 23

Exploring what he refers to as the 'living paradox' of any mode of thought that addresses itself to the future, namely, the paradox whereby the future 'demands thought, it forces us to think, yet it is by definition beyond the capture of what thinks it', Savransky seeks to reclaim speculation by problematising the modern division between guesswork and forecasting based on 'firm evidence'. By contrast, he argues that to think *for* the future always involves a wager, a leap of faith, or trust. What matters, therefore, 'is not whether one makes a wager in thought, but what *kind* of wager one makes'. By way of an innovative understanding of the pragmatist thought of William James and John Dewey, Savransky thus reclaims speculation as a thinking practice which involves the wager that the present is fundamentally unfinished, and that, while far from submissive to human reason, futures are not indifferent to the thoughts one *proposes* to them. Instead of a necessary evil in the face of uncertainty, Savransky's proposition is that to speculate is to seek to establish a particular kind of *rapport* with futures that enables thinking and futures to become responsive to each other.

Expanding on Savransky's pragmatic defence of speculative thought, Rosalyn Diprose explores the politics of speculation in the field of impact-driven agendas in higher education and in the governance of research, particularly as it concerns research in the humanities. Her attempt to reclaim the political role of the speculative in research and education prompts her to connect the aforementioned traditions of speculative philosophy with the existential phenomenologies of Maurice Merleau-Ponty, Hannah Arendt, and Jean-Luc Nancy, in order to consider the corporeal nature of speculation. In so doing, she argues that speculation operates by virtue of 'inspiration', that is, 'the pulse within the corporeal, affective, and embedded (trans-subjective) fabric of experience', a pulse that, when cultivated, leads to innovation. At a time when innovation and inspiration 'are being depleted by the managerialism and corporatization of our universities', Diprose finds in speculation an urgent political task to reopen paths for thinking, and thus proposes that 'speculative research and speculative thinking are crucial to liberal democracies and democratic pluralism'.

Resituating

Reclaiming is a difficult ethical and political challenge that requires careful modes of attention. Indeed, the chapters in this part and throughout this collection testify to the fact that to reclaim is not merely to celebrate a term as if one could feel free to ignore the histories from which one is seeking to reappropriate it. Reclaiming speculation demands care, and it requires that one devices propositions to relay the potential of this concept in practice, but also that one attends to the constraints with which such propositions may avoid falling prey to the conditions they seek to alter. Addressing 'the danger of generating and venerating an empty concept of speculation', Michael Halewood attends in the third chapter of this part to the need to *situate* speculative practices such that they be developed 'in relation to a specific ground (or problem)', and so that they can recognise the constraints that this ground places on thought. Against the

24   *M. Savransky* et al.

connotations that associate speculation with human excesses and hubris, Halewood proposes a situated mode of speculation whose constraint is that of 'realizing that the world (the cosmos) has its own concerns, some of which involve us (humans) and some of which do not'.

In this way, the chapters in this part take these, and other, questions up in different ways by devising propositions for speculative practices of thought, action, and care. Recognising that some forms of speculation may indeed 'kill', they nevertheless reclaim this notion to attune us to the possibilities that alternative understandings of the speculative may make available for cultivating other ways of thinking, acting, and feeling. In other words, for fostering other modes of *living*.

Note

1 And since judgements and threats are often not easily distinguishable, the message *'spéculer tue'* reappears again today, but no longer in the form of a warning hanging from a window. Rather it has now become the inscription of a best-selling t-shirt by a company (www.spreadshirt.fr) that offers 'personalised' clothing designs, and incites potential consumers not only to buy their designs but to 'make money [...] easy and without risk', by submitting their own.

References

Pignarre, P., & Stengers, I. 2013. *Capitalist sorcery: Breaking the spell.* Basingstoke and New York: Palgrave Macmillan.

Whitehead, A. N. 1958. *The function of reason.* Boston: Beacon Press.

Zola, É. 1900 [1891]. *Money.* London: The Caxton Publishing Company.

2 The wager of an unfinished present

Notes on speculative pragmatism

Martin Savransky

Introduction: a speculative pragmatics of thought

What might be at stake in thinking and imagining *for* a future that may be more than a mere extension of the present? This question, which constitutes the object of exploration of this chapter, demands a moment of pause. What is being asked, and therefore entertained, is neither a general question concerning how the future might be thought 'about', nor how to characterise a mode of thought that could finally hold it still, bring it closer, and interrupt its becoming. To pose the question of how one might go about thinking *for* the future already invites a different set of constraints: ones that seek not to dispel, but to inhabit, the living paradox that the becoming of a future – one that could never be reduced to the present – *demands* thought, it forces us to think, yet it is by definition beyond the capture of what thinks it. This paradox makes present that, whenever futures are concerned, what normally binds thought to principles and reasons that may claim to guarantee its success loses its hold, and we are confronted with what different modes of thinking trust in, that is, with the risks they take.

Although speculation is often disqualified as an unfounded and conjectural mode of thinking about futures, all future-oriented forms of thinking involve assumptions and wagers on the nature of the future, and on the efficacy of thinking and knowing in relation to it. Perhaps what makes those practices of anticipation based on probabilistic inferences 'modern' is thus their disavowal of their own wagers. A disavowal that seeks to replace the risk of trusting with a discourse that, claiming to be the only heir to 'reason', defines and in the process monopolises what counts as reliable 'evidence' for making assertions about social, economic, political, and ecological futures. But such practices make their own wagers too – indeed, they wager on a kind of isomorphism between present and future, whereby the present conditions *in which* the calculations are drawn will be conserved in the future *for which* these calculations are drawn (Hacking, 1990; Whitehead, 1967). Thus, they think for a future that, in relation to what is thought, must be an extension of the present.

The question, then, is not whether one makes a wager in thought, but what *kind* of wager one makes. In this chapter, I aim to explore this question by attending to speculation as a specific kind of wager that thought makes upon the

26 *M. Savransky*

future when futures demand to be thought. The latter, I suggest, prompts us to explore questions which concern the role and efficacy of thinking in and for a world that is neither submissive to human reason and mastery, nor entirely indifferent to it. A world that, as William James (1957 [1890]) famously put it, is blooming and buzzing, being shaped and transformed as its many heterogeneous actors practically intervene in it.

Thus, I want to experiment with the possibility that speculation might provide us with a key not into 'the absolute', for which relations, and their consequences, do not matter, but into a certain pragmatics of thought. A pragmatics which is not just or only an attempt to say that thinking is, alas, a practice too, but to suggest that speculation is a singular and specific thinking practice, one whose business is, as Whitehead, (1958 [1929]: 82) phrased it, 'to make thought creative of the future'. If, however, we are to inhabit the living paradox of a future that simultaneously demands thought but never allows itself to be completely captured by it, it is necessary that we pay careful attention to how this 'creative' practice might be conceived. I want to propose that, for a speculative pragmatics of thought, to be creative of the future cannot be read in the key of an idealism that would take the powers of thought for granted. Rather, it must be addressed in the manner of an experiment, whose mode of operation depends on the wager it makes, and whose success is never guaranteed. My aim here, then, is to experiment with some of the requirements and possibilities of what might be at stake in developing a mode of thought which proposes itself *to* a future that may be more than a mere extension of our present. In so doing, I will develop a reading of some aspects of the work of two thinkers who learned how to take seriously what connects thinking not to principles and foundations, but to an art of consequences – namely, the early American pragmatists John Dewey and William James – in order to elucidate and specify some of the practical dimensions of what might be called a 'speculative pragmatism' (for a connection between Whitehead's 'speculation' and Charles S. Peirce's concept of 'abduction', see Parisi, 2012).

Indeed, I will suggest that, despite what the dominant reception of pragmatism in social theory would have us acknowledge, Dewey's and James' philosophies of experience, and their discussions of the logic of inquiry, and the role of concepts in experience, respectively, may offer us a productive, experimental understanding of speculation that creates new demands, and new responsibilities, for philosophy and social theory. Conversely, a reading of pragmatism in a speculative key might provide a different understanding of their pragmatic propositions. In so doing, I will contend that speculation can be conceived as a wager on an unfinished present, whose potential is that of cultivating thinking to lure experience – at once natural, social, cultural, political – to take the risk of opening up to its own becoming.

Experience, science and thought: a pragmatist plea for speculative audacity

While pragmatism has recently undergone something of a renaissance, which has opened the work of its foundational authors to novel interpretations (e.g.

The wager of an unfinished present 27

Debaise, 2007), to seek to disclose a mode of speculation from the work of the early American pragmatists might still sound to many like a contradiction in terms. Indeed, throughout the twentieth century, pragmatism has been understood as a characteristically anti-speculative philosophy. Were not the pragmatists those who proposed that we should care for (the truth of) ideas only in relation to the 'cash-value' they report, that is, only in so far as they 'work' by 'helping us to get into satisfactory relation with other parts of our experience'? (James 2011[1907]: 33). Were they not the ones who flirted with a certain scientism, depositing a blind faith in the capacities of what they called 'the scientific method', to become a vector in the progress of thought (e.g. Dewey, 2008 [1929])? Were they not, after all, radical anti-intellectualists who proposed that concepts are, by definition, ultimately inadequate, seeking to discreetly contain a reality that is in fact continuous (James, 1996 [1911])? Even Whitehead (1978: xii), who was otherwise never short of praise for the pragmatists, expressed his preoccupation to 'rescue their type of thought from the charge of anti-intellectualism, which rightly or wrongly has been associated with it'.

In light of much of the historical reception that early pragmatist thought has enjoyed throughout the course of the twentieth century, and especially in relation to social theory (Joas, 1993), it might seem somewhat surprising to find that in a later essay by John Dewey (2008 [1927]: 10, emphasis added) titled 'Philosophy and Civilization', he makes what surely deserves the name of a cry, a plea that is *at once* speculative and pragmatic. A plea, in other words:

> for the casting off of that intellectual timidity which hampers the wings of imagination, a *plea for speculative audacity*, for more faith in ideas, sloughing off a cowardly reliance upon partial ideas to which we are wont to give the name of facts.

What, one might be tempted to ask, can possibly be the meaning of such a plea in the context of pragmatist thought? How might one put such a stark plea to the test? What kind of test might be relevant to it (Savransky, 2016)? It seems to me that, in this case, there is only one way to provide an answer to such a question while at the same time taking it seriously. To construct a relevant test for it, one must take the risk of putting it to its own pragmatic test. That is, to experiment with the possible implications of such a plea by affirming, pragmatically, that the only 'meaning' it can have is no other than the difference it makes when it is put to the test of our experience, in this case, of our experience of pragmatist thought.

In order to take the risk of thinking with the difference that Dewey's speculative plea can make, one must first recall and come to terms with what perhaps constitutes James's and Dewey's most foundational commitment. Namely, their investment in a radical empiricism that, as James (2003 [1912]: 22) famously put it, 'must neither admit into its constructions any element that is not directly experienced, nor exclude from them any element that is directly experienced'. A form of empiricism that regards experience itself as neither fixed nor fully

28   *M. Savransky*

contained in thought, as a dynamic plane on which, through which, thinking is cultivated, articulated, and transformed. Experience, James (2011 [1907]) would insist, comes in drops: it is active, dynamic, and ever-changing, producing thought and putting it to its own tests and novel demands. Experience, in other words, 'has ways of *boiling over*, and making us correct our present formulas' (James, 2011 [1907]: 142).

To approach the question of thinking in this empiricist way already makes perceptible two important consequences. First, and unlike various rationalist traditions for which thought sustains a structuring relationship to experience, for pragmatists, thoughts are felt. Thoughts, in the concrete, 'are made of the same stuff as things are' *and must themselves be experienced* (James 2003 [1912]: 20). Thus, no account of thought that seeks to take experience seriously can presuppose a thinker as an 'observer' in retreat from the flux of reality but must conceive of thinking itself as a component in the fact of experience. Thinking is always thinking with and in the midst of experience, becoming taken by an intellectual experience such that 'the thought is itself the thinker, and psychology needs not look beyond'. (James, 1957 [1890]: 401).

Second, the drop-like, processual character of experiences that have ways of boiling over forces us to resist any temptation to make thought into a final operation that might be capable of capturing experience once and for all. 'Canst thou by searching describe the Universe?' (Whitehead, 1967: 145) – while such a question is deeply ingrained in the history of modern thought, the pragmatist answer to it must be a resolute 'no.' There are no thoughts, or concepts, capable of adequately capturing the dynamic complexity of relationships in the world of experience. To claim the opposite is to incur in what Whitehead (ibid.) rightly termed 'The Dogmatic Fallacy'. One cannot produce thoughts capable of capturing experience once and for all, but in the case of pragmatism this incapacity tells us less about the finitude of human thought than about the deambulatory character of experience itself, both within and beyond the human. Error and the fallibility of thoughts pose no transcendental tragedies. Rather, they become inescapable events in every process of thought and knowledge, reminding us that experience boils over thought, and sometimes thought boils over experience. To the extent that thought is no longer outside experience, but it is part and parcel of an experienced world, all thinking is experimental. It unfolds and develops by way of connections and transitions that always involve the risk of a test whose criteria of success and failure are always immanent to the experiential mutation made possible by the connection in question.

I believe it is such a deeply empiricist account of thinking, and not any form of scientism, that explains the interest in scientific inquiry that characterises most patently the work of John Dewey, and more ambivalently, that of William James. Indeed, it is not, as commentators of pragmatism over the years have complained, that a certain scientific ethic provided the grounds for a pragmatist philosophy of life *tout court* (for a critical exploration of this claim see Manicas, 1988). Rather, it was the experimental logic of inquiry, instead of the dogmatic idealism of nineteenth-century philosophical inquiry, that pragmatists saw as

The wager of an unfinished present 29

being already modelled upon immediate, everyday experience. In other words, because for both James and Dewey all experience is experimental, the so-called 'scientific method' provided a systematic and highly developed means of approaching the question of practical and intellectual experimentation. At stake, therefore, was the audacious production of a mode of thought that instead of forcing experience to stand still in order to claim cognitive victory over it, could partake in the flow of experience, contributing to the latter's mutating, surprising, and novel drops.

In this sense, the whole of Dewey's *Reconstruction in Philosophy* (2004 [1948]), for instance, may be read as an attempt to transform the longstanding dreams of a philosophy concerned with capturing that which is 'immutable' and 'eternal'. An attempt at transforming the dreams of philosophers so that the latter might become relevant to a new world characterised by the ingression of modern scientific discoveries in technology, society, and politics. Such discoveries and operations, in his view, forced one to 'abandon the assumption of fixity and to recognize that what for it is actually "universal" is *process*' (Dewey, 2004 [1948]: vii–viii, emphasis in original):

> Until the dogma of fixed unchangeable types and species, of arrangement in classes of higher and lower, of subordination of the transitory individual to the universal or kind had been shaken in its hold upon the science of life, it was impossible that the new ideas and method should be made at home in social and moral life. Does it not seem to be the intellectual task of the twentieth century to take this step? When this step is taken the circle of scientific development will be rounded out and the reconstruction of philosophy be made an accomplished fact.

Similarly, and although James was arguably less invested in science than Dewey was (Gavin, 1992), he too thought that no philosophy, be it natural or moral, could ignore scientific discoveries and methods, nor the buzzing world they make perceptible. Thus, in his famous essay on ethics, 'The Moral Philosopher and the Moral Life', he argued that 'ethical science is just like physical science, and instead of being deducible all at once from abstract principles, must simply bide its time, and be ready to revise its conclusions from day to day' (James 1956 [1897]: 208).

The importance of reclaiming a pragmatist logic of experimentation in philosophy was not, however, only a matter of asserting the processual nature of reality. Although this remains no minor accomplishment, even to this day. Crucially, the logic of experimentation also made available an escape from the classical philosophical conundrum of trying to explain the process of knowing by means of a theory of consciousness, as if the latter would be so unproblematic a concept as to be capable of doing any 'explaining'. The 'problem of consciousness' for pragmatism is clear enough: any theory of knowledge that presupposes consciousness as an entity, as the very onto-psychological 'stuff' that makes knowledge possible, is forced to bifurcate reality into things-in-themselves, on

30   *M. Savransky*

the one hand, and the thought-of-things on the other. It is forced, in other words, to split the world into subject and object as absolute ontological terms. Radical empiricism, however, conceives of experience –'pure experience' in James (2003 [1912]); 'primary experience' in Dewey (1929) – not as that which a pre-existent phenomenological subject undergoes, but as the very fabric of which the world – including subjects and objects – is made. As David Lapoujade (2000, 2007) has rightly suggested, pure experience is neither subjective nor objective, but the 'material' out of which such distinctions are carved. As he puts it, the notion of:

> material does not allow itself to be conceived according to a matter/form relationship, no more than it can be said to be contained within the categories subject/object, matter/thought, etc. It is directly physical-mental. Material is neither Matter, nor Thought, though it is the fabric of both.
>
> (Lapoujade, 2000: 194)

In this account, consciousness cannot explain the process of knowing because it already needs to be conceived as a specific relational process – itself experienced – by which the material drops of experience become connected. A connection through which 'one of its "terms" becomes the subject or bearer of the knowledge, the knower, the other becomes the object known' (James, 2003 [1912]: 3). The thought is itself the thinker. Thought is an event of experience and as such it is not presupposed by consciousness. Rather, 'thought goes on', and it is the concept of consciousness which itself presupposes the going-on of thought (James 1957 [1890]: 225).

In this way, knowledge and thought do involve, but can hardly be reduced to, questions of cognition. They are, first and foremost, matters of practice and inquiry – of all those practices that contribute to the connection of elements in experience so that some of those elements can be said to be 'known' while others can be said to 'know'. It is this practical approach to thought that the logic of experimentation allows one to elucidate. As I will suggest, speculation, as an experimental mode of thinking, does not stand outside experience. Rather, it is itself a going-on of experience that, by cultivating its material in the mode of imaginative propositions, seeks to create the possibility of an experimental faith in the transformation of experience. Speculative pragmatism, then, designates an experimental mode of harnessing experience such that new intelligent connections among things may become possible.

The wager of an unfinished present: on speculative experimentation

To speculate, then, is to relate experimentally to experience. It is, in other words, to enable experience itself to take the risk of trusting its own becoming. Let us therefore explore in more depth just what might be at stake in this practice of 'speculative experimentation'. As Dewey put it in *The Quest for Certainty* (2008 [1929]: 63, emphasis in original):

The wager of an unfinished present 31

[Experimental inquiries] exhibit three outstanding characteristics. The first is the obvious one that all experimentation involves *overt* doing, the making of definite changes in the environment or in our relation to it. The second is that experiment is not a random activity but is directed by ideas which have to meet the conditions set by the need of the problem inducing the active inquiry. The third and concluding feature, in which the other two receive their full measure of meaning, is that the outcome of the directed activity is the construction of a new empirical situation in which objects are differently related to one another, and such that the *consequences* of directed operation form the objects that have the property of being *known*.

This is a rich and complex description, the full implications of which I hope will become clearer as this text proceeds. For the moment it is worth noting that while, for Dewey, the experimental production of ideas that might direct practices is already a crucial ingredient in any process of knowledge-making, it itself can be conceived in those terms too. In other words, what the pragmatist sense of experimentation makes present is that the experience of thought is not only one of *being felt* but also one of *feeling*. Thinking is not only passively empirical but also actively experimental, and it emerges whenever the present confronts one with perplexing facts, with difficulties that demand creative attention and the production of alternative patterns of contrast for, and of new forms of trust in, the construction of new empirical situations. As Dewey (2004 [1948]: 80) suggests elsewhere:

men *(sic)* do not, in their natural estate, think when they have no troubles to cope with, no difficulties to overcome. A life of ease, of success without effort, would be a thoughtless life, and so also would a life of ready omnipotence. Beings who think are beings whose life is so hemmed in and constricted that they cannot directly carry through a course of action to victorious consummation.

Not any problem, however, demands to be thought. In fact, for Dewey, whenever a problem is 'completely actual and present, we are overwhelmed. We do not think, but give way to depression.' (ibid.: 82) In contrast, for it to demand the practice of thought a problem needs to present itself as an 'impending problem', one that makes felt an *unfinished present* that is incomplete and developing, orienting us to what is yet to come. To that extent, ' "[t]hought" represents the suggestions of a way of response that is different from that which would have been followed if intelligent observation had not effected an inference as to the future' (ibid.: 83).

In this account, thus, speculative thought constitutes a mode of experimentation whose aim is that of producing suggestions, propositions, or ideas that, by trusting the possible, might offer the necessary guidance to produce a different mode of response to an impending problem. As an experimental practice, the aim of speculation is to transform the trajectory of transitioning between present

32   *M. Savransky*

and future by providing an alternative path towards a novel empirical situation – towards a new experience. It is characterised by a form of creative responsiveness to problems that make the future itself depend upon the propositions that may be constructed for it. As such, speculative experimentation is necessarily attentive to the facts and it seeks a going-on that may stem from the possibilities that the facts, and their relations, themselves make perceptible.

In other words, to the extent that thinking, in this experimental account, can be said to be speculative, it should not be thought of simply as a practice of wild imagination. For there is 'a distinction between hypotheses generated in that seclusion from observable fact which renders them fantasies, and hypotheses that are projections of the possibilities of facts already in existence and capable of report' (Dewey, 2008 [1929]: 63). And while the term 'speculation' often is a term of abuse, one used to pejoratively characterise a practice that respects no constraints or is unconcerned with real events, to speak of speculative experimentation is precisely to highlight the fact that the consequences of those 'imaginative speculations that recognize no law except their own dialectic consistency' may be markedly different from those 'which rest on an observable movement of events, and which foresee these events carried to a limit by the force of their own movement'. (ibid.) For while the former begin from 'arbitrarily assumed premises', and indeed rely on the dogmatic image that such premises afford in order to ascertain themselves, the ground of speculative experimentation is the problematic form that the material of experience can take, and its task is thus to set forth 'the implications of propositions resting upon facts already vitally significant'. (ibid.).

Thus, for speculation to enable experience to trust its own becoming, to develop from impending problems propositions whose implications may contribute to the construction of an alternative future, speculative experimentation retains a humility to facts without however succumbing to them. Its own internal risk is that of becoming capable of developing an imagination that combines the freedom of the possible with the stubbornness of actuality. Like all forms of experimentation, speculation involves a wager, which in this case, is perhaps the most creative one, in the sense at least that without it the meaning of very idea of 'creativity' begins to fade. *To speculate, thus, is to wager on the unfinished nature of the present.* For this reason, it encounters the facts of experience not as final but as the very material for speculation, as themselves exhibiting the possibility of an alternative that demands creative modes of intellectual experimentation. Is this speculative operation not the one that James (1996 [1911]: 65, emphasis in original) himself endowed concepts with, namely, that of '*harness[ing]* perceptual reality [...] in order to drive it better to our ends'? As he put it:

> Had we no concepts we would live simply 'getting' each successive moment of experience, as the sessile sea-anemone on its rock receives whatever nourishment the wash of the waves may bring. With concepts we go in quest of the absent, meet the remote, actively turn this way or that, bend our

The wager of an unfinished present   33

experience, and make it tell us whither it is bound. We change its order, run it backwards, jump about over its surface instead of plowing through its continuity string its items on as many ideal diagrams as our mind can frame. All these are ways of *handling* the perceptual flux and *meeting* distant parts of it.
(James, 1996 [1911]: 64)

The attention to fact and the harnessing of speculative flights by the risky development of real possibilities are thus crucial requirements of such form of experimental speculation, but as anyone who is minimally familiar with the practices of the experimental sciences might anticipate, there is yet a third element that needs to be taken into account whenever speculation is approached as an experiment in thinking. And this is that there is no experimentation, in the strong sense of the term, without a practice of putting to the test (Stengers, 2000). Indeed, as the tradition of pragmatism has always been at pains to stress, the whole meaning and value of a practice, be it intellectual or otherwise, lies in the *differences it makes.* In other words, a speculative pragmatism cannot be understood without first entertaining the question of what, following Isabelle Stengers (2011), I associate with 'speculative efficacy' – the question of the differences speculations make with regards to the experiences they connect.

The question of speculative efficacy: speculation, truth, and the test of thought

Insofar as the radical empiricism underpinning the work of James and Dewey obligates us to account for anything and everything that is experienced, it also simultaneously situates experience itself as the risk that any speculative proposition, concept, and idea must confront. Speculation emerges from the fabric of experience and its primary aim is to return to it, albeit in a transformed way. Indeed, to place experience as the very test of thought involves rescuing the latter from the hands of logicians, who have reduced the question of the efficacy of ideas and theories to a doctrine according to which 'their one function is to be judged as to their truth or falsehood' (Whitehead, 1978: 184). Instead, both for the pragmatists and for Whitehead, judgements as to the truth of a proposition are always secondary and 'very rare' components in their effects. By contrast, their primary function is that of becoming 'a lure for feeling', of effecting a transformation in experience:

> The existence of imaginative literature should have warned logicians that their narrow doctrine is absurd. It is difficult to believe that all logicians as they read Hamlet's speech, 'To be, or not to be: …' commence by judging whether the initial proposition be true or false, and keep up the task of judgement throughout the whole thirty-five lines. Surely, at some point in the reading, judgement is eclipsed by aesthetic delight. The speech, for the theatre audience, is purely theoretical, a mere lure for feeling.
> (Whitehead, 1978: 185)

34 M. Savransky

In other words, if speculative experimentations are to become worthy of attention – not to mention of actually taking the risks associated with them – it is not, primarily, because of a truth they might succeed in making manifest, but because of a difference they might be capable of effecting, a mode of becoming felt that might induce a transition into a new empirical situation.

As heirs and explorers of the experimental logic of inquiry, however, the concept of 'truth' and its meanings had actually much stronger a hold on pragmatists than it had on Whitehead. But it did not do so without at the same time undergoing a radical transformation of its implications, without a metamorphosis of the way in which 'truth' as such might take hold. For the truth of a proposition, in the pragmatic sense, is but *one particular manner in which they make themselves felt*, such that truth means nothing if not the extent to which an idea or a proposition 'agrees' with reality:

> Any idea that helps us to deal, whether practically or intellectually, with either the reality or its belongings, that doesn't entangle our progress in frustrations, that *fits*, in fact, and adapts our life to the reality's whole setting, will agree sufficiently to meet the requirement. It will be true of that reality.
> (James, 2011 [1907]: 141–142)

Such a transformation, whose apparent simplicity risks making it radically misleading, has in fact always remained a locus of contestation and resistance around their work. Indeed, while for some it represented an outrageous form of instrumentalism, for others, to whom such a definition read as a kind of quirky formulation of a classical correspondence theory of truth, the pragmatist version was seen to be a veiled flirtation with logical positivism. In this latter case, an experimental success, which constitutes the very test of the efficacy of a hypothesis, has a retroactive effect. Namely, it functions by suggesting that, insofar as the techno-intellectual operations have been successful in attracting the interest of those the hypothesis addressed and did so just in the way it had predicted their attraction, the proof that success is seen to offer is one that speaks to the truth of *the hypothesis*. A truth, then, that is antecedent to the time frame of human knowledge, which is to say, that precedes the experiment itself (Stengers, 2010). Understood in this way we might conclude – wrongly – that, as critics of pragmatism have repeatedly stated, if the proposition associated with an experimental success 'agrees' with reality it also 'corresponds' to it – its operation is that of disclosing some unchanging, intrinsic aspect of the world that precedes the experience itself. To recall Bertrand Russell's (1912: 201–202) classic formulation of the correspondence theory:

> the condition of the truth of a belief is something not involving beliefs [...] but only the objects of the belief. A mind, which believes, believes truly when there is a *corresponding* complex not involving the mind, but only its objects. This correspondence ensures truth, and its absence entails falsehood.

The wager of an unfinished present 35

Entertained against the backdrop of an attempt – itself speculative – to make a speculative pragmatism possible, however, it becomes clear that confusing James's theory of truth with a matter of 'correspondence' is a mistake. I believe the pragmatist theory of truth can be read in a different, much more interesting light. If the practice of speculative experimentation constitutes, as I argued above, a wager on the unfinishedness of the present, if it is an operation whose business is that of making thought *creative of an alternative future* by producing an inventive response to an impending problem and by putting experience to the test of its own *becoming*, then to suggest that the 'truth' of a speculative proposition depends upon its correspondence with a pre-existing complex of objects or state of affairs, would be simply absurd.

To be sure, insofar as both James and Dewey assume a processual account of experience, no operation performed upon the latter that is itself experienced can testify to a state of affairs that preceded it. To insist upon truth, then, is to retain the risk that characterises every form of experimentation while abandoning the modern metaphysics that underpinned it. Indeed, what this tension makes present, is that to the extent that speculative ideas may become 'factors in the fact of experience' (Whitehead, 1958 [1929]: 80), or 'integral factors in actions which change the face of the world' (Dewey, 2008 [1929]: 111), the test of speculative thought is not performed against a world such thinking would be said to uncover, but against the one to which it has already contributed to composing by means of its own addition to it. It is for this reason that we can say without contradiction and without cynicism, that the truth of speculative propositions is a matter of *efficacy*. A matter of the efficacy of a proposition to enter, and in its entering *infect*, the very manner in which the world 'goes on'. As Stengers (2011: 510) proposes, the concept of 'infection' designates the way in which different parts of the world enter into, and prehend, each other, and the success of such a process of infection:

> implies the co-adaptation of values. When a being endures, what has succeeded is a co-production between this being and 'its' environment. This environment is nothing other than the totality of beings taken into account and valorized in a determinate way, and each of the valorized beings prehends the taking-into-account of which it has been the object, the role that has been assigned to it, in a way that is not incompatible with the maintenance of this mode of prehension, or this role.
>
> (Stengers, 2011: 158)

To my mind, it is in this *infectious* manner that the term 'agreement' should be read in James' pragmatic theory of truth. This is also what Dewey (2008 [1929]: 109) means when he suggests that '[t]he test of ideas, of thinking generally, is found in the consequences of the acts to which the ideas lead, that is in the new arrangements of things which are brought into existence.' In other words, whenever speculative experimentation is at stake, the pragmatist theory of truth should not be thought of as a correspondence theory that would relate the success of a

36 *M. Savransky*

speculative proposition to a state of affairs that could be said to precede it, but presents itself as what I would here call, tentatively, a *corresponsive* theory of truth. For what is put to the test is the transformation of experience enabled by the speculative proposition itself – the degree and the manner in which all those parts of the world to which the proposition connects have agreed to become infected by it, to meet the requirements it poses, while simultaneously infecting *it*, forcing it to take its own world into account.

That is why:

> [t]he truth of an idea is not a stagnant property inherent in it. Truth *happens* to an idea. It *becomes* true, is *made* true by events. Its verity *is* in fact an event, a process, the process namely of verifying itself, its veri*fication.*
>
> (James, 2011 [1907]: 141, emphasis in original)

Thus, a speculative proposition becomes 'true' to the extent that it succeeds in *infecting* its environment while allowing itself to become infected by it. Indeed, it seems to me that the 'truth' of a proposition is nowhere to be found if not in the very process whereby a proposition and its world begin, little by little, drop by drop, to respond to each other. What, at the end of the day, deserves to be called 'true', is the event of the future experience that such an exchange has enabled to come into existence.

Trust in the possible: speculative pragmatism for a world of *ifs*

To characterise the test of the efficacy of speculation in this way is to suggest, then, that making thought creative of the future involves indeed a *wager* and not a process of unilateral 'production' or 'performativity' that simply takes the effect of our efforts for granted (cf. Law & Urry, 2004). To take the risk of enabling experience to be put to the risk of its own becoming is simultaneously to acknowledge that what is at stake is the very manner in which a future may come into existence, and that, as James (1996 [1911]: 229, emphasis in original) expressed it, its coming into existence depends not just on the power of the proposition itself, but on 'a pluralism of independent powers'. A speculative proposition, then, is neither self-sufficient nor almighty, but shall succeed only *if* others, with whom the proposition may be concerned, contribute to its success:

> Its destiny thus hangs on an *if*, or on a lot of *ifs* – which amounts to saying (in the technical language of logic) that, the world being as yet unfinished, its total character can be expressed only by *hypothetical* and not by *categorical* propositions. [...] As individual members of a pluralistic universe, we must recognize that, even though we do *our* best, the other factors also will have a voice in the result. If they refuse to conspire, our good-will and labor may be thrown away. No insurance company can here cover us or save us from the risks we run in being part of such a world.
>
> (Ibid.)

The wager of an unfinished present 37

Thus, speculating in a pluralistic, processual world, in a world whose destiny hangs by a lot of *ifs*, involves the wager, but never the promise, that the future itself might agree to respond to what one might *propose* to it. As I have suggested, such a wager on the possibility that a proposition and its world may begin to respond to each other itself calls for a new kind of responsibility. That of a manner of proposing that, once launched into the developing edge of the present, may itself be responsive to the world's own mode of replication, such collective responses to the impending problems that present poses may be possible. If, as Whitehead (1958 [1929]: 76) had emphatically claimed, 'abstract speculation has been the salvation of the world' such that '[t]o set limits to speculation is treason to the future', I suggest that it is not because of any guarantees that some speculative logic or method may provide. Indeed, it provides none. Rather, setting limits to speculation betrays the future because there is no 'future', that comes about without a speculative wager, without risking a thinking-experience by trusting in the possibility that a world might become responsive to our efforts.

References

Debaise, D. (2007). *Vie et Experimentation: Peirce, James, Dewey.* Paris: Vrin.
Dewey, J. (2008 [1927]). *Essays, reviews, miscellany, and 'impressions of Soviet Russia'. The later works 1925–1953, Vol. 3.* Carbondale, IL: Southern Illinois University Press.
Dewey, J. (1929). *Experience and nature.* Chicago, IL: Open Court.
Dewey, J. (2008 [1929]). *The quest for certainty. The later works 1925–1953, Vol. 4.* Carbondale, IL: Southern Illinois University Press.
Dewey, J. (2004 [1948]). *Reconstruction in philosophy.* Mineola, NY: Dover Publications.
Gavin, W. J. (1992). *William James and the reinstatement of the vague.* Philadelphia, PA: Temple University Press.
Hacking, I. (1990). *The taming of chance.* Cambridge: Cambridge University Press.
James, W. (1957 [1890]). *The principles of psychology: Vol 1.* Mineola, NY: Dover Publications.
James, W. (1956 [1897]). *The will to believe and other essays in popular philosophy.* Mineola, NY: Dover Publications.
James, W. (2011 [1907]). *Pragmatism and the meaning of truth.* Milton Keynes: Watchmakers Publishers.
James, W. (1996 [1911]). *Some problems of philosophy.* Lincoln, NE, London: University of Nebraska Press.
James, W. (2003 [1912]). *Essays in radical empiricism.* Mineola, NY: Dover Publications.
Joas, H. (1993). *Pragmatism and social theory.* Chicago, IL: The University of Chicago Press.
Lapoujade, D. (2000). From transcendental empiricism to worker nomadism: William James. *Pli, 9,* 190–199
Lapoujade, D. (2007). *William James: Empirisme et pragmatisme.* Paris: Les Empêcheurs de Penser en Rond.
Law, J., & Urry, J. (2004). Enacting the social. *Economy & Society, 33*(3), 390–410

38   *M. Savransky*

Manicas, P. (1988). Pragmatic philosophy of science and the charge of scientism. *Transactions of the Charles S. Peirce Society*, *24*(2), 179–222

Parisi, L. (2012). Speculation, a method for the unattainable. In C. Lury, & N. Wakeford (Eds.), *Inventive methods: The happening of the social* (pp. 232–244). London: Routledge,

Russell, B. (1912). *The problems of philosophy.* New York, NY: Henry Holt & Co.

Savransky, M. (2016). *The adventure of relevance: An ethics of social inquiry.* Basingstoke, New York, NY: Palgrave Macmillan.

Stengers, I. (2000). *The invention of modern science.* Minneapolis, MN: University of Minnesota Press.

Stengers, I. (2010). *Cosmopolitics I.* Minneapolis, MN: University of Minnesota Press.

Stengers, I. (2011). *Thinking with Whitehead: A free and wild creation of concepts.* Cambridge, MA: Harvard University Press.

Whitehead, A. N. (1958 [1929]). *The function of reason.* Boston, MA: Beacon Press.

Whitehead, A. N. (1967). *Adventures of ideas.* New York, NY: Free Press

Whitehead, A. N. (1978). *Process and reality.* New York, NY: Free Press.

3 Speculative research, temporality and politics

Rosalyn Diprose

Introduction: politics and the meaning of speculation

A cornerstone of the election campaign of Tony Abbott's Conservative Coalition, prior to winning government in the 2013 Australian federal election, was the promise to cut wasteful expenditure. Examples of wasteful expenditure given included specific kinds of research projects funded by the Australian Research Council.[1] Three of the four projects cited were 'speculative' in that they involved philosophizing rather than empirical research, and were engaged with (speculative) ideas and thinkers from Continental Philosophical traditions. The reason implied in the claim that such research is a 'waste of tax payers money' was that, unlike empirical research, speculative research does not yield concrete outcomes of any obvious social, public health, or economic national benefit. Against this instrumentalism and anti-intellectualism, I argue in this chapter that speculative research and speculative thinking, as defined by Isabelle Stengers following Alfred North Whitehead, are crucial to liberal democracies, partly because speculative thinking lies at the heart of political agency and is also the basis of innovation. I hope thereby to continue the task that Martin Savransky undertakes in Chapter 2 of this volume and that he eloquently describes as a practical defence of thinking and its efficacy.

What Whitehead and Stengers mean by 'speculation' departs from conventional meanings, of which there are three currently in use:

1   Hypothesizing and *thinking* as introspective reflection. In modern philosophy speculative (or 'pure') *reason* is usually defined as theoretical (deductive) thought, as opposed to practical thought (or willing). More generally, within a dualistic ontology (which Whitehead describes as the 'bifurcation of nature' into 'objective' and 'subjective' dimensions),[2] speculative thinking refers to the generation of ideas in the mind (the 'subjective' realm) about nature and the world 'out there' (the 'objective' realm) through abstract reflection rather than empirical evidence. In its Cartesian form, speculation as thinking is equivalent to 'introspection', a model of self-relation that is rejected by all the philosophers that I draw on here on the basis that it perpetuates our alienation from the worlds in which we dwell.[3]

40 *R. Diprose*

2 Speculation also means *prediction* – the act of forecasting future events based on current trends.

3 *Investing* – purchasing stocks, shares or property in the hope of financial gain, but with the risk of loss.

There is a spatial paradox that haunts the first of these three conventional meanings: even though, in its Cartesian version, speculative thinking is understood as a process that is supposedly abstracted from the empirical ('objective') world, the concept itself shares a root with 'specular' (of vision) and thereby borrows significance from the sense that, for empiricists, is the most reliable means of putting us in touch with the world for the purpose of knowledge production. Hence, speculative thinking cannot escape some kind of contact with the material world it is said to bypass. There is also a temporal paradox apparent in all three meanings. On the one hand, speculation, on any definition, is futural: it keeps open (past and present) worlds to potentiality, possibility, and the unknown. On the other hand, the second and third conventional meanings of speculation, predicting and investing, aim at foresight, that is, at knowing and thereby capturing the future in advance (which, in Nietzsche's view, is tantamount to killing off the future). Speculation in the first sense of introspective thinking also kills the future insofar as thinking remains closed to alternative ideas and paths of thinking and, therefore, to possibility per se. In *Process and Reality* Whitehead says this notion of temporality that implies a dead-end is also true of empiricism when it is set up in opposition to speculative thinking: empiricism's scientific method of 'induction' is 'a method which, if consistently pursued, would have left science where it found it' (1978: 5).

In contrast, speculation, for Whitehead and Stengers, and thinking, as understood by Martin Heidegger, Maurice Merleau-Ponty, and Hannah Arendt, are futural, without a predictable outcome. Their ideas of speculative thinking also address the spatial paradox arising from the bifurcation of nature. Whitehead, for example, brings empiricism (based on 'experience') and rationalism (based on 'ideality') together in defining 'Speculative Philosophy' as 'the endeavour to frame a coherent, logical, necessary system of general ideas in terms of which every element of our experience can be interpreted' (1978: 3). In Stengers' interpretation of Whitehead, speculative research becomes decidedly unpredictable: it is an 'adventure' in ideas, a process of reformulating problems in ways that throw up new perspectives from experience, or, in her words, speculation involves 'invention of the field in which the problem finds a solution' (2011a: 16–17). Speculative philosophy invents schemas, or what Whitehead calls 'descriptive generalizations' (1978: 14), that allow a 'flight' of 'imagination' that is 'free' but also constrained in that 'it again lands for renewed observation rendered acute by rational interpretation' (1978: 5). More in keeping with the idea of speculative research towards which I'm heading, Stengers suggests that these 'descriptive generalizations' are derived from experience but, as 'experiment[s] in which our habits are both ingredient and target', they open new ways of thinking and of interpreting experience (2011b: 294). For instance,

Speculative research, temporality and politics 41

Whitehead's speculations regarding the ontological nature of the organism provide a way of refiguring problems that remain unresolved within schemas that entrench the 'bifurcation of nature'. The point for now is that this speculative research opens up possibilities for experience, it is futural, and the outcomes are unpredictable.

This is the kind of speculation that I argue is crucial to political agency, democratic pluralism, and innovation. Yet, not only is it under constant threat from the culture of prediction and investment, it can also be undermined by politics itself. There is a tendency among conservative democratic governments to attempt to control speculation, not only by insisting that public funding of research be restricted to projects that politicians deem 'useful' with 'high (quantifiable) impact', but also by the government take-over of prediction in general. Arendt argues that a key indicator of the rise of totalitarianism is when political rhetoric of economic and territorial insecurity is combined with government insisting on its own competence in predicting the future, quelling the unpredictable, and thereby securing the future in advance (1994: 468–471; 1998: 42–45). A banal example of this in contemporary Australia is the government use of the so-called 'Intergenerational Report'. Produced every five years, this report 'assesses the long-term sustainability of current Government policies and how changes to Australia's population size and age profile may impact on economic growth, workforce and public finances over the next 40 years'.[4] Wildly speculative but apparently scientific in its predictions, the report was used in 2015, by the then Treasurer Joe Hockey, to justify budget cuts to public spending in health, welfare, and education.

While accepting the kernel of Whitehead and Stengers' approaches to speculative philosophy and speculative research, I explore the connection between speculation and politics, not via the pragmatism of James and Dewey as Savransky has done in Chapter 2, but with the help of what I think is an equally fecund resource for the practical defence of thinking: the philosophies of Maurice Merleau-Ponty, Hannah Arendt, and Jean-Luc Nancy.[5] As thinkers who emerged from existential phenomenology, their philosophical research 'methods' are also ontologies, which, like Whitehead's, challenge the distinctions between subject/object and mind/body and thereby forge a path between empiricism and rationalism. Hence, they indirectly elaborate the connection Whitehead makes between speculative philosophy (or research) and ontology (existence), but in ways that explicitly address the social and political dimensions of existence. This link to the socio-political allows consideration of how speculative research may work against totalizing government.

To get to the complexity of the relation between speculation and politics I *first* consider the *ontology* of the notion of speculation I just outlined in terms of the temporality or historicity of experience and, hence, of the meaning and trajectory of our affective relation to the perceived world in general. I argue for the dynamism and unpredictability of that relation. The political point of better understanding this dynamism is that part of what is at stake in our unpredictable relation to a world is *agency*, by which I mean the phenomenon of changing

42 *R. Diprose*

things, having an impact, beginning something new; in short: *innovation*. In ways that I go on to analyse, speculative thinking that opens up new ways of understanding experience, is historical (it involves tradition) but it is also futural and open to possibility. *Second*, I go on to address the relation between speculation and politics before offering an explanation of the role of inspiration in speculation. Inspiration is a crucial ingredient of speculation that is often overlooked in individualist approaches to knowledge acquisition and autonomous thought. I argue that speculation is ontological and political *by virtue of inspiration*, the spark that gets the 'flight of imagination' and innovation going. Inspiration, I claim is the pulse within the corporeal, affective, and embedded (i.e. trans-subjective) fabric of experience.

Innovation and the political ontology of speculative thinking

First, some account of speculation as ontology. For Merleau-Ponty, speculative research and thinking arise within the 'dehiscence' of being (e.g. 1968: 128), which he also describes as the reversible fold of 'flesh' and the simultaneous 'instituted and instituting' character of human experience (2010: 8–15). In summary, the latter account suggests that, from the time of our birth, there is an element of 'existence already instituted', where 'institution' refers to experience immersed in the (social and material) field *between* myself and others. Or, in Merleau-Ponty's words, institution refers to 'those events in experience which endow the experience with durable dimensions' (habit) such that I can share a world, my subsequent experiences will 'make sense, will form a thinkable ... history', and I will tend to perceive, think about, and respond to my world in a similar way to how I have before (2010: 76–77). But habit and preservation of tradition is not all there is to institution. Institution is 'not constitution' and experience does not consist in linear, continuous progression from an objective past toward an anticipated goal. While experience undergoes some sedimentation, meaning does *not* survive as a 'residue' in a present activity so that the past is repeated. Instead, and on the other hand, institution involves, simultaneously, institut*ing*: beginning something new, innovation, the event of 'natality' to coin Arendt's term, or what Merleau-Ponty describes as 'divergence in relation to a norm of sense, *difference* [...] deformation, which is proper to institution' (Merleau-Ponty, 2010: 11). This 'divergence' of institution, which is akin to the dehiscence of the flesh of the world, is not only true of experience and perception, but also of the ideality of language through which experience of a world is thought (Merleau-Ponty, 1968: 151–155).[6] Institution-instituting itself, every 'being exposed to ...', or receptivity to other elements and the ideas they suggest, initiates the present and simultaneously opens 'a *sequel*', 'a future' (Merleau-Ponty, 2010: 8–9), by which Merleau-Ponty means that the futurity opened in experience is *indeterminate*. This opening of the new, unpredictable, and unique within the institution-instituting character of experience is where agency arises as well as new paths for thinking and living that break with determinism.

Speculative research, temporality and politics   43

Significantly for my purposes, Merleau-Ponty also describes this event of innovation within experience in terms of the past (institution/tradition) giving way to what I have been referring to as speculative research. In the pursuit of knowledge we may reach an impasse where familiar (habitual) ideas and approaches give way to '*investigation* [also translated as 'research'] in Kafka's sense, or indefinite elaboration' (Merleau-Ponty, 2010: 7). Investigation is Merleau-Ponty's term for speculative research – investigation is not a state of being, nor is it a report, or the findings that research throws up. Rather, 'investigation' is a '*new impulse*' within experience that, instead of solving a problem directly, 'allows the obstacle to be overcome from another direction' (Merleau-Ponty, 2010: 78, emphasis added). This institu*ting* side of the experience of problem-solving 'results in a picture of diverse, complex probabilities' that are indeterminate but also tethered to, and verified by, 'local circumstances' (ibid.: 78). (Hence, like Whitehead, Merleau-Ponty thinks that genuine 'investigation' or speculation involves thinking that is also always tied to – or verified by, as Whitehead might put it – experience of the material world.) As it is inseparable from experience, speculative research also transforms experience; it is a movement beyond oneself and what was. But innovation in research is not the inevitable outcome of continuous progression or the product of the 'free' thought of an autonomous 'genius'. Experience needs to be inspired by being '*exposed to ...*' something or someone other. (I return to this point about inspiration below.)

The second point about speculative research I wish to elaborate, aside from its link to ontology and the temporality of experience, is its relation to the political. Arendt's ideas about the connection between thinking and the political are helpful here. She broadens the scope of the political from the institutions of government to include public relations between people in general. She characterizes these relations in terms of the welcoming and witnessing of the event of 'natality', which opens existence to 'potentiality' and hence beyond historical, political, and biological determinism (Arendt, 1998: 9 and 200). By 'natality' Arendt means a specifically human practice of instituting or 'beginning something new' (1998: 9), although it is possible to extend the event of natality to relations between all organisms and between humans and things.[7] But I leave that issue aside for now. For Arendt, the event of natality is about instituting a 'gap between past and future' and, hence, a break with determinism. In her later work that addresses Kant's philosophy (especially in *Life of the Mind*), Arendt tends to attribute this opening of a gap between past and future to the act of thinking as judgment: 'the insertion of man' into a world, through thinking as judgment, disrupts the present, that is, 'breaks up the unidirectional flow of [historical] time' between birth and death (Arendt 1978: 202–213 and 1977: 11–12). What Arendt means by judgment and thinking varies, it is complicated and open to debate.[8] So I will restrict my comments to what she says about thinking with regard to the political.

As with Merleau-Ponty's notion of experience, Arendt's idea of political agency forges a path between the paradigms of determinism and absolute freedom and underscores the communal character of the advent of the new. The

44   *R. Diprose*

(speculative or innovative) thinking that manifests in the political must transcend the individuality of 'introspection' and other conventional notions of speculative reason (which Arendt often says has no place in the politics). Political thinking 'cannot function in strict isolation or solitude; it needs the presence of others "in whose place" it must think', not in the sense of thinking on behalf of others, but thinking that refers to others 'whose perspectives it must take into consideration, and [most crucially] without whom it never has the opportunity to operate at all' (Arendt 1977: 220–221). The dependence of innovative and critical thinking on the stimulus and witness of others is what gives speculative thinking its political dimension. In *The Human Condition* Arendt explains how the break with determinism that I have argued is a feature of speculative research is achieved by the disclosure of agents *as such* (whether as actors, thinkers, or speakers), as beginners of the new, unique initiators of something unique within the 'togetherness of human affairs' (1998: 175–177). This space of the disclosure of natality *between* human beings *is* the political, which Arendt also describes as 'power' as 'potentiality' (1998: 200) and the 'living space of freedom' (1994: 466). The political is the space of belonging to a collectivity where everyone is treated as unique agents and nothing is decided in advance (Arendt 1998: 201 and 233–234).[9] Through this interaction with other people, whereby we contest the meaning of our experiences of the world, we transform those meanings that we inherit and that condition our experience.

We might say then that what I have been calling speculative research involves Arendt's kind of political agency in that both amount to being 'exposed to …' possibility per se.[10] Crucially though, political agency is only disclosed *collectively*. As Bonnie Honig argues, agency for Arendt, as the event of beginning something new, is 'performative' (1993: 87). Or, as Arendt puts it, public action 'disclose[s] the agent together with the act' as an unidentifiable 'who' rather than a 'what' (1998: 180). For both Merleau-Ponty and Arendt, even though we are potentially innovative and speculative all the time we are awake, effective speculative research requires that we get out there and *do it* and that we do it *with others*. Further, Arendt's political ontology indicates why it is important to think of speculative research as political in general. Her radical revision of the very concept of the political emerges from a concern with what she saw as a retreat from genuine politics of critique and contestation of the status quo, an abdication of agency, a general 'abstention from the whole realm of human affairs' (Arendt 1998: 234). This retreat from the political manifests, for Arendt, in trends that are still apparent in contemporary public life, including the domination of public life by economic concerns, bureaucratic processes, and the science of prediction. These practices and attitudes either substitute action and critique with rule-following behaviour and rote-learning and/or attempt to control the unpredictable consequences of human activity.[11] For Arendt the 'degradation of politics' that attends such trends involves attempts to eliminate or supplant the 'human ability to act [and] to start new unprecedented processes' (1998: 230–235).

This brings me to a third point about this revised political ontology of innovative experience (and hence, speculative research) that I wish to emphasize and

Speculative research, temporality and politics 45

that links the other two points (about speculation as ontology and as politics). This is a point about speculation and *sensibility*, which leads into discussion of inspiration. Besides its futural temporality and political dimension, this revised notion of experience has a specific kind of *spatiality* that rests on an idea of sensibility: affective corporeality, embeddedness in the material world, or what Merleau-Ponty calls 'the flesh'. Concepts like sensibility and the flesh are speculative, 'descriptive generalizations' in Whitehead's sense, notions aimed at overcoming the limitations of the 'bifurcation of nature'.[12] The flesh is a conceptual product of speculative research that explains speculative thinking as both rationalist and empiricist, simultaneously. With this idea of the flesh, Merleau-Ponty tries to conceive of experience in terms that emphasize the corporeal and affective aspects whilst remaining in line with his notion of 'institution-instituting': experience as a chiasmic intertwining of human and non-human elements, where we are embedded in a meaningful world without constituting it and, conversely, without being engulfed or determined by that which is not oneself. The flesh envisages experience as equally receptive as it is impactful, 'activity [that] is equally a passivity', involving vision that is seen, 'feeling that is felt' (Merleau-Ponty, 1968: 139 and 136), and thinking that is thought. As mentioned above with regard to thinking and the institution of language, it is within this chiasm of flesh that (speculative) thinking arises. Merleau-Ponty's point about thinking with regard to the notion of flesh is similar to his point about any aspect of experience: thinking is characterized by and arises from the 'dehiscence [rupture] of the sensible' (1968: 145). Sensibility or the chiasm of flesh is therefore where inspiration takes place, which, as I will explain shortly, is the spark that gets speculative research going. And sensibility is also where curtailment of inspiration and speculation will be felt. So, this sort of challenge to the dualisms of Western thought (especially subject/object and mind/body) matters because it is also a challenge to government regulation that dampens critical and creative thinking (and hence agency) by entrenching habits of thoughtlessness that characterizes a 'retreat from the political'.[13]

Innovation and speculative thinking in the humanities

Practicing speculative philosophy is one way that the humanities can reverse this retreat from the political. Another way humanities do this is through 'teaching of the other'. Teaching of the other is akin to inspiration, an idea that I will now sketch to complete this elaboration of the meaning of speculative research. University teaching, like research, is increasingly regulated by a push toward vocationalism, by instrumentalist thinking, and by efficiency measures that favour teaching methods that tend to follow the principles of Socratic *maieutics*. *Maieutics* is the Socratic method of teaching and inquiry that, while centred on dialogue and debate, positions the student or interlocutor, not as the source of new ideas, but as a sounding-board who assists in drawing out (giving birth to) ideas that the teacher or researcher supposedly already knows (rather than, as Socrates defined wisdom in the *Apology*: wisdom is knowing that one *does not know*).

46 *R. Diprose*

Emmanuel Levinas (1987), in his essay 'Philosophy and the Idea of Infinity', criticizes this notion of maieutics (and Kant's idea of heteronomy – being unduly influenced by the other) for entrenching a concept of philosophical 'autonomy' that actually works against the kind of innovation and inspiration necessary for the critique, generation, and transformation of ideas. This notion of academic autonomy consists of a denial of the historicity and the intercorporeal, affective basis of critical and speculative thinking. Paradoxically, denial of the historicity or temporality of thinking actually closes down innovation, critical and creative thinking in favour of upholding existing ideas and the status of the one who supposedly knows. And that is because, like induction in science, Reason that seeks to simply possess and defend existing ideas or to possess the world and enthral interlocutors through those ideas, suspends, not only the difference, uniqueness, or innovativeness of those others, but also the movement toward the other that fuels innovation in the first place: inspiration.

Inspiration is crucial to speculative thinking and, therefore, to political agency. It attests to the deeply communal, collaborative, and affective aspects of teaching and conceptual research that are overlooked by the usual notions of philosophical autonomy and speculative reason. For the purposes of a working definition, let us say that 'inspiration' is *both* the stimulus, the disturbance of the other, that prompts a flight of imagination that is crucial for speculative research *and* the response, the gesture, the giving, or, as Jean-Luc Nancy puts it, the 'unidentifiable inclination' toward the uniqueness or strangeness of the other (idea, thing, person) (1991: 6–7). Whereas let us say that 'innovation' is the 'divergence' of flesh, as discussed, the opening toward *a* future, equally unique and indeterminate, which results from this teaching of the other. So, in inclining me toward the other person, idea or thing, inspiration also drives the resulting divergence or deformation of meaning, the 'sensitization of an image' that opens 'a future' and drives the speculative thinking that Merleau-Ponty defines as 'investigation' or 'research' (2010: 18–19).

This idea of inspiration of the other is *not* simply the opposite of the usual notion of philosophical autonomy. The notion of inspiration that is said to oppose autonomous thinking is the kind of deterministic inspiration (or heteronomy) that worried Plato in an early dialogue, *Ion* (530a–542b) (1987: 49–65). In *Ion* Plato criticizes the kind of inspiration that he claims is at work in the art of the 'rhapsode' who performs the poetry of the great poets to an audience. Plato argues that, unlike the practice of philosophy and morality, rhapsodic performance does not require skill (*techne*) governed by reason. It requires no specialist knowledge particular to the occupation, no knowledge of activities and events depicted in the poems recited, and nor does the performance require the intellectual skills of dissecting concepts that Plato equates with reasoned thinking. Further, the performance is inherently irrational, he says, in that the rhapsode is not in control of himself (*Ion* 532e–536c; Plato 1987: 53–8). The rhapsode is out of control in three ways: he is possessed by the words of the poet whose speaking position he takes up; second, the rhapsode is not present during the performance in the sense that he imagines he is elsewhere, involved in the

Speculative research, temporality and politics 47

events he is performing; and, third, his reason no longer controls his feeling and appetite. On Plato's definition, 'inspiration' is an extreme form of heteronomy involving being inhabited by and subjected to the power of an other who is external to oneself, rather than being under the sway of autonomous reason. Moreover, rhapsodic performance involves a *chain* of inspiration in the reproduction of knowledge: the original author of the poem that is being recited was inspired by the gods and the audience who is watching the recitation is being inspired by the rhapsode. Plato's critique of inspiration typifies the way Western thought has attempted to distance reasoned thinking from feeling and from the influence of others.

While I will argue, contrary to Plato, that inspiration or being affected by the other is central to speculative thinking, I raise Plato's idea of inspiration because it aptly describes how teaching and research are misunderstood within the contemporary university: as reproducing existing knowledge. Contrary to some claims about the contemporary university, intellectual autonomy (understood conventionally in terms of the individual exercise of speculative reason) is not what is centrally threatened by the corporatization of the sector. After all, research performance indicators assume that the individual author of a published journal paper is the source of an original idea. This idea of intellectual autonomy, as Stengers points out, defines researchers 'by competition' within a race of continuous progress (2011a: 12). However, as I have argued, this notion of philosophical autonomy does not adequately account for innovation or for the kind of speculative research that Whitehead and Stengers propose. Nor does the way teaching is managed and evaluated in universities foster the opening of paths for thinking. Instead, teaching is understood in terms of Socratic maieutics and mimetic inspiration. Policies that move toward massive class sizes, online lectures and chat forums instead of face-to-face discussion, trends toward generic course structures and assessment packages in disregard of specific content, inequitable funding of disciplines that favours vocational degrees, and so on; all this reinforces the view that the teacher, and the students for that matter, are conduits of information originating somewhere else, and that they are endlessly exchangeable. Just like the players in Plato's chain of inspiration.

One problem with this way of regarding teaching is that it works against even the Enlightenment ideas of philosophical autonomy and critical thinking. Kant would have called it *heteronomy*: being subjected to the law of the other; or tutelage – learning by rote. However, while teaching and learning in this sort of environment – of speed-dating between conduits – is suffocating of agency and innovation and tends to close down critical and creative thinking, I suggest that it is not actually what happens in the classroom, the research workshop, or the reading group. Plato's worry about heteronomy or inspiration (being inhabited by and subjected to the other) is precisely that it *leads to innovation* in experience. Inspiration by the other disrupts the status quo and leads to transformations in meaning and in the reality of experience. Plato admits as much when, in *The Republic* (395a–e), he criticizes inspirational performance in the following

48 *R. Diprose*

terms: 'prolonged indulgence in any form of literature [or other so-called mimetic art] leaves its mark on the moral nature of a man, affecting not only the mind but physical poise and intonation' (1955: 134).While Kant's worry about heteronomy (being influenced by the other) was that it stifles critical thinking, for Levinas and others like Stengers, it is precisely what *leads to innovation* or speculative thinking. This being-inspired or being 'exposed to ...' and affected by the other is the heteronomy that Levinas thinks is essential to autonomy and to thinking in general. Heteronomy refers to the encounter with the 'absolutely other' or what Arendt calls 'natality', which interrupts and puts into question the posture of absolute freedom and autonomy that is characteristic of the self-contained, introspective thinker self that seems to only have a relationship with itself: for example, Descartes cogito that 'converses with itself' (Levinas, 1987: 49). The subsequent 'divergence' of flesh, not only opens me onto a world in ways beyond the familiar, it is the precondition for this relation with myself that we call autonomy and thinking.

With regard to teaching and research in the humanities,[14] there are two final ontological–political points to be made about inspiration, the communal and intercorporeal–affective basis of speculative thinking. First, the 'empirical' material of humanities research consists of this inclination toward others or the 'flesh of the world': it is the speech and action of others (coextensive with the political in its wider sense) that provides the inspiration for the transformation of ideas of which humanities research consists; and the speech and action of others also provides the field for testing the validity of those ideas. Far from being a solitary exercise abstracted from the real world, thinking in the humanities is always in touch with its world, either directly through debate and dialogue with agents of institution, or through material expression of ideas and events: through engagement with social, moral, and political issues, and through the written word and other visual and aural texts. The second point is that turning ones back on the inspiration of others (e.g. in political and public life) is also how speculative thinking is closed down. Quite apart from being expressions of uniqueness per se in the sense of being the source of innovation, all bodies are different in terms of culturally specific characteristics and these differences impact on thinking. This is not to say that the sex, race, or age of some body determines whether or how they think. Nevertheless how different bodies signify differently within different socio-political contexts does have some bearing on whether they are considered inspiring and are welcomed as such and whether their ideas are considered all-too-familiar, innovative, or nonsense. Stripping bodies of their ability to signify uniqueness (by violent means or by turning my back or just refusing to listen) is one way to deprive a person of their status as an innovator, a thinker. Humanities research is (or should be) devoted to opposing any moves to close down speculative thinking. It can do this by generating new ways of framing experience (Whitehead's 'descriptive generalizations'), ways of keeping open paths for thinking, ways of shifting our own habits of perception and those of others so that we do not deprive others of the ability to signify their uniqueness and so participate in speculation, in the cycle of innovation and inspiration

Speculative research, temporality and politics 49

characteristic of communal life. Keeping oneself and others open to the risk of thinking is (or should be) the primary 'use' of humanities research.

Teaching in universities is another important way that humanities scholars keep the world open by speculative thinking. While Arendt tends to separate education institutions from the public space of the political (for various reasons that are not relevant here),[15] she also notes that 'the essence of education is natality' (1977: 174). By this she means that, while education involves teaching traditions upon which our worlds are based (which provides some social stability), its key feature is teaching of the other, teaching the young that they are the beginners of the new, they are innovators. Teaching for a world of innovators is not aimed at ensuring that they invent new gadgets. Rather, it is aimed at saving the world from 'ruin', from stagnation and totalitarianism brought about through historical, political, and biological determinism. As Arendt puts it: 'Education is the point at which we decide whether we love the world enough to assume responsibility for it and by the same token save it from ruin which, except for renewal, [...] would be inevitable' (1977: 196). This renewal of shared worlds happens through collective engagement that generates critical and creative thinking and action. A key place for teaching and enacting this renewal is a community of scholars, particularly if that includes the inspirational enthusiasm for thinking apparent among some of the less-jaded members of our university communities, including our students. Crucially though, the task of renewing a world open to potentiality, whether through teaching or research, cannot be controlled (even and especially by government), and the outcomes are 'unforeseen'.

Notes

1 A press release of 5 September 2013, authored by Jamie Briggs MP, outlines the kinds of research projects that the Liberal Party considers a waste of money. It can be accessed at: www.liberal.org.au/latest-news/2013/09/05/ending-more-labor%E2% 80%99s-waste (accessed 10 March 2016). There were many responses condemning the statement including from some of the researchers whose grants were named (e.g. Redding, 2013).
2 For a lucid account of Whitehead's notion of the 'bifurcation of nature' see Halewood 2013: 1–22.
3 Hannah Arendt criticizes this idea of speculation as 'introspection' in *The Human Condition* (HC) (282–283). In *The Visible and the Invisible* (VI) Maurice Merleau-Ponty critiques the same notion of thinking, calling it 'reflection and interrogation' based on Descartes' dualistic ontology (3–49).
4 The Australian Government's 2015 Intergenerational Report can be found at: www. treasury.gov.au/PublicationsAndMedia/Publications/2015/2015-Intergenerational-Report (accessed 10 March 2016).
5 As I am selecting only affinities between these thinkers that are relevant to my analysis, I bypass any differences between their approaches to speculation. I am also ignoring the way some commentators of Whitehead, Deleuze, and Stengers explicitly reject existential phenomenology (as do Deleuze and Stengers themselves, on occasion), particularly Heidegger's philosophy, for its supposed anthropocentrism. As I do not have the space or inclination to enter that debate, I let others justify the connections I develop here. For example, David Macauley (1996) explains how Arendt uses Whitehead's account of science as process to account for human 'homelessness'

50   R. Diprose

(or 'earth alienation') and William Hamrick and Jan van der Veken (2011) argue that Merleau-Ponty's ontology of the 'flesh' and his later philosophy of nature develop insights from Whitehead's ontology of the organism.

6 M. C. Dillon provides an impressively clear explanation of Merleau-Ponty's condensed thesis about the relation between thinking, language, and the 'divergence' of the flesh (or the 'dehiscence' of being) (1988: 171–173).

7 For an account of how Arendt's idea of the (political) event of natality can be extended to living with the non-human, see Diprose (2011); for an account of Whitehead's take on the same phenomenon in relation to 'things' see Bono (2014).

8 For a comprehensive analysis of the concept of judgment in Arendt's philosophy, particularly in *Life of the Mind*, see Max Deutscher (2007).

9 This space for the contestation and transformation of reality does not have to be restricted to the public sphere in the narrow sense that Arendt understood it. For instance, Stengers' 'cosmopolitical spaces' (as described in *Cosmopolitics I & II*) seems to be a more complex version of this Arendtian notion of the political, applied to the landscape of practices that produce knowledge in modern science.

10 I am grateful to Martin Savransky for suggesting, in his thoughtful response to my initial draft, that I might formulate the point in this way.

11 Much of Arendt's book *The Origins of Totalitarianism* (1994 [1951]) is devoted to analysis of this 'retreat from the political' especially in Nazi Germany. But in *The Human Condition* Arendt also provides an astute summary analysis of the domination of public life in contemporary democracies with the science of prediction (1998: 40–49).

12 William Hammick and Jan van der Veken provide a convincing argument to this effect (2011: 4).

13 Space does not allow me to elaborate here on this point about the relationship between affective corporeality and the political curtailment of agency and critical thinking. For further discussion see, for example, Diprose (2008).

14 While I share Stengers' (2010: 12) scepticism about whether universities as they currently operate are conducive to speculative research, I believe strongly that the survival of each requires the other.

15 Arendt's philosophy of education is concerned primarily with the education of children in schools, which she views as institutions for training children to transition from the private to public spheres. There are problems with the private/public distinction within her approach, but her basic claims about education and natality are right I think, and so I make use of them here. For an excellent discussion of Arendt's philosophy of education that accounts for the difficulties, see James M. Magrini (2013).

References

Arendt, H. (1994 [1951]). *The origins of totalitarianism*. New Edition with added Prefaces. San Diego CA: Harcourt Inc.

Arendt, H. (1998 [1958]). *The human condition*. Second Edition with Introduction by Margaret Canovan. Chicago IL and London: University of Chicago Press.

Arendt, H. (1977). *Between past and future*. London: Penguin.

Arendt, H. (1978). *Life of the mind*. (Vols 1 and 2). San Diego: Harcourt.

Australian Government (The Treasury). *2015 Intergenerational Report: Australia in 2055*. Commonwealth of Australia (March 2015). Accessible at: www.treasury.gov.au/PublicationsAndMedia/Publications/2015/2015-Intergenerational-Report

Bono, J. J. (2014). Atomicity, conformation, enduring objects, and 'things': Science and science studies after the Whiteadian turn. In R. Faber, & A. Goffey (Eds), *The allure of things: Process and object in contemporary philosophy* (pp. 13–35). London; New York: Bloomsbury, 2014.

Speculative research, temporality and politics 51

Briggs MP, J. (2013). Ending more of Labor's waste. Press release 5 September 2013. www.liberal.org.au/latest-news/2013/09/05/ending-more-labor%E2%80%99s-waste (accessed 1 May 2015).

Deutscher, M. (2007). *Judgment after Arendt*. New Edition. London: Routledge.

Dillon, M. C. (1988). *Merleau-Ponty's ontology* (2nd ed.). Evanston IL: Northwestern University Press.

Diprose, R. (2008). Arendt and Nietzsche on responsibility and futurity. *Philosophy and Social Criticism, 34*(6), 617–642.

Diprose, R. (2011). Building and belonging amid the plight of dwelling. *Angelaki, 16*(4), 59–72.

Halewood, M. (2013). *A.N. Whitehead and social theory: Tracing a culture of thought*. London: Anthem Press.

Hamrick, W., & van der Veken, J. (2011). *Nature and logos: A Whiteheadian key to Merleau-Ponty's fundamental thought*. Albany: SUNY Press.

Honig, B. (1993). Arendt's accounts of action and authority. In B. Harig, *Political theory and the displacement of politics*. Ithaca NY: Cornell University Press.

Levinas, E. (1987). Philosophy and the idea of infinity. In *Collected philosophical papers* (pp. 47–60). (A. Lingis, Trans.). Dordrecht: Martinus Nijhoff.

Macauley, D. (1996). Hannah Arendt and the politics of place: From earth alienation to *oikos*. In D. Macauley (Ed.), *Minding nature*. New York: Guilford.

Magrini, J. M. (2013). An ontological notion of learning inspired by the philosophy of Hannah Arendt: The miracle of natality. *Review of Contemporary Philosophy, 12*, 60–92.

Merleau-Ponty, M. (1968 [1964]). *The visible and the invisible*. (A. Lingis, Trans.). Evanston, IL: Northwestern University Press.

Merleau-Ponty, M. (2010). *Institution and passivity: Course notes from the Collège de France (1954–1955)* (IP). Forward C. Lefort. (L. Lawlor and H. Massey, Trans.). Evanston, IL: Northwestern University Press.

Nancy, J.-L. (1991 [1986]). *The inoperative community*. (P. Connor, L. Garbus, M. Holland, & S. Sawhney, Trans.). Minneapolis MN: University of Minnesota Press.

Plato. (1987). Ion. In T. J Saunders (Ed. and Trans.) *Early Socratic dialogues*. London: Penguin, 1987.

Plato. (1955). *The republic*. (H. D. P. Lee, Trans.). Harmondsworth: Penguin.

Redding, Paul. (2013). Philosophy is not a 'ridiculous' pursuit. It is worth funding. *Guardian (Australia)*, 17 September 2013, www.theguardian.com/commentisfree/2013/sep/17/defence-philosophy-abbott (last accessed 10 March 2016).

Stengers, I. (2010). The care of the possible: Isabelle Stengers interviewed by Erik Bordeleau *SCAPEGOAT: Architecture | Landscape | Political Economy, 1*, 12–17, 27.

Stengers, I. 2011a. *Thinking with Whitehead: A free and wild creation of concepts*. (M. Chase, Trans.). Forward B. Latour. Cambridge MA.: Harvard University Press.

Stengers, I. 2011b. *Cosmopolitics II*. (R. Bononno, Trans.). Minneapolis MN: University of Minnesota Press.

Whitehead, A. N. (1978 [1929]). Process and reality: an essay in cosmology. In D. Griffin, & D. Sherburne (Eds), *Gifford lectures of 1927–8* (corrected ed.). New York: Free Press.

4 Situated speculation as a constraint on thought

Michael Halewood

> Abstraction expresses nature's mode of interaction and is not merely mental. When it abstracts, thought is merely conforming to nature – or rather, it is exhibiting itself as an element in nature.
>
> (A. N. Whitehead, *Symbolism. Its Meaning and Effect*: 25–26)

Is speculation a suitable method for social science? To put the question in this way is, perhaps, problematic. It assumes that speculation, whatever that turns out to be, is to be understood as operating on the same level as other social scientific methods such as interviewing, surveys, participant observation and so on. This would be to flatten out the specific contribution that speculation could make and to presume that it is just another method within social research. It may turn out that speculation could be used within such research but to equate it immediately with other, already existing, methods is, I would suggest, over-hasty. This is why I have started with this question: in order to introduce some caution when considering the relation of speculation to social science or social theory more generally. My worry is that there is a danger that those engaged with social analyses might move too quickly in adopting some concept of speculation without paying due attention to the very specific milieu within which it has been formulated in recent years. My aim in this chapter is to outline the particularity of speculation. It may well be a productive approach but it also implies constraints. Moreover, speculation is not a method.

It seems that there are at least two major sources for the renewed interest in speculation. One is the contemporary philosophical 'movement' of Speculative Realism as variously developed by writers such as Quentin Meillassoux, Graham Harman, Ian Hamilton-Grant and others. Another source is the work of Alfred North Whitehead. In his book *The Universe of Things*, Shaviro (2014) has provided a comprehensive and enlightening analysis of the interrelations and tensions between these two approaches. For my purposes, I will concentrate on the writings of Whitehead and two others who are sympathetic to him – Stengers and Haraway. I have chosen elements of Haraway's work to provide some kind of bridge, or at least an example, of how the philosophical question of speculation might be deployed within other fields. I will, however, start with another problem.

The problem of speculation

One major problem with the concept of speculation is that it might seem to offer anyone the chance to think whatever she or he wants. Our dictionaries seem to agree that 'speculation' means something like 'conjecture without all available evidence or facts'. Does this allow us to think whatever we want? Surely, that would be the role of imagination. I can imagine a fish playing cricket. If this is all there were to speculation then neither philosophy nor social theory will have gained very much. None of us want, in our academic lives at least, to be accused of idle speculation. Speculating what would happen to the economy if we were invaded by aliens might not be the most productive way to spend an hour. This raises the important question of how are we to judge whether a given instance of speculation is worthwhile or not? In the two examples just given, is it really clear when we are imagining and when we are speculating? To justify speculation within philosophy or sociology, we need to do some more work; we need to set out some conditions and constraints that might make speculation worthwhile and effective. It is not a question of making speculation one method among others. This would run the risk of viewing it as just another tool in the social researcher's tool-box; one that is to be taken out and utilized at will, rather than a constraint upon thought, as something which almost imposes itself upon us.

Whitehead on speculation in *process and reality*

> It is the ideal of speculative philosophy that its fundamental notions shall not seem capable of abstraction from each other. In other words, it is pre-supposed that no entity can be conceived in complete abstraction from the system of the universe, and that it is the business of speculative philosophy to exhibit this truth. This character is its coherence.
>
> (Whitehead, 1978: 3)

Speculation will involve abstraction, but this abstraction does not mean a complete dislocation from other notions. Speculative philosophy is not the invention, out of nowhere, of strange concepts with no relation to other concepts, since 'no entity can be conceived in complete abstraction from the system of the universe'. Moreover, speculation is not completely abstract as it is implicated in the 'system of the universe', in the world. This is the first constraint that Whitehead puts on speculation. We must recognize that it emerges from and is immersed in the world, and is not completely dislocated from it. Is this a full definition of all that is involved in speculation? Whitehead is clear that it is not. And, in order to explain how speculation operates, he continues by reintroducing a very specific account of the role of imagination, one which retains some of the usual connotations of the term but asks more of it, and of us.

Speculation does involve imagination, but imagination of a very specific kind. Whitehead makes this point forcefully when he discusses the attempt to

54   *M. Halewood*

generalize from a given set of facts or data. His argument is set against the 'rigid empiricism' (Whitehead, 1978: 4), and the 'method of induction' (Whitehead, 1978: 5) that some, following Francis Bacon, claim to be the basis of natural science. According to Whitehead, if these approaches had been rigidly adhered to, then this 'would have left science where it found it' (Whitehead, 1978: 5). What has been ignored is the role of what Whitehead calls 'imaginative generalization':

> What Bacon omitted was the play of a free imagination, controlled by the requirements of coherence and logic. The true method of discovery is like the flight of an aeroplane. It starts from the ground of particular observation; it makes a flight in the thin air of imaginative generalization; and it again lands for renewed observation rendered acute by rational interpretation.
>
> (Whitehead, 1978: 5)

The image of a plane taking off from some ground, enjoying its flight of fancy, then returning to earth, is lucid but if it is taken as saying no more than there is a need for empirical observation to be followed by some play of abstract imagination, which then returns to the world to confirm or deny these thoughts, then we have not really found anything very radical. Whitehead's position might seem like a rather limpid compromise between empiricism and rationalism. But, as is often the case with Whitehead, the importance is in the details. The key detail here is 'free imagination' and 'imaginative generalization'.

Whitehead was not a dogmatic thinker. He does not want to tell us that we are not allowed to think or imagine as we wish. But he does insist that imagination is not a faculty that is inherent in the human subject. Imagination does not arise from the operation of consciousness. This only becomes clear later in *Process and Reality*, when Whitehead is talking about his specific concept of 'propositions' (Whitehead, 1978: 256–265). Propositions express, for Whitehead, the way in which the world that we encounter is not a mute facticity but is comprised, in and of itself, of actuality and potentiality. The world we encounter acts as 'a lure for feeling' (Whitehead, 1978: 25). Shaviro has succinctly described this position as one where 'potentiality or difference is always anchored in some "particular actuality", in an actual thing or group of actual things' (2014: 54). Moreover, 'When I respond to a lure [...] I am led to envision a possibility, or to "entertain a proposition", and thereby to *feel* something that I would not have felt otherwise' (ibid.: 55, emphasis in original). It is in this response that imagination finds its place. But 'Imagination is never very free' (Whitehead, 1978: 132) as it always proceeds from particular actualities with their accompanying possibilities. These possibilities do not proceed from our mind or consciousness but from the world and our relation to it. Whitehead puts this a little more technically when he states, 'In the case of the imaginative feeling, this emotional pattern reflects the initial disconnection of the predicate from the logical subjects' (Whitehead, 1978: 273).

It is now possible to reconsider Whitehead's initial thoughts on speculation and imagination as set out at the start of *Process and reality*. Once acts of

Situated speculation as a constraint on thought 55

imagination and imaginative generalization have been firmly located within the world, we can return to their relation to speculation and what makes speculation different to the simple imagining of any possibility. The word that Whitehead chooses to differentiate speculation from mere imagination, while incorporating acts of imagination as a crucial element of speculation, is 'success':

> The success of the imaginative experient is always to be tested by the applicability of its results beyond the restricted locus from which it originated. In default of such extended application, a generalization started from physics, for example, remains merely an alternative expression of notions applicable to physics.
>
> (Whitehead, 1978: 5)

It is notable that Whitehead here talks of the 'success of the imaginative experient', a slightly peculiar phrase, but one which reminds us that the act of imagination comes not from some enduring faculty of imagination but is a specific event. Furthermore, the word 'experient' connotes both experience and experiment. What moves this instance of speculation beyond mere imagination is 'the applicability of its results beyond the restricted locus from which it originated'.

An astrophysicist needs to imagine. For example, they might imagine how we could better understand the formation of the planets of our solar system if we do not assume their orbits are fixed but that planets are free to roam. However, this is not, according to Whitehead, true speculation as the application of such an instance of imagination remains within the specific field of astronomical physics. Interesting exercises in imagination do not constitute proper philosophical speculation if they remain within their own domain. This applies to all academic fields:

> the conditions for the success of imaginative construction must be rigidly adhered to. In the first place, this construction must leave its origin in the generalization of particular factors discerned in particular topics of human interest; for example, in physics, or in physiology, or in psychology, or in aesthetics, or in ethical beliefs, or in sociology, or in languages conceived as storehouses of human experience. In this way the prime requisite, that anyhow there shall be some important application, is secured.
>
> (Whitehead, 1978: 5)

The constraint on imagination comes not from disallowing any particular thought. We can think what we want, if we like. But to call our acts of imagination truly speculative, we must move beyond the field from which they originate. It is at this point that Whitehead seems to be suggesting that speculation is resolutely philosophical insofar as it necessarily leaves the ground provided by any particular field of study. In other words, 'the partially successful philosophic generalization will, if derived from physics, find applications in fields of

56 *M. Halewood*

experience beyond physics' (Whitehead, 1978: 5). Whitehead's example of the flight of the aeroplane becomes clearer and more demanding. We leave the immediate realm that provided the ground (airfield) for our imaginative flight. When we return, the test of the success of our flight, of our speculation, is not that we return to the ground (airfield). Rather, if we have been successful, our understanding of the world will have changed, it will have broadened, as successful speculation requires that our findings are applicable beyond their initial ground. Ultimately, 'The task of speculative philosophy is to demonstrate that all entities are involved in interactions which make them what they are and which enable them to go beyond what they are' (Whitehead, 1978: 20).

At this point it might seem that Whitehead has gone against his own prescription and engaged in, or insisted upon, a form of philosophical speculation without describing or acknowledging the ground from which his thought arises. However, I would suggest that it is possible to set out an implicit location from which Whitehead makes his initial jump; it is the context of early twentieth-century philosophy, especially that of Russell and the early Wittgenstein, one where speculation and the associated taint of metaphysics were deemed irrelevant if not impossible. I would suggest that Whitehead does not make this location of his thought explicit for two interlinked reasons. If he stated at the outset that his question was only that of 'how to justify a form of speculation which goes beyond what is allowed by the empiricism of Russell and Wittgenstein', then his work would be constantly judged within the limited domain of how far he responds directly to the points of Russell and Wittgenstein. This leads to a second, related, point. To frame his argument as only an attempt to counter Russell and Wittgenstein would prevent his readers from fully immersing themselves in the suggestions and imaginative leaps that Whitehead offers us. It would be to reduce the range of possibilities of *Process and Reality*, to limits its power to act as a 'lure for feeling'.

Taken in this light, the status and role of Whitehead's discussions of speculation assume a different hue. It is, in one sense, a more local problem. It is one that is situated. This is an important point. To be situated does not mean to be unimportant or to lack wider relevance. Rather, it means recognizing that which generates a philosophical problem and the ground from which our thinking of this problem departs. It also indicates what is at stake in any claim that departs from this ground and the requirements that must be met in order to go beyond this problem. With this in mind, it is worth turning to a consideration of the work of Stengers to situate these ideas within a more contemporary arena, and to approach the implications of Whitehead's thought for social theory.

Stengers and speculation

> Speculative philosophy addresses what exists as part of a Cosmic adventure, while sciences address the order of nature [...]. What is the difference that matters for Whitehead between the Cosmos and the order of nature? The difference is that the order of nature is a problem for the thinkers, scientists

Situated speculation as a constraint on thought   57

and philosophers, while the Cosmos must include the thinker. Thinking itself must become part of the Cosmic adventure.

(Stengers, 2013: 193)

The argument that I have just set out has outlined Whitehead's rigorous rules for speculation. Stengers aims to assess the extent to which these could sit with the procedures of a good scientist who might, indeed must, hypothesize with regard to a specific problem. In doing so, a scientist should stay faithful to that problem in her or his conjecture and experiment, and provide responses and evidence that validate (or not) the hypothesis in light of these. Does this constitute speculation?

According to Stengers, scientists, philosophers and sociologists who simply deal with the 'order of nature', that is with the world considered as real and external to thought, might appear to speculate about such a world. But in doing so, they tend to miss out the thinker and the thinking involved; the thinker and its thinking play an active part in the world, and in the speculation. Many sociologists would, at this point, strongly object to this characterization of their activities. They might raise issues of reflexivity, notions of identity or certain understandings of the Hawthorne effect, as central to contemporary sociological approaches. Good sociologists always reflect on their situation and how it contours their thought, or so it is claimed. Whitehead would not dismiss such responses out of hand. He might simply say that in focussing on the identity of the researcher, such sociologists have missed out the other side of the problem, that is – the 'objective' world as posited by philosophers and scientists.

The great demand that Whitehead sets himself and his speculative philosophy is to make it possible to think both sides of these at once. Thinking, identity, reflexivity must not be seen simply as subjective, as social, as creations of a specifically human realm. They too must be made a real part of existence, of the world in its fullest sense, of, as Stengers puts it, the 'cosmos'. And, this is why the subtitle of *Process and Reality* is subtitled *An Essay in Cosmology*:

We should hear two things with this idea of Cosmology. The first is that now everything that may be told to exist will be concerned. And the second is that a Cosmos is not just a Universe, some kind of a matter-of-fact ensemble of everything that exists.

(Stengers, 2013: 195)

'Real' speculation does not involve simply speculating about a world that exists placidly and allows us to think what we want about it or about ourselves. 'Worthwhile' or 'successful' speculation involves realizing that the world (the cosmos) has its own concerns, some of which involve us (humans) and some of which do not. This is one of the roles of 'propositions' for Whitehead. Furthermore, our (human) concerns are part of the world (cosmos) and not elements of some separate realm of sociality, made up of gender, ethnicity, class, etc. The world is having its own adventure:

58   *M. Halewood*

> For Whitehead what matters is that we do not think and feel this adventure either in terms of a promise that everything will eventually turn well, or in terms of fate, of sin, of human guilt. Novelty and possibility are for the better of for the worse.
>
> (Stengers, 2013: 197)

Speculation, again, is not some kind of free-for-all, some liberation of thought, where we can indulge our imagination, or our fancy. Speculation is a demanding and rigorous procedure. There is an openness involved in speculation, so that it does not simply report on what we already consider the world to be. But this openness is not a simple liberation. It implies a real constraint:

> Keeping the doors and windows open is a constraint on thinking. It does not only demand that the thinker leave the solid ground of agreed human conventions, which affirm the legitimacy of certain possibilities and condemn others. In order to leave this ground, it also demands that the thinker not aim at what would transcend the conventions that give its consistency to this ground.
>
> (Stengers, 2009: 18)

Speculation, on this view, becomes a matter of 'keeping the doors and windows open'. Clearly this notion suggests that speculation entails an openness, a refusal to sit within what Whitehead elsewhere calls 'grooves of thought' (Whitehead, 1932 [1925]: 245). We must not simply repeat the past or stick within the parameters given to us by our own areas of specialization.

But why does this make such openness a constraint on thinking? Stengers' version of openness involves a jumping out of those certainties that provide our usual academic setting. But, in jumping, we must not imagine that we have freed ourselves from the world in which we are situated. The jump does not come from nowhere. We jump from a specific place, a specific ground. It is not possible to jump from anywhere (see Halewood, 2011, for a further discussion of this). We should, therefore, recognize what it is that enables us to jump and the limits that this puts on us. We do not 'transcend' the problems that provide us with the ground from which to jump. We must stay faithful to this ground, to what enables us to jump, to speculate, at the very moment that we make our jump. We must also consider where we are going to land:

> We can and we may, as it were, jump with both feet off the ground into or towards a world of which we trust the other parts to meet our jump and only so can the making of a perfected world of the pluralistic pattern take place. Jumping off the ground [...] transmutes the question of choice. It is no longer a worldly choice – what should one choose to be or do in this world? – but a choice for the world to which it is a matter of contributing. This choice doesn't only imply a world in the making; it affirms a world whose components are themselves indeterminate, whose 'perfectibility' depends on

the jumper's trust that he may connect with 'other parts' that may become an ingredient in its fabric.

(Stengers, 2009: 11, emphases in original)

This relates to Whitehead's apparently innocuous description of the process of speculation as 'like the flight of an aeroplane'. As opposed to those philosophers who wish to leave the earth behind and transcend the limits that it imposes (Descartes, for example), the task is to make a jump, knowing that one must return to earth and that this return should justify or validate that jump, that speculation. Again, this might not seem so novel. What is new, according to Stengers (and Whitehead) is the faith and the risk that is involved in the jump. The faith is that the world will do what it should, it will meet us after our jump. Yet, this is only part of the story, for we need to accept that the world to which we return is not the same as the world from which we launch ourselves. This is the whole point of speculation; it is not to confirm what we already believe (or know) but to create new thoughts and new realities. Obviously, these new realities do not, and cannot, emerge simply from the speculation itself (from human thought about the world). Instead, the world itself must be trusted to have its own concerns and as rising to meet us when we land, but not as a placid resting place. To view the world as simply there, the same as it was when we jumped, is to view it as exhibiting an 'order of nature' (as do traditional scientists and philosophers). That which enables speculation is a faith in novelty; a novelty that is not restricted to our thought but is implicit in the change which characterizes the process of reality. In this sense, the world is a 'pluralistic pattern', it is a 'world in the making'. Our thought, our speculation, our jumping, are not separate from this world, they are part of the making of the world. In Whitehead's account, speculation is not simply imaginative thinking about an external world. It is a located, situated, jump which recognizes the conditions which enable that jump, views the world as 'in the making', and, crucially, views that thought, jump and speculation as a vital element of that world in the making.

Speculation, risky thought and capitalist sorcery

Speculation is always related to a specific problem. In their book *Capitalist Sorcery*, Pignarre and Stengers (2011) set themselves the problem of describing the character of contemporary capitalism. This involves locating our thought, our speculation, both as proceeding from a specific milieu and also as involved in the world that is being made. But, crucially, this locating of our thought does not imply mere reflexivity where one's own gender, sexuality, ethnicity, class, age, etc. are discussed at the beginning of the text, because:

such a reflexive mode still makes of us the brains, that which confronts the ultimate dilemmas without ever interrogating itself about what feeds it, attributing to itself a force that it testifies to but that it doesn't know how to honour.

(Pignarre and Stengers, 2011: 142)

60   *M. Halewood*

Making ourselves into 'brains' means that we do not ask what it is that feeds or produces a position where such reflexivity is seen as necessary, nor does it ask where the categories of gender, class, sexuality, age, etc. derive their supposed explanatory power. These categories, or the problems of these categories, are not made part of the problem, of the speculation itself, and of a world in the making.

As opposed to such somewhat 'superficial' reflexivity, as Pignarre and Stengers might describe it, they take the risk of speculating in the mode of witches: 'To end with witches, for example, exposes us – and we know it – to the conclusion that that is the model that we are proposing, that that is where we are surreptitiously leading.' But this 'has not prevented us from taking risks that prudence would have advised us to avoid' (Pignarre and Stengers, 2011: 142). Pignarre and Stengers are not simply saying that they are adopting the stance or methodology of witches. Rather, they view witches as prime exemplars of a true and radical pragmatism (Pignarre and Stengers, 2011: 138). This is a demanding form of pragmatism. It renounces any faith in a settled world that can be immediately known. Instead, it launches itself from, and returns to a world-in-the-making, where one's speculations can only be assessed in terms of the effects and consequences that they produce as part of the making of the world. This decision to frame their analysis of capitalism by reference to neo-pagan witchcraft is also risky. They risk having their arguments and works dismissed out of hand by (us) serious minded heirs of the Enlightenment who would grant no place to witches within academia. They also risk being too readily accepted by those with woolly new-age sentiments.

Conclusion: situated speculation and situated knowledge

The previous example of Pignarre and Stengers' invocation of the practices of neo-pagan witches as offering a novel approach to analysing capitalism, and our relation to it, is not to be viewed as a crucial step in the argument that I am trying to set out. It is only an example. I would like to conclude, by making one further point and, in doing so, returning to the question set out at the start of this chapter regarding the status of speculation as a method for social science or social theory.

One productive example of this can be found in the work of Haraway, especially in her concept of "Situated Knowledges" (Haraway, 1991: 183–201) as a description of speculation, or even situated speculation:

> I think that my problem and 'our' problem is how to have simultaneously an account of radical historical contingency for all knowledge claims and knowing subjects […] and a no-nonsense commitment to faithful accounts of a 'real' world, one that can be partially shared and friendly to earth-wide projects of finite freedom, adequate material abundance, modest meaning in suffering, and limited happiness.
>
> (Haraway, 1991: 187, emphasis in original)

Situated speculation as a constraint on thought 61

Although I do not want to 'reduce' Haraway's insights to those of Stengers, there are clear resonances between their ideas. A comparison between the two could shed new light on both approaches. For example, in her essay on 'Situated Knowledge', Haraway argues against the traditional academic position of 'seeing everything from nowhere' (Haraway, 1991: 189), which she describes as the 'god-trick'. As with Whitehead and Stengers, speculation cannot transcend or deny the ground that enables such speculation or act of thought. We must pay attention to that which allows us to think, in order to avoid the 'god-trick'. Haraway also reminds us that thought is always situated within worlds, but the kinds of worlds that Haraway invokes are more familiar to social theorists. These are worlds immediately concerned with 'modest material abundance', 'meaning', 'suffering', and 'happiness'. This is not to make Haraway a traditional sociologist, but it does give specific flesh to the philosophical bones. Similarly, Whitehead and Stengers' concept of speculation breathes new possibilities into our understanding of Haraway. For example, the emphasis on speculation reminds us that 'knowledges' are not passive, are not made up of things that lie in some objective reality, waiting to be uncovered by rational thought. Speculation resolutely introduces the activity, the production, the process of thought, and includes thought within such processes, as signalled in the 'epigraph' from Whitehead, which was given at the very start of this chapter.

In this respect, it is possible, perhaps, to see Haraway's 'Cyborg Manifesto' (Haraway, 1991: 149–181) as a piece of successful speculation. In this compelling piece, Haraway describes a world that is both familiar and strange. It is one with complex gender relations, technologies, power, the military, capitalism and real individuals. The risk that Haraway takes, the speculative movement, is to ask us to jump and leave the stable ground of two genders (masculine and feminine) in order to land back in a world where such stabilities have been transfigured into the image of the cyborg. This is not to deny gender or power or capitalism, but to invite us to inhabit a new cosmos, a new world, where the cyborg provides a coherent, logical, more adequate account of the world-in-the-making within which we are embroiled. The world and us have changed through this speculative moment. The risk that Haraway runs is that of leaving the safety of established understandings of gender, and incurring the ridicule of those might feel that Haraway has betrayed sociology and feminism by making us all into cyborgs. As such, the Cyborg Manifesto is a strong exercise in speculation.

With this final example, I think it is now possible to conclude by identifying three main forms of speculation. (It should be noted that financial speculation could, perhaps, be subsumed under the first two:)

1 'Traditional' speculation, which conjectures without the full available facts. It means we could, if we want, think what we like. This might run close to imagination, sometimes. Does Boris Johnson want to be Prime Minister?

2 'Scientific' speculation, which generates hypotheses that are to be tested in the future, following certain 'experiments'. This will put some

62   *M. Halewood*

constraint on what is thought. However, this form of speculation only treats the world as exhibiting an order that lies in wait to be discovered. Furthermore, the thought that constitutes such speculation is treated as separate from that world and not part of the content of the speculation (or the order exhibited by the world). This is not full-blown speculation.

3   'Situated' speculation, which arises in relation to a specific ground (or problem) which is the starting point for the 'jump' of speculation, and also recognizes the conditions that this ground places on such a jump. This is a first form of constraint. But it is one that will allow for productive speculation. This situated speculation involves a faith in the world, not as a fixed, external world, but a world-in-the-making. Situated speculation entails seeing an act of speculation as part of that world-in-the-making. This introduces a second form of constraint: situated speculation involves risk. It is not a question of confirming a hypothesis as this form of speculation is inherently and radically pragmatic. This is a third form of constraint. Speculation is only to be judged in terms of its consequences and effects. There is no 'right' or 'wrong', 'good' or 'bad' only what happens next.

Such constraints on situated speculation do not render it weak or insipid. Quite the contrary. But it does mean that examples of this third form of speculation are likely to be scarce. In this respect, I will finish where I started. It may well be that speculation is relevant for social theory and social science but only if it is recognized to be a demanding exercise and not easy to achieve. Speculation in social theory is likely to be rare, rather than a new but easy methodological tool.

Speculative boldness must be balanced by complete humility before logic, and before fact. It is a disease of philosophy when it is neither bold nor humble, but merely a reflection of the temperamental presuppositions of exceptional personalities.

(Whitehead, 1978: 17)

References

Halewood, M. (2011). Science, concepts and the social environment. *Theory of Science*, *33*(1), 3–31

Haraway, D. (1991). *Simians, cyborgs, and women. The reinvention of nature.* London: Routledge.

Pignarre, P., & Stengers, I. (2011). *Capitalist sorcery. Breaking the spell.* Basingstoke: Palgrave.

Shaviro, S. (2014). *The universe of things: On speculative realism.* Minneapolis: University of Minnesota Press.

Stengers, I. (2009). William James. An ethics of thought. *Radical Philosophy, 157*, September/October 2009, 9–19.

Stengers, I. (2013). Whitehead and science: From philosophy of nature to speculative cosmology. *Journal of Political Criticism, 13*(12), 179–204

Situated speculation as a constraint on thought 63

Whitehead, A. N. (1927). *Symbolism. Its meaning and effect*. New York: The Macmillan Company.

Whitehead, A. N. (1932 [1925]). *Science and the modern world*. Cambridge: Cambridge University Press.

Whitehead, A. N. (1933). *Adventures of ideas*. Cambridge: Cambridge University Press.

Whitehead, A. N. (1964 [1920]). *Concept of nature*. Cambridge: Cambridge University Press.

Whitehead, A. N. (1978. [1929]). *Process and reality. An essay in cosmology*. (Gifford Lectures of 1927–8). (Corrected edition) (D. Griffin, & D. Sherburne, Eds). New York: The Free Press.

Part II
Speculative lures

Introduction
Speculative lures

Marsha Rosengarten, Martin Savransky, and Alex Wilkie

If speculation is to craft an alternative to a pervasive preoccupation with the aversion to risk and, hence, calculable futures in order to induce a departure from such patterns of the present, what might entice this venture? What might constitute a lure away from the logic, rationalities, and habits of the present that would otherwise prevail and, by doing so, delimit possibilities? Indeed, what might such a lure offer by drawing us to embark on the adventure of thinking otherwise?

It is perhaps this last question that foremost puts on notice that the speculative orientation of this collection has political intent. To be sure, this intent has a different quality to that which we find in the response to many of 'the problems' now said to extend across the globe. Wherever we find a problem – whether it is inequality, climate change, a lethal epidemic, a fascist regime or terrorist organisation, indeed, even the application of method – the conventional response is the imposition of an ideologically and hence *pre*-defined aim for the achievement of a 'solution'. In practice, the solution-response demands a sustained conformation in conduct to what has already been determined in advance to matter.

By contrast, the 'openness' to possibilities that we entertain here through the speculative notion of the lure has a different flavour. It is, on the one hand, no more than a humble invitation to cultivate a conduct elicited by exposure to the matterings that compose the problem (Savransky, in this volume). That is to say, it is an invitation to attend to the expression of the problem and partake in its experience. On the other hand, to take up such an invitation already requires a shift open to the exposure in unforetold ways. That is to say, it is an invitation to become differently that cannot be orchestrated from the outset and, thus, remains indicative only of a learning otherwise that must transpire. Indeed, it is a learning that comes with a pause – a reflection that holds back on usual habits – in the presence of the explosions, resistances and momentary accommodations that may come with the enlivening of connections that constitute the encounter (Savranksy, 2016).

For Whitehead, the lure that would or could break with habits is the proposition itself: 'A proposition is an element in the objective lure *proposed for feeling*, and when admitted into feeling it constitutes *what is felt*' (Whitehead, 1978: 187). Without expounding on the breadth of experience and array of technical terms

68 *M. Rosengarten* et al.

that Whitehead provides in extending feeling to all modes of a connected existence, it may suffice to state that when propositions are posed to entreat speculation in the presence *of* different 'matterings', they are not the measure of what would be taken as an existing state of affairs. As Gaskill & Nocek (2014: 6) claim from their reading of Whitehead, what is important is not that propositions speak of existent truths but that they 'energize and direct feeling'. It is through propositions that we may be lured from a reliance on and, hence, conformation to what has become established as the contours of the given. This does not mean that we depart wholeheartedly from the given as we know it, a task that is in fact futile because unlike what is being proposed here it has no possibility. As Stengers (2011: 313) has argued, 'a speculative possibility does not simply fall from the sky of ideas. Speculation originates in unique situations, which exhibit the possibility of an approach by the very fact they have already undertaken it.'

The proposition of speculative lures comes with a pluralist politics. More specifically, as Stengers (2016) terms it 'a politics of ontology': 'a world where many worlds fit'. For the social scientist or any inquirer interested in the adventure that comes with exposure to other worlds, this politics has perhaps one key guide rail: to avoid judgements by one world of another and, instead, construct what Stengers (2005) proposes should become 'an ecology of practices'. Although conflicts of interests are the more usual state of affairs, this does not mean we should settle for such makings. To accept the world on such terms – the terms of given 'problems' – is to ignore the creativity and hence novelty that comes of the 'weaving of co-evolutions' (Stengers, 2016).

Co-evolutions are the making of connections between 'beings' whose interests, whose ways of having their world matter, diverge. Two entities with different 'reasons' but who, in their encounter, constitute an ecology (Stengers, 2005). As Gilles Deleuze states, it involves a 'double capture, of non-parallel evolution, of nuptials between two reigns' (Deleuze and Parnet, 2007: 2). The orchid lures the wasp whose pleasure seeking activity achieves for the orchid the process of pollination, yet all the while they remain differently 'reasoning' co-evolving species (Deleuze & Parnet, 2007: 2, 3). They do not need to share a 'common definition of understanding' to refer to each other and, in doing so, participate in the creativity of their and our co-evolving worlds (Stengers, 2016).

But given what we have already described in the introduction to this collection and flagged in our opening above, that is, the prevalence of reasons that foreclose on the co-evolution of an ecology of practices, how or by what means might the proposition be practically posed? If, as Stengers proposes, 'lures' in their turning of attention vectorise the concreteness of what comes to matter, by what means might this turn for a politics of ontology come about? For Stengers, it is the figure of the diplomat. A figure somewhat modified from the sort we find in contemporary political practice where tolerance is the aim. Tolerance, Stengers stresses, serves only to enable the acquiring or maintaining of the hegemonic machine that refutes divergence. By contrast, the charge for Stengers' (2016) diplomat is to become a 'creature of speculation'. Intervening for 'a peace that *might* be possible'.

Introduction: speculative lures 69

Becoming a creature of speculation is, however, by no means straightforward if the latter would imply a formula or model of adherence. There is no method to diplomacy. It is the doing of what it proposes. That is, it comes about through and expresses what is felt in the encounter with the interests of those whose presence has been overlooked, excluded or quashed and whom, as a 'speculative creature', the diplomat as such has come to know. The lure of 'peace' – as it underscores a present of war and, more specifically, of antagonistic commitments – is the lure for an ongoing but inevitably transformative and possibly transforming experiment, a *process* that is emergent and has no finite end as would be the expectation of seeking a solution – 'a secure chain of its and thens and thuses' (Stengers, 2016). The diplomat is thus a type of liminal figure whose own precarity bears the possibility of giving presence to those otherwise subject to an authoritative neglect, indifference or, indeed, genocide.

Diplomatic manoeuvres for a pluralist research

In this part of the collection on *Speculative Research* we introduce our own proposition, that of placing the social researcher in the role of Stengers' diplomat. If the diplomat is a creature of speculation, opening the way to a process of co-evolution by putting forward what matters for those otherwise made absent from the table so, we venture, might the researcher be figured in this manner. To be sure, the research field is rife with antagonist relations. Too often we see these displayed in the arrogance of mounting critique, damming the efforts of others and, as such, may be part of the very problem that the critique is claimed to surmount. In short, the possibility of supplanting such antagonisms itself poses the proposition for a plurality and hence co-evolution of the very practice of inquiry.

In the chapters that comprise this part, we see the authors treading carefully amongst their fellow researchers to bring forward other worlds to augment what may be made of the field of inquiry. Each chapter exhibits a concern for the relations between researcher and researched as these play out in prior uncontested claims of what is at stake. In each case, the speculative orientation of our authors unsettles the force effect of antagonistic relations, relations that would otherwise attribute a one-sided irrationality to those whose worlds have become subjugated by the worlds of what present as scientific, social scientific/'speculative' design and historical research. Indeed, this quashing might be said to give cause to our proposition that the researcher be called to the role of the diplomat.

More specifically, the three chapters provide a rethinking of the situating and consequent obfuscation of other 'reasons' found in the work of the lauded randomised control trial which serves as the basis for evidence-based medicine (Rosengarten); corporate endeavours that have appropriated the notion of speculative research for the design of healthcare devices (Wilkie & Michael); and non-relational capitalist critiques of the origins of money (Deville). In the context of this rethinking, 'methods' themselves become exposed for the work they do in sustaining a hegemonic view of the world, whether they are explicit in their

70   *M. Rosengarten* et al.

intention of achieving probablistic estimates to guide the future (Rosengarten); the practice of 'brainstorming' in routine design work that promises openness but inevitably returns to a pre-determined account of what matters by the researchers (Wilkie & Michael); or historical studies that are already inscribed by versions of Marxism blind to the relationality in the co-evolving of different worlds (Deville).

Although each chapter engages with a different 'problem' and thus examines methods employed by researchers located in disciplinary fields, the chapters share one particular feature that is worthy of a pause itself: the challenge they take up is not only that of doing speculative research but the nature of the lure to do so.

While Rosengarten's chapter proposes a lure for a more complexified science, attentive and able to learn with the 'reasons' of its recalcitrant research subjects, Wilkie and Michael provide through their 'ethnography of ethnography' a counter to the fallacious lure of an inquiry premised on the all too quick claim that an innovative method will do the work of speculation, a method shown to foreclose precisely on its promise of new possibles. Deville, by contrast, tackles the unanswerable question of the origin of money. Here, through a review of an anthropological account of human-becoming, we find again a world that resists accommodation within the conformationist data of another. Drawing on a series of encounters between white Australian colonialists and indigenous peoples of Papua New Guinea, Deville shows how money itself is speculative. It is not simply an object with which to speculate but what becomes money is already a matter of speculation. Not unlike what could be said of the research process or the intervention that comes of research, value (money or shells) is disclosed as co-constitutive – becoming a value in the relations that it partakes in shaping while situated between different worlds. Thus serving as a lure for feeling in its capacity to make connections between: 'beings' whose interests, whose ways of having their world matter, diverge.

References

Deleuze, G, & Parnet, C. (2007). *Dialogues* (2nd Revised ed.). New York, NY: Columbia University Press.

Gaskill, N., & Nocek A. J. (2014). Introduction. *The lure of Whitehead* (N. Gaskill, & A. J. Nocek, Eds). London, Minneapolis, MN: University of Minnesota Press.

Savransky, M. (2016). *The adventure of relevance: An ethics of social inquiry*. London: Palgrave Macmillan.

Stengers, I. (2005). Introductory notes on an ecology of practices. *Cultural Studies Review, 11*(1), 183–196

Stengers, I. (2011) *Cosmopolitics II*. Minneapolis, MN: University of Minnesota Press.

Stengers, I. (2016) The challenge of ontological politics. Paper delivered at *The Insistence of The Possible Symposium*. Goldsmiths, University of London.

Whitehead, A. N. (1978). *Process and reality*. New York, NY: Free Press.

5 Pluralities of action, a lure for speculative thought

Marsha Rosengarten

> I am convinced that we need other kinds of narratives, narratives that populate
> our worlds and imaginations in a different way.
>
> (Stengers, 2011a: 371)

I begin this chapter with a story from Michel Serres's book *The Troubadour of Knowledge*, which has served as a lure for my own thinking on the possibilities afforded by the attention to different ways of knowing. I use the story to pose a question about whether the practitioners of science might be similarly provoked and in such a way that, borrowing here from Isabelle Stengers (2005: 994), leads them 'to shrug their shoulders' at the modes of modern scientific inquiry that foreclose on learning from difference. My question thus turns on the possibility of a lure to speculation: leaving off the grip of knowing what has already been determined in advance to matter.

Serres's story begins with an account of a group of sailors who find themselves shipwrecked on a Polynesian Island in a strange but wonderful paradise. We learn of intense exchanges between contrasting cultures, inclusive of discussions 'about each other's gods [...] about the rules followed in given matters by each of the two communities, their advantages and disadvantages':

> The natives nourished a strange passion for words: they asked for the precise translation of their terms and were tireless in their explanations [...]. They [the shipwrecked and the natives] wore themselves out on parallels: the constraints differed, but each was subjected in his country to equally complicated rules, incomprehensible to the point of laughter to his interlocutors, but on neither side were these rules neglected.
>
> (Serres, 1997: 127)

Eventually, we are told, the shipwrecked sailors were rescued only to return again, this time by their choice. They were welcomed with a large feast and, most relevant to what I want to extract from the story, an almost never-ending soccer match. Each time the game finished with an uneven score – precisely what we would regard as indication of a winner and loser – the game was

72 M. Rosengarten

replayed. Only when the score was even did the Islanders stop playing and celebrate. The game, Serres (1997: 130) narrates, had been played according to the usual rules of soccer with only one single rule change: the absence of a 'conqueror and a conquered'. The Islanders explain the alteration through the example of a pancake that would usually be divided according to the numbers needing to eat it: 'This pancake, did it occur to you not to share it?' 'That wouldn't mean anything', the sailors protest. 'But yes, as in soccer. Someone will eat the whole thing and the others won't eat anything, if you don't share it.'

The Islanders elaborate:

> We do not understand that which is neither just nor human, because one gets the upper hand. So we play the game for the time you taught us. If at the end the result is nil, the game ends on true sharing [...]. If not, the two teams, as you say, are decided between, which is something unjust and barbaric. What is the point in humiliating the vanquished if one wishes to pass for civilized like yourselves? So, one must begin again, for a long time, until sharing returns. Sometimes the game lasts for weeks. Some players have even died from it.
> Died from it? Really?
> Why not?

Serres concludes the story with a type of postscript. He says the sailors again left but now with the question of what it means to win. It led them to wonder if they had actually 'won' the Second World War, given the event of Hiroshima. In turn, one sailor offers the following insight as the group reflected on their experience:

> Are you trying to determine the true conquerors? [...] I know them well, from having taken them sometimes in my boat.... Ethnologists, sociologists, I don't know their title, but they study the natives of the islands ... and in general take men for the subject of studies, that is, for objects.

And a final comment from another:

> They sing of victory: who can conceivably be above those who explain and understand others who, from this point of view, will never again be their fellow creatures, what is more their neighbours?
>
> (Serres, 1997: 130, 131).

The story enables us to ponder on the stakes of play and, by changing one rule only, exposes how what matters to a community may be vastly different to that to another. In this case, taking some forms of dying for granted (those for conquering) in contrast to others (those for sharing). It also alludes to a willingness or an ableness by all the characters – and potentially us, as readers – to be exposed to other possible modes of existence. They key example being the

Pluralities of action 73

contrasting modes of the game of soccer. The sailors' response proffered by Serres's imaginative play may be tentative but, in his telling, they became privy to the investment we – those of us who do not live in a paradise-like world – have in the act of conquering or, as I want to understand it, in the assertion of a knowing that closes down on possibles obtained from the experience of others.

For now I shall leave off this tale to offer a little back story to what leads me to be so enchanted by Serres's narrative. I begin with a group of biomedical scientists, more specifically those who would go to distant lands in order to test – by way of the method of the randomized control trial, hereon referred to as the RCT – a pill called PrEP (pre-exposure prophylaxis) for preventing HIV infection. Although aligning paradise and science might seem for now somewhat outlandish, I do so in order to ask what the RCT might become if a challenge to the purpose of its rules was seriously contemplated. A challenge that I suggest has already been mounted and, arguably, not entirely unlike the provocation to the sailors on witnessing the unfolding of a remarkable remaking of the parameters of *their* game.

The biomedical story I want to tell comprised over 14,000 research subjects enrolled in five RCTs spanning the continents of Africa, Asia, North and South America. All of these trials, each including a series of different country sites, were designed to test the probabilistic efficacy of PrEP. Central to the narrative is that the findings from these trials were surprisingly contradictory. According to the conventions of trial design and measured outcomes, PrEP pill efficacy was demonstrated in iPrEX, a trial that specifically enrolled men who have sex with men (MSM); in The Partners PrEP Study that enrolled heterosexual couples (one HIV positive and one HIV negative, with men and women of both categories); and, also, in a significantly smaller and therefore not considered efficacy RCT, TDF2 that enrolled young heterosexual men and women. By unexpected contrast, lack of efficacy and therefore said trial 'failure' occurred in both the Fem-PrEP and VOICE RCTS that had specifically recruited only 'young single women.'[1] Explanation for Fem-PrEP and VOICE's failure has been deemed to rest squarely on 'young, single women' due to the very characteristic attributed to the reason for their recruitment. Young single women are an epidemiological category that has been shown to experience exceptionally high rates of vulnerability to HIV infection.[2] That is to say, the characteristic of being young, single and female was deemed warranting intervention. However, in the scenario I am relating, it not only retained what warranted intervention – indeed, it continued to do so as significant numbers acquired HIV in the course of the trials[3] – it also incurred failure to the activity of intervention. Not only did the category of 'young single women' – unlike those of different epidemiological characteristic – fail to adhere to the trial protocol *and* falsely reported about being so, they left the trials without the statistical probability of efficacy necessary to trial success. Further, with evidence shown simply to be a case of failure the women themselves are left without possibility of an intervention.[4]

74   *M. Rosengarten*

The 'problem': non-compliant female research subjects

Initially on the release of the contradictory findings of the above five trials, 'biological' and/or 'social/behavioural' causal factors associated with femaleness were proposed to explain the apparent anomaly across the RCTs (Van der Straten, Van Damme, Haberer, & Bangsberg, 2013). The biological factors were conjectured as related to hormones: an unexpectedly high number of women became pregnant in the product arm of Fem-PrEP and also some others were taking injectable hormones. Contraception is a requirement of all women of reproductive age when entering an HIV trial and because both pregnancy and injectable contraceptives are *suspected* of increasing HIV susceptibility (Mascolini 2012; Mugo, et al., 2011), they were considered for their effect on the metabolic achievement of PrEP. But since neither the finding of hormonal contraceptives or pregnancy was considered pertinent to the women in the successful trials, this has not to date been taken further.[5]

An article by Koenig et al. (2013: S92), published after that of Van der Straten et al. (2012) cited above, noted that women in one of the other 'successful' trials, 'The Partners Study', had HIV positive partners who made the risk of HIV acquisition apparent and provided support for their HIV-negative partner to adhere to the dosing regime. But, ultimately, this too was disregarded along with hormones and other suggestions proffered by Koenig et al. (2013: S93) based on studies elsewhere that have included forgetting, depression, anxiety, poor quality of life, misperceptions about treatment efficacy and those noted by Wilton et al. (2015) including mucosal inflammation or differential drug penetration in the female genital tract. In sum, the interesting question of what was happening in the trials and hinted at in the commentaries post their findings, has been reduced to the positivist inference that young single women cannot be trusted or, more palatable perhaps, cannot be relied upon.

A final component to the story, as it can be told from science narrated sources, is the manner in which the trialists have needed to exonerate themselves from the said cause for 'failure', that is, from the situation of lack of adherence and false reporting. An article by Mack et al. (2013). details the efforts made in the preparation for and during the Fem-PrEP to ensure 'good' trial relations with the research subjects as well as their communities. Outreach work involved making personal contact with individuals in bars, women's groups, sex-worker 'hot spots' as well as at formalized meetings in order to achieve community 'research literacy', and plans were put in place for 'issues management', 'trial closure' and 'results dissemination'. Research literacy – which might in some respects be said to encompass the other criteria of issues management, trial closure and results dissemination – refers to an understanding of the trial aims and processes by those enrolled and possibly by their communities. These strategies and others specifically in place were intended to avert or quash 'misunderstandings' about the trial, for instance: claims that the drugs might be harmful and/or that the trialist intentions were underhand and risk inducing (Mack et al., 2013: 133).

Pluralities of action   75

It is the care taken by the trialists to ensure co-option to the agenda of the RCT that I think highlights what is taken to matter by those conducting the trials, and it is a curious turn in the intended effects of bioethics. Adherence to the set protocols follows from the presumption that scientific authority is right and proper. Hence it is the role of those instituting the RCT to achieve a conversion in their research subjects to scientific requirements. Although I do not want to denounce the effort to engage with the targeted community as such (some say the Fem-PrEP trial offered more forms of care than have many other trials), the efforts themselves were very much intended to shore up the trialists' own version of the world. The quote below, especially the last line, underscores how 'the community' is viewed as a potential source of disruption to a trial and, by implication, to the generalized need for the methods of modern science:

> Even though the primary analysis of clinical trial data revealed that adherence to the study product was too low to demonstrate the effectiveness of Truvada [drug combination in PrEP] for HIV prevention among the study population, we do not believe that the community program failed. The community program was intended to create a supportive environment for women participating in the clinical trial, including for women who wanted to take the study drug, through community education about the purpose of the trial and by addressing the community's concerns about the trial. The FEM-PEP researchers are currently exploring the reasons for low adherence among former FEM-PrEP participants, including any role that the community may have played.
>
> (Mack et al., 2013: 135)

There is a history to the concern for research subject and community acceptance of RCTs that follows from community protests mounted against an early set of PrEP trials bringing about their closure (see McGrory, Irvin, & Heise, 2009; Rosengarten, & Michael, 2009). On the one hand, this has generated a guide now taken as a form of 'gold standard' in itself for instituting a RCT in locales where there may be doubts about the intentions of scientific research as suggested in the account above by Mack et al. (2013).[6] Although well-intentioned, the guide may be considered part of the problem I am wanting to illuminate and I will come back to this. On the other hand, it also seems that community protests may have provoked individual scientists involved at the time to a more cautious and, thus, interested engagement with research subjects' experience. When participating on a conference panel on speculation that I organized not so long ago, one such scientist – who went on to become the Principal Investigator of the iPrEX trial – recounted his recent learning that what constitutes the end of a night and beginning of a day varies with the activities that come to comprise the temporal distinction. His reflective approach raised for me not so much the problematic of imposing repetitive clock time on lives that are not ordered in this way – something I could ascertain from my own direct experience – but that

76 M. Rosengarten

scientific interest can extend, not unlike the interest of Serres's sailors, to different modes of doing.

Needless to say, for the most part the method of the RCT – as it is currently deployed – functions as a mode indifferent to matters other than statistical probabilities. That is to say, the method itself works against other modes of knowing. Its capacity to do so, in a manner that I am suggesting rides roughshod over the experiences of its research, is no doubt because of the hold of modern science. Above I mentioned that the guide to good participatory practice might well aid this situation. What I mean by this is that it has extended the reach of scientific logic and authority into communities in a manner specifically for the purpose, as indicated above, of avoiding disruption to what has already been deemed to matter. To put this rather more bluntly, the RCT has no truck with experiences that differ to those determined in advance. Sense-making *of* science from the standpoint of existing 'local' logic is not a matter for trial learning.

By contrast other sections of the HIV field inclusive of social scientists as well as advocacy groups have posed questions that suggest a need for more understanding, if not an entirely different account of the 'failed' trials. A short online opinion piece on VOICE with some reference to Fem-PrEP by the highly regarded treatment information non-government organization, NAM, took up the question of why the women chose to enroll in the trials given their later non-compliance to the protocol:

> Thousands of women went to the bother of signing up for a large clinical trial and often travelling to attend day-long clinic visits every three months, but the majority never took a single pill or used a dose of microbicide [vaginal gel also tested against HIV] – and perhaps never intended to. Yet there was excellent retention … the benefits of joining a trial like VOICE in a resource-poor setting may be so large as to make the disclosure of non-adherence feel very difficult for participants, who may fear being excluded from the trial.
>
> (Cairns, 2013)

Later in the piece, Cairns drew on commentary by Judith Auerbach, a prominent social scientist in the HIV field, to posit that payment for trial participation and health benefits may have been important. Unfortunately, so far, these aspects of the trial have not provoked a more extensive reflection on the possible presence of different interests in the making of HIV RCT research outcomes. This is despite the complex nexus of factors that have been identified in effecting the trial outcomes elsewhere (Auerbach, Parkhurst, & Caceres, 2011; Michael & Rosengarten, 2013) and that gesture toward a broader scope of situated constraints. Here I am referring to what I have noted above of the pattern of low contraception and the apparent significance of having an HIV positive partner supportive of pill taking. These and/or other phenomena may well have been integral to the achievement of what has been reduced to 'lack of adherence'. That is to say, the absence of adherence and false reporting needs to be

Pluralities of action 77

considered as part of a situated achievement composed of dynamic interconnected and thus ever emergent biological, social, economic, cultural milieus specific to the individual research subject (Savransky & Rosengarten, 2016).

Recalcitrant subjects

Without discounting the various explanatory accounts offered on the contradictory PrEP trial outcomes but, nevertheless, wanting to see what might be learnt from rather than explained of the research subjects of Fem-PrEP and VOICE, I want to put forward the proposition that the research subjects – and with some similarity to Serres's Islanders – were provocateurs for a change in authoritative rules of thinking.

The term 'recalcitrant' has been taken up by both Bruno Latour (1999) and Isabelle Stengers (2011b) to characterize the resistance exhibited by a scientific non-human entity to the research agenda of the scientist and, as such, from which something new may be learned. Latour and Stengers make the point that such learning is difficult to achieve with human research subjects because the latter are likely to give the answers they believe are expected.

> [H]umans, as soon as they are in a scientific lab, agree ... to answer questions or produce performances that reproduce lab dissymmetry: scientists are wondering, learning, hesitating about the relevant interpretation while the object performs without questions.
>
> (Stengers, 2011b: 83)

By complying to what they anticipate is expected, human research subjects leave the scientist unknowing about what actually matters, precisely what might be assumed as the rationale for inquiry. For Sorensen et al. (2001), this suggests that it is the role of social inquiry to *cultivate* recalcitrance. But I wonder whether the very problematic of doing so, as is indicated by Latour and Stengers, may be rendered unnecessary if we relinquish a priortising of the verbal and attend also to action. Here I draw on Martin Savransky's illustration of recalcitrance in the form of a withdrawal. He describes the case of an analysand who leaves in the middle of a therapy session because she experiences a comment or question by the therapist as inappropriate. The act, he states:

> affirms the relational engagement that makes it possible – i.e. the therapeutic or 'scientific' relation – and forces the vectors that configure that relation to change, to become other, by putting the questions posed by the respective authority to the test.
>
> (2014: 106)

In this scenario, the change that is induced by the resistance or recalcitrance to what is put by the therapist – indeed, what might be considered a generative dynamic that is already doing the work of cultivating – is a possibility for

78 *M. Rosengarten*

novelty. Recalcitrance is induced but, in becoming so, it works as a force for alteration in the dynamic of the encounter, shifting the terms that would otherwise leave the analyst without exposure to something more or different in the evolving relationship.

To be sure, the therapeutic encounter is already premised on the existence of a provocative relationship and a 'good' therapeutic analysis can be argued to depend on the analyst's capacity to reflect on the challenge posed by the act. Here the notion of reflection might be understood as the pause that Stengers calls for if a cosmopolitics is to acquire possibility (Stengers, forthcoming). That is to say, a politics where relevance – that is, that which has come to matter through the event –is allowed to emerge through the expression of what more usually involves toleration if not unequivocal refusal. Reflection in this sense is then an opening to something other than what has been put in place, a possibility for something other than what has been imposed. Recalcitrance is an opportunity for such reflection. I wonder if it might even be considered part and parcel of the ethical sensibility of any practitioner including that of the RCT scientist. 'Ethical' because it is concerned with one's own conduct and with what that conduct induces as a practitioner of inquiry. And of a sensibility that is speculative in the sense that the concern is of a nature beyond what the practitioner has determined in advance. That is, it is open to novel possibilities that come with an inquiry intent on desisting from imposing 'turtles' if not all the way down, then even a couple of layers.

In place of victory or failure

To reconcile the RCT mode with the speculative properties afforded by recalcitrance is an ambitious task, well beyond the confines of this chapter. However it is not beyond the need to make an attempt, even if in only some small way to an articulation of the stakes involved. Having proposed that the research subjects' recalcitrance suggests a different conception of HIV prevention may be available to those who would seek to predetermine what matters, I draw on A. N. Whitehead to first consider more closely the conventional RCT as anti-speculative. Second, again with Whitehead, I consider whether recalcitrance itself might be a lure to speculation.[7] As we shall see, the RCT depends on a logic that believes in the possibility and necessity of closing down on precisely the plurality that Serres celebrates with the togetherness of shipwrecked sailors and inventive locals. Perhaps surprising to those unfamiliar with Whitehead's work, I will use it as a means of according respect to the concern to inquire, a concern I see present and in a rigorous, albeit seriously curtailed, manner by the RCT. By this I mean that I do not presume to denounce the RCT and in its place propose a radically alternative mode. Rather and I hope consistent with how I began this piece, I want to pursue the lure of different ways of knowing – here that of the mode of the RCT and that of the research subjects' – in a manner that does not eventuate in the imposition of one mode on another but, rather, has a more pluralist force. A force that attends to more divergent worlds: 'empowering a

Pluralities of action 79

difference between relevant questions and unilaterally imposed ones' (Stengers, forthcoming).

In *The Function of Reason*, Whitehead outlines two forms of reason: that which derives from Plato and is about understanding, in contrast to that derived from Ulysses which is very much about method for the achievement of a specific purpose. Although the latter form prevails – and is evident in the acceptance of the technology of the RCT as the gold standard for generating evidence-based research in the health and medical field (Michael & Rosengarten, 2013) – Whitehead advocates that the two modes of reason be brought together. He explains: 'The conduct of human affairs is entirely dominated by our recognition of foresight determining purpose, and purpose issuing conduct' (1929: 9). This domination is, he states, a 'dodge' to live, a mode of seeking to stabilize phenomena that is, in fact, the creation of 'a relatively slow process of atrophied decay' (1929: 66). According to Whitehead, this deadening effect is not surprising, though no less worrying for being so. He states that the prevailing orientation toward purposive reason is due to an inclination by human nature to 'obscurantism':

> Obscurantism is the refusal to speculate freely on the limitations of traditional methods. It is more than that: it is the negation of the importance of such speculation, the insistence on incidental dangers.

> (1929: 34)

Needless to say, Whitehead does not desist from recognizing speculation as that which has mostly been 'foolish, brutish, and nasty' (1929: 65). Speculation for a better life, as he poses it, requires discipline, systematic modes of undertaking: 'the interplay of thought and practice is the supreme authority. It is the test by which the charlatanism of speculation is restrained' (1929: 64, 65). We might deduce from this that speculation requires some form of method or, perhaps better noted, a systematic, coherent mode. The mode of inquiry may proceed from a knowing in advance of what matters and its design will inevitably provide constraints that participate in what comes of the work. But if the work, itself, is responsive to what the research comes upon, then there is the possibility for the constraints themselves to be reviewed and the initial premises revised:

> The speculative Reason works in two ways so as to submit itself to the authority of facts without loss of its mission to transcend the existing analysis of facts. In one way it accepts the limitations of a special topic, such as a science or a practical methodology. It then seeks speculatively to enlarge and recast the categoreal ideas within the limits of that topic. This is speculative Reason in its closest alliance with the methodological Reason.

> (1929: 68)

Throughout this chapter I have been explicit in stating that the 'failed' trials invite review of a mode that, to date, is premised on a very specific win at the

80 *M. Rosengarten*

cost of other possibilities. I have wagered that the recalcitrance exhibited by the research subjects in these trials might lure those involved in RCTs to rethink the nature of what is posed as the trial's 'failure'. It remains a wager no matter how I conclude this chapter because I cannot retain any certainty that what I propose could make even a dint in the prevailing reasoning of the HIV biomedical research field. This is not to deny that the field will change. Indeed the field of HIV inquiry can be viewed as always in a process of change with the transformation and thus becomings of bodies, virus and interventions that come with multiple diverse encounters including research encounters (Michael & Rosengarten, 2013; Rosengarten, 2009; Savransky & Rosengarten, 2016). But this type of change may serve only to complexify an existing tendency to frame the problem in terms similar to what we already have: *Who or what failed?* Rather than: *how did the RCT matter to all those whose actions were so crucial to its outcomes?*

In the Whitehead sense, I hope it may serve as a 'lure for feeling' that is called for if the game involves HIV prevention rather than a reductive reliance on consistent dosing adherence or any other strategy conceived as if to work in isolation from the situation in which it takes place (see Rosengarten & Savransky, 2015). Or, to rephrase, if it is understanding that may cultivate an intervention and not a predefined research method, then what is called for is a shift in *feeling* research: in coming to experience what matters in the process that constitutes its taking place. To date, the efforts by the trialists to ensure their research subjects accepted the trial resembles, in some crucial respects, the 'ethnologists, sociologists ...' who, in Serres's story, prioritized their study *of others* to achieve a knowing *of* those whom they have not taken the time know *as* 'fellow creatures' (1997: 131). In practical terms, acceptance for the trial was imported into a home territory with the intention of dodging what research subjects can do besides or in response to 'domination' (Whitehead, 1929: 66).

If we apply Savransky's (2013) call for a speculative approach that involves 'making relevant the experiences that ... [existing] habits oppose', then the experiences of the research subjects are yet to be considered. To return again to Serres's narrative, like the Islanders it can be claimed that the female research subjects in Fem-PrEP and VOICE changed *a* rule, the rule of what must be done according to the authority that imposes it. A rule in the reasoning of the RCT that is premised on thinking that a product – in this instance, a pill – can be isolated from the situation in which it is experienced (Rosengarten et al. 2013; Savransky & Rosengarten, 2016). As things stand, the RCT is dependent on compliance such that when its authority fails, its endeavour fails. But by implication, failure is not the failure of an isolated product but, rather, failure to grasp the situated relations in which its effects are or are not achieved.

In keeping with the epigraph from Stengers (2011a: 371), the research subjects involved in the pursuit of HIV prevention offer a different narrative, possibly plural in content if we were to also consider differences in adherence now documented across the 'failed' trials (see for example, Koenig et al., 2013: S91–S93). If treated as a provocation, their recalcitrance offers the possibility of

Pluralities of action   81

countering 'the atrophied decay' that comes with the imposition of rules that are, themselves, the creatures of habit. Another way of saying this is that it may be possible to rethink the rules of HIV prevention without assuming that the effects of the user-reliant intervention – in this instance, a daily pill – are to be judged according to pre-determined criteria. If the rules are those set by the scientists, we could deduce that their logic has been a provocation for their research subjects and, hence, in place of winners or conquerors 'failure' has opened the possibility for a more pluralist approach to inquiry. To date, it has been an inquiry into an entity curiously posed by the mode of the RCT as if *in* people's lives, yet known in exclusion from them.

Notes

1 It may be of interest to know that all were conducted independently of each other by public health organizations and funded by public and/or philanthropic monies. The drug manufacturer did not run the trials but provided the pills and consistent exchange involving pharmaceutical expertise. Later, the data from the successful trials was used to obtain licensing of PrEP in the United States and is in now in process of acceptance across the world.
2 According to the UNAIDS GAP Report, there are almost 380,000 new HIV infections among adolescent girls and young women (10–24 years old) around the world every year. Globally, 15 per cent of all women living with HIV aged 15 years or older are young women 15–24 years old. Of these, 80 per cent live in sub-Saharan Africa. In this region, women acquire HIV infection at least 5–7 years earlier than men. Young women 15–24 years old in sub-Saharan Africa are twice as likely as young men to be living with HIV.
3 During the Fem-PrEP trial, 33 HIV infections occurred in the product arm and 35 in the placebo/control arm. www.fhi360.org/news/final-results-fem-prep-hiv-prevention-study-indicate-great-attention-adherence-will-be-required [accessed 18 March 2016]. A similar effect occurred in the VOICE trial where the same number of infections occurred in the product and placebo arms. NAM AIDS Map (2013).
4 Koenig et al. (2013: S91) state: 'Self-reported adherence was high in all of the PrEP trials, but it was not a valid measure it is did not correspond with more-objective measures of medication adherence such as pill counts or measurable drug levels.'
5 Medical testing on pregnant women is always a concern if there are deemed to be unknown risks to the fetus. Hence the requirement that women research subjects of reproductive age be using some form of contraception such as the contraceptive pill or an intrauterine device (IUD).
6 The guide is titled 'Good Participatory Participation Guidelines' and was initially produced by AVAC and UNAIDS after the above mentioned controversy over the early PrEP trials. AVAC/UNAIDS (2011).
7 Unfortunately the term speculation has come to be associated within the HIV field with unsubstantiated claims about the cause of HIV that led to the delay of prevention and treatment in South Africa (see Fassin, 2007).

References

Auerbach, J. D, Parkhurst, J. O., & Caceres, C. F. (2011). Addressing social drivers of HIV/AIDS for the long-term response: Conceptual and methodological considerations. *Global Public Health*, *1*(17: 6) Suppl. 3, S293–309.

82   M. Rosengarten

AVAC/UNAIDS (2011). Good participatory practice: guidelines for biomedical HIV prevention trials', second edition. www.avac.org/resource/good-participatory-practice-guidelines-biomedical-hiv-prevention-trials-second-edition [accessed 11 November 2016].

Cairns, G. (2013). VOICE trial's disappointing result poses big questions for PrEP. *www.aidsmap.com/VOICE-trials-disappointing-result-poses-big-questions-for-PrEP/page/2657862/* [accessed 1 April 2014].

CDC Fact Sheet. *www.cdc.gov/hiv/prep/pdf/TDF2factsheet.pdf* [accessed 7 March 2015]

Fassin, D. (2007). *When bodies remember. Experience and politics of AIDS in South Africa*, (Amy Jacobs and Gabrielle Varro, Trans.). Berkeley: University of California Press.

Koenig, L., Lyles, C., & Smith, D. K. (2013). Adherence to antiretroviral medications for HIV Pre-Exposure prophylaxis lessons learned from trials and treatment studies. *American Journal of Preventive Medicine, 44*(1S2), S91–S98.

Latour, B. 1999 When things strike back – A possible contribution of 'science studies' to the social sciences. *British Journal of Sociology, Special Millenium Issue* (John Urry, Ed.), *51*(1), 105–123.

McGrory, E., Irvin, A., & Heise, L. (2009). Research Rashomon: Lessons from the Cameroon pre-exposure prophylaxis trial site. Washington, DC: Global Campaign for Microbicides at PATH.

Mack, N., Kirkendale, S., Omullo, P., Odhiambo, J., Ratlhagana, M., & Masaki, M. et al. (2013). Implementing good participatory practice guidelines in the FEM-PrEP pre-exposure prophylaxis trial for HIV prevention among African women: A focus on local stakeholder involvement. *Open Access Journal of Clinical Trials, 5*, 127–135.

Mascolini, M. (2012). Poor adherence may explain FEM-PrEP failure to find protection from HIV with Truvada. *19th Conference on Retroviruses and Opportunistic Infections, March 5–8, 2012*. Seattle.

Michael, M., & Rosengarten, M. (2013). *Innovation and biomedicine: Ethics, evidence and expectation in HIV*. England: Palgrave Macmillan.

Mugo N.R., Heffron R., Donnell, D., Wald, A., Were, E.O., & Rees H., Celum, C., Kiarie, J. N., Cohen, C. R., Kayintekore, K., & Baeten, J.M. (2011). Increased risk of HIV-1 transmission in pregnancy: A prospective study among African HIV-1 serodiscordant couples. *AIDS, 24; 25*(15), 1887–1895.

NAM AIDS Map (2013). www.aidsmap.com/VOICE-%ADtrials-disappointing-%AD result-poses-%ADbig-questions-%ADfor-PrEP/page/2586636/ [accessed 18 March 2016].

Rosengarten, M., & Michael, M. (2009). Rethinking the bioethical enactment of drugged bodies: On the paradoxes of using anti-HIV drug therapy as a technology for prevention. *Science as Culture, 18*(2), 183–199.

Rosengarten, M., & Savransky, M. (2015). Situating efficacy: HIV and Ebola RCTs and the care of biomedical abstractions. Paper presented at *Situating Efficacy: Biomedicine, Interdisciplinarity, and the Politics of Intervention Symposium*, Brocher Foundation, 16–17 February 2015.

Rosengarten, M., Michael, M., Mykhalovskiy, E., & Imrie, J. (2008). The challenges of technological innovation in HIV. *Lancet*, 2 August, *372*(9636), 357–358.

Savransky, M. (2013). Speculative methods. Paper presented at Goldsmiths, University of London.

Savransky, M. (2014). Of recalcitrant subjects. *Culture, Theory and Critique, 55*(1), 96–113.

Savransky, M., & Rosengarten, M. (2016). What is nature capable of? Evidence, ontology and speculative medical humanities. *Medical Humanities*, *42*,166–172.

Serres, M. (1997). *The troubadour of knowledge*. (Sheila Faria Glaser, & William Paulson, Trans.). Ann Arbor: University of Michigan Press.

Sorensen, C.,Whitley, E. A., Madon, S., Klyachko, D., Hosein, I., & Johnstone, J. (2001). Cultivating recalcitrance in information systems research. In Nancy L Russo, Brian Fitzgerald, & Janice I. De Gross (Eds), *Realigning research and practice in information systems development. IFIP advances in information and communication technology* (pp. 297–316), (Vol. 6). Dordrecht, the Netherlands: Kluwer Academic Publishers.

Stengers, I. (2005). The cosmopolitical proposal. In B. Latour, & P. Weibel (Eds), *Making things public: Atmospheres of democracy* (pp. 994–1003). Cambridge: MA MIT Press.

Stengers, I. (2011a). Wondering about materialism. In L. Bryant, N. Srnicek, & G. Harman (Eds), *The speculative turn: Continental materialism and realism* (pp. 368–380). Melbourne: re.press.

Stengers, I. (2011b). Sciences were never 'good'. *Common Knowledge*, *17(*1), 82–86.

Stengers, I. (2015). *In catastrophic times*: *Resisting the coming barbarism* (Critical Climate Change). (Andrew Goffey, Trans.). London: Open Humanities Press.

Susser, I. (2015). Focus on social and behavioural factors just as important as the medication itself. *Aljazeera America*. Retrieved 7 March 2015 from http://america.aljazeera.com/opinions/2015/3/blame-research-design-for-failed-hiv-study.html

UNAIDS Gap Report (2014). www.unaids.org/sites/default/files/en/media/unaids/contentassets/documents/unaidspublication/2014/UNAIDS_Gap_report_en.pdf [accessed 18 March 2016].

Van der Straten, A., Van Damme, L., Haberer, J. E., & Bangsberg, D. R. (2013). Unraveling the divergent results of pre-exposure prophylaxis trials for HIV prevention. *AIDS*, *26*, F13–F19.

Whitehead, A. N. (1929). *The function of reason*. London: Humphrey Milford, Oxford University Press, copyright Princeton University Press.

Whitehead, A. N. (1978). *Process and reality: An essay in cosmology*. New York: Free Press.

Wilton J., Senn, H., Sharma, M., & Tan, D. H. S. (2015). Pre-exposure prophylaxis for sexually-acquired HIV risk management: a review. *HIV/AIDS – Research and Palliative Care, 7*, 125–136.

6 Doing speculation to curtail speculation

Alex Wilkie and Mike Michael

Introduction

We begin with an extract from an 'in-home' interview conducted by a Design Researcher with Ron, an elderly man living in the Pacific Northwest of the US and coping with diabetes mellitus (type-2), amongst other acute and chronic health conditions:

DESIGN RESEARCHER: *05:01* Okay, all right. And, were you experiencing, you weren't experiencing any more symptoms or anything like that that drove you to the doctor or...

RON: *05:11* Well, I had a swelling in my legs and feet and as a matter of fact I had a lot of problems with my right foot and it was hard to walk even, and although I came to find out later when they removed a toe from the diabetes that, err, there's a little metal spring in my foot. Aliens put it there. Now, I had an operation way back down when, dunno, when I was somewhat out of my teens or something like I'd had problems with my feet and apparently they did it then and I didn't even remember it.

DESIGN RESEARCHER: *05:47* Oh.

RON: *05:48* That's why I like the aliens story better.

DESIGN RESEARCHER: *05:50* Yeah, that does sound more exciting. Umm so, uh... and so did they think that that was the reason for your pain in your foot?

RON: *06:00* Yeah, that's why my pain hurt. But, there again, they'd such as short time afterwards that this is a December [counts] 04, December 05, five six. I had a major heart attack and died and, uh, they gave me mouth to mouth and my wife worked my chest until the ambulance got here. But they were able to save my life and keep my head on straight still and, uh, shortly after that, after the after I'd gone to the hospital and then they noticed my leg had turned black and there was gangrene, so they had to remove my leg, uh, and that was early January.

DESIGN RESEARCHER: *06:47* Early January?

DESIGN RESEARCHER: *06:50* Okay.

In this brief passage, Ron, for whatever reasons, ascribes the metal implant in his foot to extra-terrestrial origins. The excerpt is five minutes into the interview,

Doing speculation to curtail speculation 85

and the Design Researcher is struggling to establish exactly when Ron developed type-2 diabetes along with other details of his medical biography. His physician had died and Ron, a veteran of the Korean War, had subsequently been diagnosed with type-2 diabetes by clinicians working for the US Department of Veterans Affairs (VA). The interviewer was aiming to derive 'thick' descriptions, but even in this brief extract we get indications of a multiplicity of interpretive viscosities, ranging from the thinness of vague and uncertain testimony through to the difficult solidities of 'fantasy'. Taken together with the rest of this 'ethnographic' engagement with Ron, and from the perspective of the design researchers, it is difficult to see how a uniformly thick description can be produced that yields a 'stratified hierarchy of meaningful structures' (Geertz, 2000: 7). As we shall see, this 'multiplicity' of interpretive viscosities which could serve as a basis for speculation, especially when mediated by a putatively speculative method – the brainstorm – ends up being the precise opposite: a reinforcement of prior entanglements.

From 'ethnography' to 'product'?

This interview is one of a series, conducted by members of a team of user-centered designers working on behalf of a multinational semiconductor manufacturer and tasked with exploring the societal and market potential for an end-user healthcare technology.[1] More specifically, this technology would be designed to intervene in the management of acute and chronic health conditions including cardiovascular disease, obesity, high-risk pregnancy, post-operative rehabilitation and diabetes. The in-home interviews, where members of the design team ethnographically engage with research subjects in their 'natural' domestic habitat in order to occasion situated visual (photographs) and narrative data, were envisaged as a nimble means to empirically include patient experience and knowledge in the research and development process. The data produced during the interviews was viewed as a complement to expert medical views, market 'intelligence', recent developments in software and electronic hardware, telecare services as well as the ergonomic possibilities of mechanical technology. Taken together, this heterogeneous set of perspectives was employed to resource the design team's speculations on a viable future healthcare technology for global consumer markets, co-extensive with the corporation's silicon markets and strategic vision. The interview was also an element in the first author's fieldwork, conducted in 2006, as a part of an ethnographic study of 'users' enacted in design practice within the organisational milieu of the aforementioned corporation. Put another way, both prior and current analyses can be considered in terms of an ethnography of the deployment of ethnography as a means to occasion the voice of the patient as a practical resource for commercial biomedical invention and innovation (see Pols, 2014).

Not long after the interview, the design team convened for a 'brainstorm' meeting to reflect on and scope out the latent social, technological and commercial opportunities that might be present in the everyday management of type-2 diabetes. This process was meant to draw on the interdisciplinary views of and research conducted by those present. As is now common practice within large corporate research and development (Nafus & Anderson, 2009; Wilkie, 2010), especially in the IT sector, the participants of the meeting produced and employed visual and handwritten material to both evidence 'empirical reality' and chart emergent sociotechnical developments. So, by transferring descriptive traces of this data onto Post-it® notes, material was rendered open to visual and spatial combination and recombination. In other words, the design team arranged printouts of internet-sourced photographs depicting existing and emerging technologies with handwritten Post-it® notes indicating 'insights' drawn from their own expert knowledge or from the collected interview data. In arranging this material, the design team, at first, sought to make visible existing healthcare services and patient experience as a loose-knit patterning of visual and textual elements on the wall of the meeting room. To this end, notes included handwritten inscriptions such as 'poor adherence', 'reasons to exercise', 'I dislike needles', 'support groups', 'complexity of routine', 'VA' and so on, spatially organised around a set of categories including 'Routine', 'Education and Self-knowledge', 'Self-monitoring', 'Psychological Triggers', 'Support' and 'Psychological and Emotional'.

As the brainstorm progressed, however, the notes and visuals were moved, and new material added, as the patternings on the wall and conversations provoked new associations between aspects and elements of the research. Here, for example, the addition of the note 'Blogs & Online Groups' was introduced and placed under the category 'Support', indicating the potential of online lay-communities to deliver care. Crucially, however, this note was also placed under other categories, engendering conjecture about other modes of engagement with online interest groups – exercise communities, body-monitoring communities or collectives organised around sharing experience and practical knowledge.

Initially Ron figured as a non-user (see Wyatt, 2003), as a person unlikely to incorporate disease management technology effectively into his everyday life. In part, this could be put down to his, not untypical, erratic struggles of living with/in a body-with-diabetes (Mol, 2008; Mol & Law, 2004,). Notwithstanding this, aspects of Ron's situated medico-technological practices came to permeate the material on the wall. That is to say, the design team extracted recognisable and useful features of the interview from the design researcher's recounting of the data. At the same time, other details were downplayed, overlooked or omitted. Thus, on the one hand, descriptions of Ron's pillbox, his handwritten medication list, a bathroom drawer containing his various medications, his reliance on healthcare insurers such as the VA, as well as his diet all made it onto Post-it® notes as transcribed evidence of a 'lived patient reality', out there. On the other hand, a whole range of that 'lived patient reality' didn't make the cut, for instance: going back to bed mid-morning; playing cards with a friend; his involvement with a local journal dedicated to the Bigfoot Sasquatch Yeti; a squirrel feeder; routine observations of a gaggle of ducks in the back yard; the sorrowful and tragic loss of his wife; the struggles of a close daughter who was informally providing care for Ron whilst also enduring a return to school as a

Doing speculation to curtail speculation 87

40-year-old. Here, it seems, Mol and Law are correct in arguing (2004: 58), that 'smooth' and coherent narratives succeed, or get prioritised over 'jagged' accounts of patients everyday experiences elicited in order to inform medical knowledge, or, as in this case, corporate knowledge seeking to *territorialise* the technological platforms and computational standardisation of global healthcare delivery. The accounts that are privileged in informing 'creative' innovation practices are those that link together those seemingly disparate entities – pill-boxes, medications and medication lists, organisational drawers and regimes – that nevertheless align with medical and technological expertise. Those entities and phenomena that don't fit in with this programme, or those that promise interference, get screened out.

From 'brainstorm' to 'creativity'?

Unsurprisingly, the literature on brainstorming as a designerly practice is oriented to problem solving and the generation of new 'ideas' for developing computational systems is underpinned by theories and accounts of human cognition and the engineering of group dynamics. According to accounts by experimental psychologists (e.g. Taylor et al., 1958) and researchers in human-computer interaction design (e.g. Bao et al., 2010; Gabora, 2002; Faste et al., 2013) the genealogy of brainstorming can be traced back to the advertising executive Alex Faickney Osborn's books (1942, 1957) on techniques apparently first employed in 1939 at the prominent advertising agency BBDO (Barton, Batten, Durstine, & Osborn), which Osborn headed at the time. For Osborn, human 'ideation' as a cognitive and collaborative process of problem solving could be formalized, organized and managed through 'brainstorm' (1957: 151) sessions. The key aim of Osborn's brainstorms was to produce many ideas, rather than a single solution, and group effectiveness could be facilitated by way of the reinforcement principle associated with the psychologist and behavioural scientist B. F. Skinner. Thus, Osborn's (1957: 156) rules for brainstorming sessions included: (1) the withholding of adverse judgment (only positive stimulus); (2) encouraging the occasioning of 'wild' ideas; (3) the more ideas the better – quantity as a way to get to quality, and; (4) the combination of ideas to create 'better', more useful ideas. These rules could then be applied to the 'creative problem-solving process', which, for Osborn (1957: 86), would follow a three-step procedure comprising: 'fact-finding' in order to define or invent a problem; 'idea-finding' as the process of producing provisional ideas and; 'solution-finding' as the process of evaluation of ideas and the prioritization of a single solution.

For Osborn, brainstorming techniques were applicable to many domains of research and development, and not the preserve of advertising or design. He sees creativity, as might be expected by an advertising executive working across diverse brands and interests, as present within various disciplines and domains of knowledge including, but not limited to: policy; engineering; experimental science; manufacturing; education; military strategy, operations and affairs (according to Osborn, ideation techniques were used in 1954 by the then

88   *A. Wilkie and M. Michael*

Veterans Administration, now the aforementioned VA). Incidentally, and despite Osborn's emphasis on the cognitive processes of human collectives and his reliance on the behavioural sciences, there appear four references to Whitehead in his book 'Applied Imagination' (1957).[2] While Osborn does not draw directly on Whitehead's conceptualization of 'creativity', nor acknowledge the centrality of the concept to Whitehead's speculative metaphysics, he employs excerpts from Whitehead's work to support his arguments concerning the emphasis placed on creativity in education (64), the importance of hobbies as 'creative exercise' (76), the profuse production of ideas during ideation (130), and finally, the centrality of 'imagination' in scientific method and knowledge production (354).[3]

Thus, at base, Osborn and Whitehead share an interest in the production of ideas as the basis of applied problem-solving and innovation, for the former, and the aim of inventive philosophy, for the latter (Whitehead, 1968 [1938]: 173). For the purposes of this chapter, we make three further points regarding Osborn's detailed formulation of brainstorming in 'Applied Imagination', over and above his advocacy of various cognitive techniques. First, Osborn stresses the importance of material devices and settings to support ideation. Second, and this throughout his book, Osborn emphasises the principle and practice of 'combination', where ideas are commingled in order to develop, evaluate and validate emerging propositions.[4] Lastly, the novelty of Osborn's formulation of managing creativity lies partly in the way that the productivity of working groups can be linked to creative problem solving and enterprise. That is to say, he regards the peculiar 'making' of the group as a mechanism for the production of ideas. Having said that, it is also, of course, much more: a governmental medium of industrial relations and productivity (Rose, 2008: 456–458); a mechanism for the engineering of particular democratic forms (Lezaun and Calvillo, 2013); and, in its spread across innumerable fields and practices, lauded operator in the knowledge economy of late capitalism (e.g. Thrift, 2005; Shaviro, 2009).

From 'brainstorm' to 'design'

In common with other contemporary 'creative' practices, designers of computational and information systems have adopted and operationalized brainstorming as a technique with which to formalize, manage and coordinate inventiveness and knowledge production, not least in relation to human-computer interaction design practices predicated on 'user' engagement and involvement. Here we see a preoccupation with methodological innovations in order to enhance collaborative productivity amongst interdisciplinary design teams and experts from various fields (e.g. Bødker et al., 2000), but also through drawing on 'users' in one form or another. These innovations generally feature the deployment of experimental digital communication technologies into the brainstorm process, including: online text and video conferencing to explore cultural differences amongst participants (Wang et al., 2009); tabletop and whiteboard interfaces as a means to counter agonistic 'dominance' (Bautista et al., 2012); a digital 'picture space' for visually stimulating group activity and the production of ideas (Wang

Doing speculation to curtail speculation 89

et al., 2010); and the development of web-based tools and story-telling techniques for pre-sessional priming (Bao et al., 2010). As such, within the field of interaction and systems design the brainstorm itself becomes a practice and milieu to be problematized and enhanced by way of 'experimental' and organized design research.

These studies in design and brainstorming carry on longstanding efforts in cognitive psychology to quantify, systematize, order and discipline, in both senses of the word, the process of ideation (e.g. Dunnette, Campbell, & Jaastad, 1963; Diehl & Stroebe, 1987; Taylor, Berry, & Block, 1958) as well as early efforts to explore digitally mediated group ideation (Dennis & Valacich, 1993). Put another way, these studies entail a turning of method upon itself; method becomes the object of experimental and observational method. This should come as no surprise given Osborn's enthusiastic endorsement of Whitehead's (1997 [1926]: 96, emphasis in original) aphorism 'the greatest invention of the 19th century was the invention of the *method* of invention'. Indeed, in keeping with this, Osborn (1957: 209) himself turns brainstorming into the 'problem' of brainstorming.

From 'design' to 'creativity'

So, according to accounts of brainstorming we have seen that the technique seems to be an open process – the proliferation of ideas, non-judgmental reinforcement of suggestions etc. And this ethos is carried into later iterations and versions of brainstorming in Interaction Design and other sub-genres of design (Lehrer, 2012).

But if we look back at the brainstorm featuring Ron, that's not what we see. Instead, we see a limitation of brainstorming through a limitation of 'materials' or entities that enter into the event of brainstorming and the techniques of brainstorming that actually do not especially allow for the transformation of the elements within it (even though we might expect non-judgmental practice to allow for mutual change). Here, we are not arguing, as others have done, for a more 'expanded' version of brainstorming, where, for example, the tools or spaces can be designed to precipitate or enhance 'creativity'.[5] Or, in other words, that creativity remains a cognitive property of individuals that can be stimulated and enhanced by material tools and settings. Instead, and to clarify the notion of creativity we deploy in this chapter, we turn back to Whitehead and recover an alternative version of creativity. A version inextricably linked to the notion of the 'event', where creativity is generic and mundane feature of ontological processes that are unfastened from purely human capacities i.e. the view that ontological creativity is a fundamental and principal feature of existence.

Recent work on the notion of event as a way to illuminate design practice (e.g. Michael, 2012a, 2012b; Wilkie, 2014; Wilkie, Michael, & Plummer-Fernandez, 2015) draws on the view that an event is a process of transformation, or happening, where various diverse elements come together and in coming together change one another. Here, entities acquire their identity and capacities

90 *A. Wilkie and M. Michael*

through actualisation within an event. For Whitehead, the principle of process, or becoming, is foundational for the emergence of all new entities and phenomena: '*how* an actual entity *becomes* constitutes *what* that actual entity is.... Its 'being' is constituted by its 'becoming' (1978 [1929]: 23, emphasis in original). Thus, interviewees, ethnographic interviews, interview data, patients, prospective users, brainstorm inscriptions, novel sociotechnical means of enacting healthcare as well as Yetis, geese and extraterrestrial implants are viewed as elements (or prehensions) that are undergoing continual change.

Rather than rehearse the significance of the event, ground covered by the aforementioned accounts, we draw on Isabelle Stengers (2005) to emphasise three key characteristics of the event, in relation to brainstorming and creativity. First, brainstorms bring about 'nonsymmetry' between a past and present where new sociotechnical arrangements are proposed and new virtualities open up. Second, brainstorms can be understood as undetermined or open – what arises out of a brainstorm cannot be known in advance. Third, brainstorm events mark a difference between a before and after where novel healthcare practices, patient knowledge and orientations to the problem of computationally supported disease management are brought into being.

So far so good, however what we have just described fits rather too neatly with idealized and human-centered accounts of brainstorming and speculative practices in design i.e. that 'innovation' actors (e.g. designers) retain a privileged role in bringing about novelty.

Here, Whitehead's ontological principle, i.e. 'there is nothing that floats into the world from nowhere. Everything in the world is referable to some actual entity' (1978 [1929]: 244), suggests another understanding of the parameters and scope of the interview–brainstorm event. What at one level of analytic engagement looks like creativity, from the perspective of 'the event' it does not. That is to say, from a Whiteheadian perspective the brainstorm session actually serves to filter out all those entities and phenomena – gaggles of geese, Yetis, alien implants, and so on – that were evident during the ethnographic engagement, and were potentiality available to the brainstorm event. For Whitehead, creativity does not reside in cognitive processes only but in the coming together of all the diverse entities involved in an event. Arguably, then, what we see is a doubling of constraint in ordinary design practices, where 'speculation' proceeds with certain assumptions about what can enter into and operate in the brainstorm as well as the capacity in which entities operate, e.g. the situated possibilities for those entities that do enter into the event to become-with others.

There are a number of issues to draw out from this, which we gather under two sub-headings: the 'what' of an event, and the 'how' of an event.

The 'what' of an event. The constraints on the brainstorm's creativity, the 'under-speculation' evident in its process can in some ways be put down to the fact that the 'problem' it addresses is 'pre-ordained'. It sits, as it were, 'outside' of the event of brainstorming – untouched by the unfolding eventuation of the brainstorm. Or rather, we could say that the brainstorm event is situated within a larger eventuation, say of the corporation (e.g. developing a market sector),

Doing speculation to curtail speculation 91

which itself is within a nexus of eventuations, such as semiconductor roadmaps, the dynamics of various healthcare industries, emerging forms of patient-centred technologies and so on and so forth. Put another way, the various participants in the brainstorm bring with them a series of 'feelings' about what the brainstorm is about – feelings that reflect their emergence from other events (e.g. as engineers interested in particular platforms, as employees of a corporation etc.) and which are 'consonant' – they reinforce each other to direct the brainstorm in some directions rather than others. Now, this pattern of feelings mean that only certain prehensions can come together and mutually change. Not just any prehension can enter into a concrescence – this is the teleological element in Whitehead's schema. As such, the event's satisfaction (its momentary 'internal cohesion', for want of a better phrase) obviates certain trajectories of creativity. In particular, arguably, creativity (and speculation) is directed in a particular direction, toward the finding of a solution to a broad question of how to use a range of technologies and platforms to intervene in the management of diabetes, as opposed to generating more inventive problems (Fraser, 2010).

So, what we are actually witnessing, as part of designers' routine speculative practices in defining a novel healthcare technology, is the practice of brainstorming as a constraint on the event of the brainstorm (and the virtualities that this might yield). The 'milieu' of the brainstorm has placed limits on what elements or phenomena (or 'prehensions') could 'enter into' the brainstorm, notably those elements that eventuated during the ethnographic interview with Ron that got left out.

'Milieu', 'feelings', 'satisfaction': all these terms point to the problem of the 'what' that can enter into an event of brainstorming. But they also point to whether the event we are observing can simply be described as that 'of brainstorming'. The event might encompass a series of other actual entities that are not simply the ostensible elements of that event. Thus, the feelings that attach not least to the human participants – which might well be unconscious or visceral – might be indicative of different sources of prehension. The event that might look like a 'brainstorming event' might thus be a 'tacit market sector identification event', or a 'platform development event'. Each of these suggests a different composition, but also a different 'shape' to the event: the event's siting between prior and subsequent events changes. That is to say, its creativity shifts, and, to reiterate, the virtuality it affords reconfigures. Put yet another way, this raises the issue of the 'extent' or 'extensiveness' of an event – what are its parameters?

The 'how' of an event. Let us think a little more carefully about the limitations of 'what' entered the brainstorming event. Commonsensically, we might suggest that there could always have been a way of 'recalling' those elements that failed to make the cut. As a brainstorming event, one might think it not unreasonable that memories of Ron's 'eccentricity' could have received some sort of expression. That is to say, accounts of Ron's 'eccentricity' were latently 'present' or 'available', were not accommodated within the brainstorm's eventuation, yet, given the techniques of brainstorming, might have featured.

92   *A. Wilkie and M. Michael*

Our argument is that the 'how' of the brainstorming event works against this eventuation, whilst reproducing normative expectations. Let us take the use of Post-its®. These devices were used to specify particular features of Ron's experience in particular ways. Their ready availability means that they can mediate the proliferation of text: lots of snippets of text can be generated (and, indeed, discarded). Post-its® are of a limited size – they can contain only so much text, which means that extended text needs to cover a number of Post-its®, or else needs to be condensed. Post-its® are sticky: they can stick to a variety of surfaces and to each other. But their stickiness is also 'partial' – they can be unpeeled and re-stuck. That is to say, they are highly mobile – they can be moved from one site to another with ease. All these various features suggest that text can be rapidly generated, moved, combined (with other text and other materials such as photographs), accumulate at certain sites (under given headings), migrate across headings, be reproduced under different headings. More abstractly, they can mediate connections, cohere as groups based on this or that criterion (form sets and sub-sets), trace lines and mark borders.

As Michael (2006: 95–96) notes Post-its® enact a sort of 'pure communication' in being a discrete and convenient medium for messages. The ease of movement might suggest speculative fecundity. Combining and recombining, categorising and re-categorising, associating and re-associating (with other materials) – surely in the Post-its®' properties we have the prospect of rampant creativity. Yet, drawing on Michel Serres (1982, 1995), we can treat the Post-its® as 'blank dominoes' or 'jokers'. How they mediate relationships amongst the other elements within the brainstorming event is under-determined. They do not betray or problematise or structure or disturb those relations in any discernible way. Nor do they suggest the becoming of entities, rather, they imply connection without deformation – 'user' (or non-user) and technology retain particular attributes and capacities in combination. And, in part because of this, they do not trouble the existing 'what' that has entered into the event. The elements from the ethnographic engagement with Ron, filtered by the 'feelings' of the human participants circulate and combine in search of 'satisfaction' – the right pattern of Post-its® – which solves the problem of demarcating a computationally supported diabetes management system.

So, the Post-it®, along with the other technique and materials that come under the rubric of brainstorming, mediate apparent 'freedom of (ideational) association' (that is one of the promises of brainstorming). And this is a key shortcoming. The 'what' that enters simply combines – concresces – in ways that reflect the peculiar 'extensiveness' of the brainstorming event ('tacit market sector identification event', or a 'platform development event'). The apparent speculativeness of brainstorming events embodied in the extreme 'freedom of association' (mobility of text in our case study) in actuality undercuts the process of speculation, which might lead to more inventive problems or the becoming of more inventive entities.

Some modifications of the Post-it's® design might illustrate what we mean. Imagine notes whose stickiness was variable: some would become immovable or

Doing speculation to curtail speculation   93

completely lose their tackiness after a certain (random) period. Or consider a note sheaf where some notes are primed to spontaneously combust, or to render any writing invisible, or to replace added writing with pre-composed messages. There is of course no guarantee, but these little disturbances, parasites, idiocies problematise the how of the brainstorming event. They interrupt the 'all too smooth' recombination and re-categorisations of text, and, in the process, open up the possibility of a recovery of those waylaid 'memories of Ron'.

Concluding remarks

Clearly then, our case of brainstorming, which to some degree typifies other examples, can be said to be speculative in its formal operations, loosely following the rules and procedure first codified by Osborn. The designers' undertaking of prior-research, the collation and communication of research materials, the inscription of data derived from this material and their use of Post-its® and visual material to support the situated production of multiple ideas. The designers' orientation to a pre-specified problem – identify and specify an end-user healthcare opportunity at a scale that aligns global microprocessor markets. As such, the designers end up working against speculation and creativity in that their practices are constrained by the obligations and requirements placed on them as employees of a corporation committed to particular strategic vectors, the mixture of disciplinary and epistemic expertise and the historicity of brainstorming as a technique with implicit codes of conduct. As such, the future of computationally supported healthcare is latent within a present set of highly restrictive and confined assumptions and problems. In other words, brainstorming as practised in our data suggests that creativity is enacted through a limited speculation – ironically a limited speculation mediated by unlimited communicational possibilities (of say the Post-it®). Thus, rather than insisting on a generic or absolute definition of speculation, this chapter outlines a practical emergence of the speculative through the case of user-centred designers formatting biomedical futures. In other words, a situated and working definition taking flight *with* the empirical. In relation to Halewood (this volume), we see speculation as a practice specific to a particular milieu and changeable in the context of broader eventuations.

Another view of brainstorming, although it could be any sort of creativity mechanism, would allow for the co-becoming and intra-action of elements to yield, not an actualisation of a restricted virtual (a solution to a problem), but a proliferation of virtualities (inventive problems). In the present case, this suggests that additional elements occasioned in the interview, such as traces of Ron's interest in other life forms, such as extraterrestrials, Yetis or geese as well as more troubling and difficult to rationalise phenomena, such as the complex and lived actuality of his healthcare provision, where the formal and informal fold into one another, might explicitly enter into the brainstorming event. In addition, if the 'extensiveness' of that event could be expanded to incorporate not only the actual entities associated with silicon markets but also with 'blue

94 A. Wilkie and M. Michael

skies' for instance, the brainstorm might beget mutual change (e.g. how to understand diabetes in terms of Yetis or unearthly implants) and the production of more interesting and more inventive problems. Finally, against the easy circulation of entities within the brainstorm event (in our case the circulation of texts via Post-it® notes), a little disruption and waywardness might not go amiss. This contrast between the two versions of brainstorming can be put more formally in this way. The first, as described in our account of the 'Ron' brainstorm, entails a 'constrained' speculation where a pre-specified problem passes (unscathed) through a set of, ironically, 'open' practices characterised by a 'freedom of association'. The yield is a 'solution'. The second, incorporates a series of other 'components' (a divergent 'extensiveness', 'punctualised' circulation and fragmentary 'freedom of association') that allow for heterogeneous elements to come together and change one another to support the propagation of new virtualities. Of course, our ideal view of brainstorming also includes the potential becoming of sociological accounts, such as this.

So, as we have tried to make obvious, it is not the aim of this chapter to debunk brainstorming and to deny that the technique exhibits the production of novelty. Unlike those that do, we accept that brainstorms and 'creative' practices are concrete parts of social life that operate by virtue of the becoming together and actualisation of various human and non-human participants. What we have argued, and illustrated by way of the case of the interview with Ron and the subsequent brainstorm, is that speculation in design (practice) proceeds by way of a limitation of 'what' can enter into the brainstorm, and the 'ease' with which these whats can be recombined and re-categorised.

Notes

1 We are careful, here, to distinguish between speculation as an ordinary feature of commercial design practices, as discussed in this chapter, and 'Speculative Design' as a development of 'Critical Design' closely associated with the work of Anthony Dunne and Fiona Raby (2013), or, as a speculative approach to interdisciplinary engagements between design and sociology drawing on the work of Whitehead and Stengers (e.g. Michael, 2012a, Wilkie et al., 2015).
2 Whitehead (1978 [1929]) is cited in the first instance, and latter excerpts and citations are left unreferenced.
3 Incidentally, Whitehead is credited with coining the term 'creativity' (Ford, 1986; Halewood, 2011: 35; Meyer, 2005).
4 Shaviro (2009) points to the importance of Whitehead's (1978 [1929]: 184–207) theory of propositions which describes entities that entice feeling, connecting the latent to the actual. Thus, propositions are hybrid entities that combine 'hypothetical futures beyond that actual entity' (ibid. 188).
5 The view that the production of ideas (and economic prosperity) can also be stimulated and enhanced through the design of interior settings and the built environment (e.g. Cooke, 2008; Hall, 2004) or the concentration of 'talented' workers (Florida, 2002) has preoccupied architects, urbanists, educationalists and organisations for some time, though, arguably, such approaches are based on the very idea that creativity resides within the cognitive capacities of the individual acting alone or as part of a collective (cf. Csikszentmihalyi, 1996). The plethora of literature on these topics is far too excessive to cite, so we provide exemplars.

Doing speculation to curtail speculation   95

References

Bao, P., Gerber, E., Gergle, D., & Hoffman, D. (2010). *Momentum: Getting and staying on topic during a brainstorm.* CHI'10 Proceedings from the *SIGCHI Conference on Human Factors in Computing Systems.* Atlanta, GA, April, 1233–1236.

Bautista, M., Crane, J., Largent, J., Yu, J., & Bardzell, S. (2012). *Understanding designer brainstorms: The effect of analog and digital interfaces on dominance. CHI'12 Extended Abstracts on Human Factors in Computing Systems.* Austin, Texas, May, 1481–1486.

Bødker, S., Nielsen, C., & Petersen, M. G. (2000). *Creativity, cooperation and interactive design. DIS '00.* Proceedings of the *3rd conference on Designing Interactive Systems: Processes, Practices, Methods, and Techniques.* Brooklyn, NY, August, 252–261.

Cooke, P. L. L. (2008). *Creative cities, cultural clusters and local economic development.* Cheltenham, UK; Northampton, MA: Edward Elgar.

Csikszentmihalyi, M. 1996. *Creativity: flow and the psychology of discovery and invention.* New York, NY: HarperCollins Publishers.

Dennis, A. R., & Valacich, J. S. (1993). Computer brainstorms: More heads are better than one. *Journal of Applied Psychology, 78*(4), 531–537.

Diehl, M., & Stroebe, W. (1987). Productivity loss in brainstorming groups: Toward the solution of a riddle. *Journal of personality and social psychology, 53*(3), 497–509.

Dunne, A., & Raby, F. (2013). *Speculative everything: design, fiction, and social dreaming.* Cambridge, MA: MIT Press.

Dunnette, M. D., Campbell, J., & Jaastad, K. 1963. The effect of group participation on brainstorming effectiveness for 2 industrial samples. *Journal of Applied Psychology, 47*(1), 30–37.

Faste, H., Rachmel, N., Essary, R., & Sheehan, E. (2013). *Brainstorm, chainstorm, cheatstorm, tweetstorm: New ideation strategies for distributed HCI design.* Proceedings of the SIGCHI Conference on Human Factors in Computing Systems. Paris, France: ACM 2013, 1343–1352.

Florida, R. L. (2002). *The rise of the creative class: and how it's transforming work, leisure, community and everyday life.* New York, NY: Basic Books.

Ford, L. S. 1986. Creativity in a future key. In R. C. Neville (Ed.), *New essays in metaphysics* (pp. 179–197). Albany, New York: State University of New York Press.

Fraser, M. (2010). Facts, ethics and event. In C. B. Jense, & K. Rödje (Eds), *Deleuzian intersections: Science, technology and anthropology* (pp. 57–82). New York, NY; Oxford: Berghahn Books.

Gabora, L. (2002). *Cognitive mechanisms underlying the creative process.* Proceedings of the *4th conference on Creativity & Cognition.* Loughborough, UK, 2002, 126–133.

Geertz, C. 2000. Thick description: toward an interpretive theory of culture. In *The interpretation of cultures: selected essays by Clifford Geertz* (pp. 3–30). New York, NY: Basic Books.

Halewood, M. (2011). *A. N. Whitehead and Social Theory: Tracing a Culture of Thought.* London; New York, NY; Dehli: Anthem Press.

Hall, P. (2004). Creativity, culture, knowledge and the city. *Built Environment (1978–), 256–258.*

Lehrer, J. (2012). *Groupthink.* The New Yorker.

Lezaun, J., & Calvillo, N. (2013). In the political laboratory: Kurt Lewin's Atmospheres. *Journal of Cultural Economy,* 1–24.

Meyer, S. (2005). Introduction. *Configurations, 13*(1), 1–33.

Michael, M. (2006). *Technoscience and everyday life*. Maidenhead, Berks.: Open University Press/McGraw-Hill.

Michael, M. (2012a). De-signing the object of sociology: toward an 'idiotic' methodology. *The Sociological Review, 60*(S1), 166–183.

Michael, M. (2012b). 'What Are We Busy Doing?' Engaging the Idiot. *Science, Technology & Human Values, 37*(5), 528–554.

Mol, A. (2008). *The logic of care: Health and the problem of patient choice*. London and New York, NY: Routledge.

Mol, A., & Law, J. (2004). Embodied action, Enacted bodies: the example of hypoglycaemia. *Body & Society, 10*(2–3), 43–62.

Nafus, D., & Anderson, K. (2009). Writing on the walls: The materiality of social memory in corporate research. In M. Cefkin (Ed.), *Ethnography and the corporate encounter* (pp. 137–157). New York, NY; Oxford: Berghahn Books.

Osborn, A. F. (1942). *How to think up*. New York, NY; London. McGraw-Hill Book Company, Incorporated.

Osborn, A. F. (1957). *Applied imagination: Principles and procedures of creative problem-solving*. New York: Scribner.

Pols, J. (2014). Knowing patients Turning patient knowledge into science. *Science, Technology & Human Values, 39*(1), 73–97.

Rose, N. (2008). Psychology as a social science. *Subjectivity, 25*(1), 446–462.

Serres, M. (1982). *The parasite*. Baltimore, MD: The Johns Hopkins University Press.

Serres, M. (1995). *Angels, a modern myth*. Paris: Flammarion.

Shaviro, S. (2009). *Without criteria: Kant, Whitehead, Deleuze, and aesthetics*. Cambridge, MA: MIT Press.

Stengers, I. (2005). Events and histories of knowledge. *Review (Fernand Braudel Center), 28*(2), 143–159.

Taylor, D. W., Berry, P. C., & Block, C. H. (1958). Does group participation when using brainstorming facilitate or inhibit creative thinking? *Administrative Science Quarterly, 3*(1), 23–47.

Thrift, N. (2005). *Knowing capitalism*. London; Thousand Oaks, CA; New Dehli: SAGE Publications.

Wang, H.-C., Cosley, D., & Fussell, S. R. (2010). *Idea expander: Supporting group brainstorming with conversationally triggered visual thinking stimuli*. CSCW'10 proceedings from the *2010 ACM conference on Computer Supported Cooperative work*. Savannah, GA, February, 103–106.

Wang, H.-C., Fussell, S. F., & Setlock, L. D. (2009). *Cultural difference and adaptation of communication styles in computer-mediated group brainstorming*. CHI'09 proceedings from the SIGCHI *Conference on Human Factors in Computing Systems*. Boston, MA, April, 669–678.

Whitehead, A. N. (1929). *The aims of education and other essays*. New York, NY: The Free Press.

Whitehead, A. N. (1968 [1938]). *Modes of thought*. New York, NY: The Free Press.

Whitehead, A. N. (1978 [1929]). *Process and reality: an essay in cosmology*. Gifford Lectures of 1927–8 (corrected ed.). New York, NY: The Free Press.

Whitehead, A. N. (1997 [1926]). *Science and the modern world*. New York, NY: The Free Press.

Wilkie, A. (2010). User assemblages in design: an ethnographic study (PhD). Goldsmiths, University of London.

Wilkie, A. (2014). Prototyping as event: Designing the future of obesity. *Journal of Cultural Economy, 7*(4), 476–492.

Wilkie, A., Michael, M., & Plummer-Fernandez, M. (2015). Speculative method and Twitter: Bots, energy and three conceptual characters. *The Sociological Review, 63*(1), 79–101.

Wyatt, S. (2003). Non-users also matter: The construction of users and non-users of the internet. In N. Oudshoorn, & T. J. Pinch (Eds.) *How users matter: The co-construction of users and technologies* (pp. 67–79). Cambridge, MA: MIT.

7 Retrocasting

Speculating about the origins of money

Joe Deville

How did money become money? This simple question has aroused intense debate amongst a group of thinkers interested in the role that money plays in contemporary social and economic life. The problem is that the answers are lost in the mists of deep human time. No one really knows. This has not always, however, been seen as an insurmountable obstacle. It's just that overcoming it has involved a considerable amount of speculation. This is speculation that is interested in how to connect an ultimately unknowable time and place to the present, not in relation to uncertain futures (at least, this is not the focus), but uncertain pasts – not forecasting but what I call 'retrocasting'.

Acts of monetary retrocasting are given force by the drive (the need? the desire? the pull of a lure?) to pin down what exactly money is, and what it does for us, as societies, as economies. They are, following Dick Bryan and Michael Rafferty, acts of ontological decomposition and recomposition, breaking down money into sets of constituent parts (in each case, an act itself predicated on understanding money as singular and sharing consistent features), to be then recombined 'to produce a credible explanation of a (often ahistorical) universal money' (2016: 28; see also Dodd 2014). What usually fails to be recognised in such practices, however, are the ways in which analysts themselves become inserted into these newly de- and recomposed monies.[1] They, their explanations, their propositions, their speculations, become part of the glue that binds together the newly assembled monetary object.

In search of a way through such debates, one capable of recognising the role of the analyst in challenging and reinforcing monetary ontologies of various kinds, the chapter begins by outlining three retrocasting activities. The first is associated with mainstream economic thinking, the second with heterodox economics, with the third informed by a hybrid of sociological reasoning and a neglected strand within economic theory. As we will see, across these three accounts, the degree to which retrocasting is subject to empirical and theoretical scrutiny can vary. Sometimes, it is a form of speculation – much like the more familiar future-oriented forms of speculation – that is a rather under-theorised practice, with parallels to many of the more conventional modalities of speculation (see Diprose, this volume) that are routinely mobilised in social situations (e.g. the future-focused practices of high finance).

Speculating about the origins of money 99

With this in mind, in the final section, I undertake some retrocasting of my own, one informed at once by an analysis of a colonial and exploitative monetary encounter and by speculative philosophy. The latter has put the creative potential of acts of speculation to the fore, as a way to explore inventive forms of problem making. In particular, I will examine the potential of seeing monetary objects, acting through particular settings, as 'lures for feeling'.

The spontaneous outcome of individual 'efforts'

There exists a somewhat obscure debate between heterodox economists and sociologists about how money came into being. Although tetchy at times, if there is one a point of agreement, it is that conventional economics has got it wrong.

From the point of view of conventional economics, the question is barely worth asking. Money is generally understood according to what appear to be its instrumental functions (see Carruthers, 2005: 356; Dodd, 1994: xv; Gilbert, 2005: 358; Ingham, 2004: 3–4), as something akin to a 'super' commodity, capable of performing the full range of procedures that are needed to ensure that market exchanges are as smooth and frictionless as possible.

Because of the emphasis on describing money's functions, conventional economic accounts of what money is – its ontology in other words – spend little time focusing on money's origins. The tendency is to look back to an account provided by Carl Menger, economist and founder of the influential Austrian School of economics. Menger reasoned that money emerged to supplant the cumbersome nature of barter-driven exchange. From this point of view, money emerges because, rather than individual goods being compared with and assessed against each other in isolation, it becomes far more 'efficient' (and less, to quote one standard economic textbook, 'troublesome' (Hardwick, Langmead, & Khan, 1999: 430)) to redirect a realm of continual 'higgling' in the direction of a standard more flexible commodity, whether shells, animals, or precious metals.

Some, however, have picked up a tension in Menger's work, operating around what Dodd refers to as 'the curious phenomenon of inevitable spontaneity' (Dodd, 1994: 6), which can be best illustrated with reference to the original text; Menger writes:

> [W]e can only come fully to understand the origin of money by learning to view the establishment of the social procedure, with which we are dealing, as the spontaneous outcome, the unpremeditated resultant, of particular, individual efforts of the members of a society, who have little by little worked their way to a discrimination of the different degrees of saleableness in commodities.
>
> (Menger, 1892: 250)

From a sociological perspective this account is somewhat irritating, in that both the emergence of money and 'the social' are rooted in the interaction between rationally maximising individuals, or individual 'efforts' as it is termed here.

100   *J. Deville*

Both money and society emerge 'spontaneously' whereas the economically max-imising individual is assumed to be an ahistorical, pre-formed figure.

The spontaneous outcome of commodity trading

A detailed challenge to orthodox economic theories of money has been developed by Costas Lapavitsas, at times in collaboration with others (Fine & Lapavitsas, 2000; Itoh & Lapavitsas, 1999; Lapavitsas, 2000, 2003, 2005). His reappraisal attempts to counter conventional economic monetary theory via a Marxist-inflected economics, while also seeking to bring out more clearly in the latter the 'social functioning' of money (Lapavitsas, 2000: 366).

This heterodox economic approach shares one key conclusion about money with its orthodox sibling: that money is rooted in commodity value.[2] However, whereas in conventional economics, the origins of money are assumed to be a product of interactions between pre-formed, maximising individuals, Lapavitsas aims to build on Marx in order to examine the historical emergence of money, and its transformation into the very essence of capitalist social relations. It is an approach that aims to account both for the emergence of money and its ontology. He sums up the argument as follows:

> the universal equivalent represents absolute ability to buy that emerges spon-taneously and necessarily out of commodity exchange relations. The essence of money is monopoly over direct exchangeability among commodities. None of money's functions dominates the rest, but all flow from money's essence.
>
> (Lapavitsas, 2006: 144)

Money's 'essence' is therefore rooted in its ability to both 'act as' a commodity and its 'spontaneous' emergence not from relations between maximising indi-viduals, but from commodity relations.

As with many monetary theorists, Lapavitsas is keen to demonstrate the uni-versality of his approach by also accounting for money's origins. The apparent absence of empirical evidence means having to engage in a considerable amount of speculation. Specifically, a particular social theory – Marxist economics – becomes situated in relation to, and provides the analytical structure for, a reim-agined, retrospective field setting.

This turn to speculation is provided with explicit methodological justification: Lapavitsas suggests that he is mirroring Marx's advocacy of a speculative method (or methodological retroaction) in *Grundrisse*, in which the 'theoretical analysis of a social phenomenon should focus on its most developed form, even if less developed forms appear independently, or earlier in historical time' (Lapavitsas, 2003: 13; see Marx, 1973: 105). The argument goes that as the commodity form is at its most developed under capitalism, traces of its previous, non-capitalist forms can be read from the present; as he writes, 'trading produced under capital-ist relations is assumed to constitute the fully developed form of *all* trading' (Lapavitsas, 2003: 13; emphasis added). Retroactive speculation is thus an

Speculating about the origins of money 101

explicitly teleological practice, which attempts to develop an ahistorical account of commodities and money 'in general', alongside an account of the historically specific manifestations of capitalist money and commodities 'in particular'.

If Marx's retroactive method provides the structure for this form of speculation, then its object becomes a reimagined set of pre-capitalist 'social and historical conditions under which the transformation of products into commodities takes place' (Lapavitsas, 2003: 11). This, for Lapavitsas, marks the beginning of a transition from a social world that operates without the market, mediated entirely by reciprocal (social) non-economic relations, towards the complex coming together of the social and the economic that will characterise capitalist relations.

The speculative challenge Lapavitsas is faced with is how in pre-modern, what he identifies as 'embedded' economies, the disconnected structures necessary for the transformation of products into commodities could have arisen, in a manner analogous to, but not equivalent to, those disembedded structures held to be present under capitalism. This is a situation in which commodity producers are assumed to operate as autonomous, competitive, and 'foreign' to one another.

The solution is to propose that in the early, pre-modern development of commodity production and trading (which would eventually lead to money), there had to have existed a form of social 'outside', a disconnected socio-economic interaction beyond the embedded face-to-face interactions that make up his imagined pre-capitalist, pre-monetary community (Lapavitsas, 2003: 28). Lapavitsas speculates that this would have begun with an initial 'accidental' stage of human socio-economic history, one populated by unstable, fleeting moments of transaction, held to occur 'at random', resulting in isolated moments of barter between what are assumed to be two 'mutually alien, independent and essentially "foreign" commodity owners'. In this process individuated subjectivities are imagined as emerging (although he doesn't put it in this way), between an active (or 'relative') party, and a passive (or 'equivalent') respondent.

Lapavistsas also mobilises some historical evidence in support of his speculation, partly as provided by the Greek historian, Herodotous, writing in the fifth century BC, who describes a phenomenon called 'silent trade'. The extract is worth quoting in full:

> On reaching this country, they unload their goods, arrange them tidily along the beach, and then, returning to their boats, raise a smoke. Seeing the smoke, the natives come down to the beach, place on the ground a certain quantity of gold in exchange for the goods, and go off again in the distance.... There is perfect honesty on both sides; the Carthaginians never touch the gold until it equals in value what they have been offered for sale, and the natives never touch the goods until the gold has been taken away.
> (Herodotus, 1954: 307; cited in Lapavitsas, 2003: 62)

The phenomenon fits Lapavitsas's argument well by seeming to demonstrate the form of paradoxically disconnected social connection that he reasons is a prerequisite for early commodity trading. Such transactions are characterised as fleeting,

102 J. Deville

limited in scope, and with no necessary logic to which of the two parties adopts which role, and setting no precedent beyond the immediate confines of that transaction (2003: 57–58, 2005: 392). This is thus not only a description which attempts to demonstrate the essentially economic *and* social nature of exchange, but which also assumes trade as a 'natural' process, predicated on individuated trading subjects that end up leaving one another disconnected. It is this very disconnection that is seen as a crucial first step on a more or less linear path that Lapavitsas traces towards pre-capitalist money, and then eventually capitalism.

The logical outcome of social relations

The sociologist and theorist of money Geoffrey Ingham disagrees with much of Lapavitsas's account (see: Ingham, 2001, 2006; Lapavitsas, 2005). What the two share, however, is the desire to develop a general monetary theory capable of challenging conventional understandings of money as a neutral facilitator while also showing how it can play a role in the contemporary (re)production of forms of social stratification. The key difference between the two is the specification of what 'underlies' money's generality. Ingham writes: '[i]n the most elementary terms, there are two distinct and incompatible theories of the origins, development and nature of money' (2006: 261); on one side there are theories which see money as a type of commodity, and having developed 'spontaneously' through exchange, and on the other which 'sees money as an abstract claim, or credit, measured by a money of account' (ibid.). Ingham places Lapavitsas, and Marxist theories of money more generally, as well as orthodox economic theories of money, on the former side, with his and other so called 'Chartalist' credit/state theories of money on the latter.

Ingham argues that what makes all money 'money' is ultimately not related to underlying commodity value, but to the existence of an a priori abstraction – more specifically, a 'money of account', an abstract 'conceptual basis' for calculating and comparing value that must (logically) exist external to, and prior to the possibility of monetary exchange. Put simply, what lies behind money are ultimately not commodities, but the acts of *counting* these commodities (Ingham, 2004: 89, 105, 309). It is this abstraction that provides the numerical framework which sits *behind* money and indeed all forms of trading.

To make this case Ingham also has to argue that, rather than being disconnection that makes money money, it is the relation, specifically relations of credit. The value of money comes not from the value held in commodities (such as the value of precious metals), but from sovereign promises to pay.[3]

Ingham's object of speculation is the character of early relationships between people, reasoning that there must have been a form of 'elementary social obligations' (or, more particularly, '[t]he primordial debt ... owed by the living to the continuity and durability of the society which secures their individual existence' (Ingham, 2004: 90)). For Ingham, the stage upon which the emergence of money was historically played out already contains all the actors it needs; communal social relations, constituted by the bond between individual and society which

Speculating about the origins of money 103

contain the originary 'substance' – communal social relations conceptualised as a form of debt – necessary for money to emerge. There is thus no need to resort to 'foreign' actors coming in from beyond communal boundaries.

Like Lapavitsas, Ingham also finds some historical evidence to support his claim: not 'silent trade' but '*Wergeld*': tightly defined, publicly agreed compensation payments for forms of societal transgression in early tribal communities, including injuries or damage. Early historical examples of these practices, argues Ingham, provide suggestive evidence of one early manifestation of an a priori 'social' concept of 'worth', or value calculation, 'elementary monies of account', that, Ingham argues, could not have simply emerged from the exchange of commodities (Ingham, 2004: 92–93).

'Foreign' 'disinterested' socio-economic relations as a precondition for the 'spontaneous' emergence of money are thus replaced by 'local' 'interested' social connections which lead, in turn, to the emergence of money. 'Social', face to face interactions and their resulting social structures are held to precede the market. Instead of money being seen as having its origins in exchange, Ingham attempts to describe the ways in which money is rooted in person to person social relations which then ultimately become codified into systems of accountability, potentially enforceable through violence.

Lures for feeling

What we have in these arguments are speculative 'slopes' (see: Stengers, 2011: 180): in each case a speculative argument is mobilised, heading backwards in time, guided by ways of understanding the world that the authors were quite confident about when they started (see also Bell, Halewood, Savransky, this volume). What, however, if we take retroactive speculation – or 'retrocasting' as I have called it – a little more seriously? What consequences follow for debates about monetary origins?

To answer these questions, I will undertake some retrocasting of my own. As with the examples above, this will mean mobilising fragments of historical evidence, although in my case from the far more recent past. On the one hand, it examines the coming into being of a new monetary form around groups of people who were apparently previously disconnected. This is, as I will argue, very much a monetary origin. On the other, it shows quite clearly the way in which relationality might come to matter in the (re)composition of monetary objects. However, as we will see, the register of relationality I will examine is somewhat different.

At the same time, I want to suggest that acts of past (or future) speculation need to also account from some of the diversity of speculative activities that surround any situation. Entities of all kinds can act as 'speculative propositions' (Stengers, 2011: 267) or what the philosopher Alfred North Whitehead has called 'lures for feeling' (Whitehead, 1978). When they do so, such entities provoke/propose different ways to relate to one another, to 'feel with' one another. Feeling, to draw on Whitehead, is not a quality limited to people or

104   *J. Deville*

even the organic, but is a way of describing the generic process of mutual relation and 'reaching out' that occurs between entities of all kinds, even if the lasting achievement of connectivity and ongoing interrelation is far rarer.[4]

One result of this attention to speculative diversity, cutting across times and places, across observer and observed, the requirement to take more seriously the object that is at the centre of the debate between Lapavitsas and Ingham but is actually in many ways absent: money itself. For what is almost totally elided in their accounts are the agential capacities of the objects that do the work of transferring value from place to place and person to person. Yet there are hints from both that monetary objects could be doing something very powerful indeed: they could either be resisting relationality in their entirety (this would be quite impressive) or they could be totally accommodating it to it. What follows are some alternate propositions concerning monetary relationality.

Monetary lures

The empirical case I want to introduce is the aftermath of a moment of so-called 'first contact' between Australian explorers and the previously isolated indigenous Hageners of the Wahgi Valley of Papua New Guinea in 1933. Here I draw on and partially reinterpret an analysis of this encounter provided by Marilyn Strathern (1992). Through this we can hopefully begin to find ways to work through the binary of either ubiquitous relation or absent relation, while putting both speculative philosophy and retrocasting to work.

Strathern's interest is in tracing what this encounter reveals about two different ontologies: that of the (white colonial) Australians and that of the Hageners. There was, she suggests, a double confusion. On the part of the Hageners, this centred on their identification of the Australians as ghosts, not humans. On the part of the Australians, this centred on the confusion around why the Hageners would not engage in trade with them for their more obviously prized items, especially pigs, despite the Australians offering the Hageners a myriad of new and strange items (see also: Gammage, 1998).

The 'problem' (seen from the point of view of the Australians – at this point at least, there was certainly no problem for the Hageners, who, after all, were the ones holding the pigs) – Strathern asserts, was not the absence of a shared language – one of the Australians grunting like a pig seemed enough to get the message across; enmity (despite the later maltreatment of the Hageners by the Australians) was also no barrier. It was rather that in Australian life sociality was an absolute property of the body. Relations flowed, certainly, but these were between autonomous, preformed beings. Hagener life, however, involved different forms of relationality in which sociality was distributed across bodies and sets of material attachments. This, argues Strathern, results in the Australians being recognised as analogous, but ultimately different kinds of being; they appeared 'by themselves', and offered nothing that connected them to the Hageners' past and future.

The conditions for this interaction ultimately shifted. And this occurred around a particular monetary object. The Australians noticed that the Hageners

Speculating about the origins of money 105

attached particular value to a type of shell: the gold-lip pearl shell. After sending for some of these shells, they offered to trade them for pigs. This, suggests Strathern, caused the Hageners to rethink their initial conclusion, a moment for which she draws on Connolly and Anderson's retelling of Ndika Nikints' (one of the Hageners) account of the event. We join it at the point Nikints addresses an old man he finds in his urgent hunt for a pig to trade, as he is too far away from home.

> I said to him, 'Bring this pig quickly!' He was afraid, and he hesitated, 'Give it to me! I'll take it!' So I took the pig to the camp and the white man saw it. He picked the big shell up and gave it to me. I took it to the old man and said, 'Take this and give it to Ndika Powa [who owns the pig]. And tell him the people-eating spirits wanted to eat the pig and gave this shell in return.' You all ran off, thinking he was a spirit. Well, what do you think now? He is the shellman! And I'm with him! Go and bring Powa! … This strange man that came, he's not a spirit, he's the shellman! Hurry quickly, there's a lot more shells!
>
> (Connolly & Anderson, 1987: 121–122; Strathern, 1992: 248)

Strathern suggests that the Hageners' conclusion that the Australians did share humanness with them comes not from a slow realisation of the underlying 'reality' of the situation, but through a process of analytical work, ultimately leading to the conclusion that, in offering to trade the gold-lip pearl shells, the Australians were 'shellmen' like them. The shells were part of the past and future of what the Hageners saw as the realm of the human social and, in making the offer of exchange, the Australians connected themselves to it. Trade could now begin.

There are ways in which Strathern's account of Hagener life might be nuanced (see, for instance: LiPuma, 1998). I would like to shift her account of our life alongside objects and, in particular, monetary objects to think more about their potential to act as lures (see also Deville, 2015: 35–39). Strathern writes:

> The Australian men found that the small shells and steel goods and other trade goods were just not acceptable. *That was to change over night. Noting the pieces of gold-lip pearl shell people wore*, Leahy and Taylor sent a message back with the first pilot to bring some in his next load. And of all the 'things' that the newcomers brought, *these were the things that made Hageners change their mind.*
>
> (Strathern, 1992: 248; emphasis added)

One way to reread this account is to suggest that the gold-lip pearl shells are not just 'noticed' by the Australian explorers, but offer themselves up as a solution to the problem in relation to which they were posed. Such a reading may help destabilise the familiar trope of explorers 'discovering' an exotic people and

106   *J. Deville*

practices, something that Strathern is also keen to do (see p. 251). But it also allows for a more nuanced account of the relations surrounding such objects and their capacity for emergence or, after Whitehead, 'prehension'. This would see the gold-lip pearl shells worn around the Hageners' necks intersect with a series of wider prehending/ed entities: human bodies; twine; the analogy (presumably) drawn by the Australians to Western practices of adornment; the technological capacity to acquire and deliver more shells; Hagener understandings of Australians, contemporary Western understandings of the practices of indigenous peoples etc. These elements do more than simply provide the context for this encounter, they problematise it in distinct ways, each becoming anew with the 'resolution' of the difficulties of trade between the two parties.

The shells can therefore be themselves seen as reaching out: they 'call out' to the Australians as much as the Australians notice the shells. In a situation of seemingly irretrievable difference, they provide a solution to the particular series of problems posed by the coming together of these two previously largely disconnected peoples. Indeed, we might speculate that it is their very capacity to reach out in this way, perhaps by catching the light in a certain manner for instance, that fed into their use as both a form of personal adornment and money within Hagener society.

What might seem a small, ostensibly insignificant encounter ends up having important consequences for both Australian and, in particular, Hagener life from this point forwards. As Ian Hughes (1978) documents, the 'lure' of these shells, and others like them, was resolutely grabbed by the region's new colonial power. They started to be used by the colonial administrators to pay for the food they needed for them and their troops, in particular for pigs, as well as to pay manual labourers, indentured servants and sex workers (pp. 312–314). Many millions of these shells were freighted in, often by air, from other parts of Papua New Guinea and from islands surrounding the Australian shore. This led to significant inflationary pressure, as shells that once had been rare and highly prized were rapidly devalued. As a result of this, attempts (albeit unsuccessful) were even made to develop a new payment technology: the 'imitation' shell (both dog whelks and egg-cowries) (p. 313).

A set of initial, localised trades between individuals had thus grown into a major enterprise, involving government institutions, new infrastructural networks, a particular set of non-human actors (the creatures producing all these shells – one has to wonder about their fate in the face of this new threat), as well as those doing the work of collecting these shells in the first place. This significantly disrupted patterns of local exchange: pigs, the main local source of protein, now tended to end up in the hands of Australians and Europeans rather than being traded across the different communities in the valley, in turn affecting patterns of agriculture as well as a range of relationships between communities, not only of trade, but also marriage and war (ibid.).

Conclusion: speculating about monetary origins

The account that I have (re)described of a set of encounters between Australians and Hageners, clustered around a set of monetary objects, is an account of monetary origins, if we hold an origin to be an instance of becoming. It involves the coming into being of a new monetary object, one able to connect previously disconnected social groups and that enables relations, including, in due course, relations of power and exploitation, to flow between them more readily. Such new monetary becomings are by no means a thing of the past. Recent developments in forms of contactless payment, the emergence of online currencies such as Bitcoin, the ongoing threats to the future of the Euro: all these bear witness to the ways in which new monetary forms are always on the cusp of emerging, while at the same time their status is never wholly secure.

Money, 'in general', seems so total a social fact that these kinds of emergent properties are usually hidden from view. In particular, what remains hidden is that money's permanence is and can only be the result of a highly situated process in which what it is to 'share' a particular universal, as a population, is being constantly reperformed. It is the coming into being of a new more universal monetary form that I have traced in the historical interactions between Australian and European settlers and the existing population of Papua New Guinea.

And, as we have seen, what comes into being is not only a shared monetary form, but particular forms of conjoined human and monetary subjectivity. The eventual Hagener identification of the Australian as 'shellmen' is in many ways quite apt: it points to the indelible connection between the fact of their presence and the value relations their presence also entails. In order for a shared monetary form to come into being, each party has to accept the other not simply as someone to give value to or take value from, but as intimately associated with the ongoing becoming of value into the future, from the immediate past. Each has to become aware of each other 'in perception'. This is quite far, for instance, from individuals interacting with each other solely on the basis of their individual best-interests, as assumed by conventional economic theory or, as in Lapavitsas and Ingham, as being either wholly embedded or disembedded. Describing the spin of entwined sets of dancers, Stengers writes that it

> is only possible because each of them trusts the others 'precursively' at the moment when they accept that their own body is put off balance: they all accept to no longer define themselves by their own means but by supposing the others, in the precise sense in which, taken in isolation, these others would be quite incapable of giving what is asked of them. None is a guarantor, as a pillar would be. Each one presupposes the others.
>
> (Stengers, 2011: 239)

In the dance between Hagener and Australian, one laden with asymmetry, violence and forms of expropriation, there is nonetheless just this kind of presupposition of the other. Moreover, this presupposition will have to be repeated

108 *J. Deville*

constantly, in this case being reinforced and constantly refreshed by the specific technologies the Australians have at their disposal (air freight, etc.).

Menger, Lapavitsas and Ingham might well object: the account I have provided does not speak to *the* origin of money. Both parties come to this dance already possessing their own medium of exchange – the coin, the shell – the challenge was only to find some equivalence between the two monies.[5] But, I want to suggest, this is exactly what tends to be missed in the search for the origin of money. As this example has shown, money is and always will be a local, situated solution to a local, situated problem, even if the problem being posed concerns a particular money's claim to generality. This is not because there is anything that makes money particularly different from any other thing, other than the ambitions ascribed to its objects (of exchange). Indeed, the propositions I have developed about money could easily be extended to the historical traces mobilised by both Ingham and Lapavitsas – both the phenomenon of silent trade and *Wergeld* can be seen as distinct, creative solutions to other again quite distinct sets of problems, that then act as lures for their respective analysts in much the same way that monetary objects have done for their users at innumerable moments in history. The same could also be said about the status of the Hagener-Australian in the account I have provided.

This complex web of relations between monies, their users and the analysts that observe them also suggests that I would be overly hasty to dismiss in their entirety the various accounts of monetary origins against which I have situated my own. For instance, while the idea of monetary emergence depending on any form of 'pure' spontaneity depends on an untenable absence of relation as an originary condition, if we rethink spontaneity as novelty, then the grasping by the Australians of the lure of the gold-lipped pearl shell can be seen as an apparently spontaneous, novel instance of recomposed relationality. Writing about the way in which the now historically distant Battle of Waterloo continues nonetheless to haunt the present, Whitehead discusses the role played by those 'imaginative historians' that provide hypothetical alternatives, what you might call the 'what-if' scenario. We may not think it of any practical importance, he writes, '[b]ut we confess their relevance in thinking about them at all, even to the extent of dismissing them' (Whitehead, 1978: 185). They are, he continues, part of the 'a penumbra of eternal objects, constituted by relevance to the Battle of Waterloo. Some people do admit elements from this penumbral complex into effective feeling, and others wholly exclude them' (ibid.). I am unable to wholly exclude some of the accounts against which I have presented my own. They hang over this account just as the search for an origin hangs over theirs.

Notes

1 This does not, however, have to be a purely analytical and/or academic endeavour: as Bryan and Rafferty make clear, various practical activities (the Breton Woods agreement, for example, or the dominance of monetarism) have arisen out of, and had a direct impact on, how money is understood and, crucially, acted upon.

Speculating about the origins of money 109

2 Even if, from a Marxist perspective, there is less interest in seeing money as a commodity itself and rather in capitalist 'commodity relations' mediated by money as a universal abstraction.
3 The key difference between this and Marx's analysis of credit money, is the degree of emphasis placed on the role of credit. For Ingham and credit theorists, *all* money is rooted in credit relations between people, and between people and their structures of governance, whereas for Marx, credit money is a specific instance of the 'universal equivalent' of money more generally (see Lapavitsas (2005) for a more detailed account of this distinction). Ingham also adds some theory to his account, drawing on Weber's neglected sociology of money. This can be summarised as an attempt to incorporate a theory of power into a theory of monetary value that is not, as with Marxist analyses, rooted in a labour theory of value.
4 Constraints on the length of this chapter do not allow for a fuller exploration of this theoretical architecture. Alongside Whitehead's own work, and his particularly important *Process and Reality* (1978), see overviews by Halewood (2011) and Stengers (2011).
5 Indeed, we may want to think more generally not in terms of money but monies: money is always, as Viviana Zelizer (1994) has demonstrated, multiple.

References

Bryan, D., & Rafferty, M. (2016). Decomposing money: Ontological options and spreads. *Journal of Cultural Economy, 9*(1), 27–42.
Carruthers, B. (2005). The sociology of money and credit. In N. Smelser, & R. Swedberg (Eds.), *The handbook of economic sociology* (pp. 355–378). Princeton and Oxford: Princeton University Press.
Connolly, B., & Anderson, R. (1987). *First contact: New Guinea's highlanders encounter the outside world*. New York: Viking Penguin.
Dodd, N. (1994). *The sociology of money: Economics, reason and contemporary society*, Cambridge: Polity Press.
Dodd, N. (2014). *The social life of money*. Princeton, NJ: Princeton University Press.
Fine, B., & Lapavitsas, C. (2000). Markets and money in social theory: What role for economics? *Economy and Society, 29*(3), 357–382.
Gammage, B. (1998). *The sky travellers: Journeys in New Guinea 1938–1939*. Melbourne: The Miegunyah Press and Melbourne University Press.
Gilbert, E. (2005). Common cents: Situating money in time and place. *Economy and Society, 34*(3), 357–388.
Halewood, M. (2011). *A. N. Whitehead and social theory: Tracing a culture of thought*. London: Anthem Press.
Hardwick, P., Langmead, J., & Khan, B. (1999). *An introduction to modern economics*, Harlow: Longman.
Herodotus. (1954). *The histories*, Harmondsworth: Penguin.
Hughes, I. (1978). Good money and bad: Inflation and devaluation in the colonial process. *Mankind, 11*(3), 308–318.
Ingham, G., 2001. Fundamentals of a theory of money: Untangling Fine, Lapavitsas and Zelizer. *Economy and Society, 30*(3), 304–323.
Ingham, G. (2006). Further reflections on the ontology of money: Responses to Lapavitsas and Dodd. *Economy and Society, 35*(2), 259–278.
Ingham, G. (2004). *The nature of money*. Cambridge: Polity Press.

110   *J. Deville*

Itoh, M., & Lapavitsas, C. (1999). *Political economy of money and finance.* Basingstoke: Palgrave Macmillan.

Lapavitsas, C. (2000). On Marx's analysis of money hoarding in the turnover of capital. *Review of Political Economy, 12*(2), 219–235.

Lapavitsas, C. (2003). *Social foundations of markets, money and credit,* London: Routledge.

Lapavitsas, C. (2005). The social relations of money as universal equivalent: A response to Ingham. *Economy and Society, 34*(3), 389–403.

Lapavitsas, C., 2006. Relations of power and trust in contemporary finance. *Historical Materialism, 14*(1), 129–154.

LiPuma, E. (1998). Modernity and forms of personhood in Melanesia. In M. Lambek, & A. Strathern (Eds), *Bodies and persons. Comparative perspectives from Africa and Melanesia.* Cambridge: Cambridge University Press, 53–79.

Marx, K. (1973). *Grundrisse.* London: Penguin/NLR.

Marx, K. (1976). *Capital.* Harmondsworth: Penguin.

Menger, C. (1892). On the origin of money. *The Economic Journal, 2*(6), 239–255.

Stengers, I. (2011). *Thinking with Whitehead: A free and wild creation of concepts.* Cambridge, MA; London: Harvard University Press.

Strathern, M. (1992). The decomposition of an event. *Cultural Anthropology, 7*(2), 244–254.

Whitehead, A. N. (1978). *Process and reality.* New York: The Free Press.

Zelizer, V. (1994). *The social meaning of money: Pin money, paychecks, poor relief, and other currencies.* Princeton, NJ: Princeton University Press.

Part III
Speculative techniques

Introduction

Speculative techniques

Alex Wilkie, Marsha Rosengarten, and Martin Savransky

Engaging with speculative thought entails questions around the tools, instruments and devices that are used in the application of social and cultural research and the nature of the empirical that is encountered therein. Recently, the social sciences have become preoccupied with the constitutive, performative and non-representational dimensions of research methods, including the inclusion of non-human agency (e.g. Law, 2004; Lury & Wakeford, 2012; Savage, 2013). Much of the debates in this area have also touched upon questions around interdisciplinarity and the broadening of the techniques through which the 'social' is grasped as a relational and underdetermined process that, in part, involves a mutual shaping of the empirical and method. In this part introduction we outline how approaches inspired by speculative thought resonate with contemporary methodological debates in social and cultural research and how a change to the speculative register necessarily involves a number of shifts: from the probable to the possible; from neutrality to a 'constructivist' approach that 'actively and explicitly relate[s] any knowledge-production to the question it tries to answer ...' (Stengers, 2008: 92), and; from reacting to pre-defined research questions to devising questions and research techniques that may engender the emergence of novel and inventive responses. The following chapters in this part detail how the speculative can inform inventive approaches to the tuning of research techniques and engagements through three interdisciplinary empirical cases.

By using the term 'technique' in contrast to that of method we aim to invoke the artful kinds and combinations of skills, crafts and technologies, in the broad sense of the word, that are used in the occasioning of speculative research. Although mostly indistinguishable to the notion of research practice as situated practical action we propose that research techniques, evoking Foucault, can be productive, constitutive and associated with the emergence of novelty. For our purposes, the notion of research technique has further advantages. First, techniques are not burdened with, and drawing on Gad and Jensen (2014: 10), the 'magical properties' of methodological practices so often presented as 'self-delimiting self-reproducing or self-explaining', nor do they necessarily provide a 'cause, an effect, or an explanation' (ibid.: 1). Second, although research techniques can be bound into configurations of conduct or *dispositifs* (e.g. education, government, medical, penal, therapeutic) that produce subjectification, they

114   *A. Wilkie* et al.

evoke the care that is required in developing interventions that may be capable of diagnosing human and non-human novelties into existence. That is to say, they may function not as a mere question of (re)production, but as an ethico-aesthetic event that is always situated, and never guaranteed.

The notion of techniques therefore invites us to modify practical questions and address methodological problematics. As the chapters in this part relay, speculative techniques are indexical and respond to the demands and requirements of a particular empirical situation – a situation that is never indifferent to the research technologies that are deployed to interrogate it. So, rather than ask of the data and the findings 'is this repeatable?', 'is this valid?', or 'is this reliable?' – questions that arguably remain within the epistemic and representational idiom of the probabilistic – such techniques invite the researcher to wonder about how to begin to formulate, and reformulate, questions that may prove more germane to the research encounter at hand. If the challenge of speculative research is to explore and make perceptible futures by experimenting with possibles, the task of empirical research shifts from the capture of measurement, determination and regulation which effectively foreclose possibilities, to questions around and efforts towards the luring of the potentiality of experiences.

In Lisa Adkin's chapter, experimenting technically with possibilities involves an exploration of the different modes of rapport between techniques of social research and the potentialities that certain forms of data enable. Exploring the shifting history of the relationships between the discipline of Sociology in Britain and the development of the Mass-Observation project, a para-academic endeavour concerned with producing recordings of everyday life – including diaries, open-ended questionnaires and other techniques for eliciting responses from 'Observers' – by ordinary people living in Britain, Adkins interrogates the varying sensibilities that have informed social research practices concerned with the archived data produced by the project. Originally perceived as a threat to the discipline, she suggests that the Mass Observation archive has now become something of a sociological resource for drawing distinctions between past and present and producing accounts of social change. While charting these mutations, Adkins simultaneously seeks to disclose and to cultivate an alternative mode of relating to the archive. Instead of approaching it as evidence of a bygone past, she articulates and proposes a relationship to the archive whereby the recorded data may be approached as a technique for folding and refolding time itself, by arranging and transforming the distances and proximities between events. In this way, Adkins proposes that, other than a repository of 'pastness', the Mass Observation archive may become a site of speculative research and experimentation with eventful temporalities – a site whose interest resides not in holding data of what was and is no longer, but 'of active presents in which potential or possible futures might subsist'.

For Rebecca Coleman, the chosen technique for grasping and exploring the probabilistic workings of Amazon's anticipatory shipping is mail art which she places in, or displaces to, the field of visual sociology. The patented system employed by Amazon harnesses location-based ordering and fulfilment data to

Introduction: speculative techniques 115

predict geographic product demand and thereby compete with local retailers in terms of the immediate acquisition of merchandise. As a setting for speculative research, Amazon's logistics system offers Coleman (this volume) the opportunity to explore, or in her own words, 'unsettle' the calculative opportunities that algorithmic deployments provide for maximizing the competitive efficiency of Internet-based retailing whilst simultaneously enhancing the experience of consumption. The seeming failure of Coleman's mail art inspired postcards to elicit more than one meaningful response out of twenty-six cards could suggest the incompatibility of two distinct logics of speculation. Although both are expressly aimed towards enhancing a consumer's experience of online fulfilment, Amazon's shipping assemblage would appear to be highly resistant to variability: unanticipated interference, uncoded intervention and the occasioning of novel and un-programmed experience. In other words, the felicity conditions for novelty in this instance were not present, demonstrating that the efficacy of speculative techniques is often fragile and not assured.

In contrast to Coleman's engagement with a somewhat impervious logistics system, Michael Guggenheim, Bernd Kräftner and Judith Kröll report on the sandbox which they employ as an experimental set-up with which to occasion and explore non-expert responses to disaster. The difference, here, lies in how Guggenheim et al., echoing Garfinkel's (1967) breaching experiments, manifest the very device and setting with which to speculate rather than rely on the capacity (or not) of an existing sociotechnical ensemble to be impinged upon. Here, the role of the sandbox is to provide an artificial and isolated environment with which 'players' can model material–semiotic worlds, play out calamitous 'ruptures' and imagine emergency provision as a technique to exceed the norms of disaster preparedness and management. This opens the way to explore the possibilities of disasters e.g. what counts as and what constitutes a disaster. In so doing, we are asked to consider how speculation 'works' as an approach to empirical research, a feature that the authors argue is missing from literature which typically concentrates on defining the speculative as a method (e.g. Parisi 2012). The practical rejoinder to the question of *how* speculative research works in the case of the sandbox takes the form of certain accomplishments including the capacity of props to acquire names, attributes, and to do this alongside other props. In other words, the elements that compose the sandbox worlds are amenable to and involved in a process of mutual becoming together where a sociological experiment simulates the manifestation of virtual catastrophes. The theoretical response to the how question comes in the form of the *idiot*, a conceptual personae (Deleuze & Guattari, 1994: 62; Stengers, 2005: 995) that is now commonly invoked (e.g. Horst & Michael, 2011; Michael, 2012; Wilkie, Michael, & Plummer-Fernandez, 2015) to theoretically grasp how speculative research aims to resist common sense and customary explanation. The concept of the idiot also gestures towards the challenge of conceiving alternative conceptual personae (cf. angels, coyotes, cyborgs, diplomats, ethnographers, parasites, shamans, stammerers etc.) that conform to the processual demands and novel immanent modes of existence produced by the situation at hand.

116 *A. Wilkie* et al.

In Michael Schillmeier and Yvonne Lee Shultz's contribution, speculative thought is brought to bear on artworks that entertain playful and non-violent possibilities of handguns by way of the Walther PPK. Through chocolate and porcelain 'replicas', the works of Lee Shultz are considered as devices that incite, what might be called, speculative publics around an issue that is unresolved and perhaps unresolvable. The proposal here, is that another sociology or anthropology of art is possible, one that avoids the empirical catch-22 of artist-object analysis and, instead, suggests that the deployment of artworks can be part of an empirical and speculative engagement with sociality. In other words, what Schillmeier and Lee Shultz ask us to entertain (echoing other contributors) is the possibility of a speculative sociology and anthropology with, rather than of, art.

References

Deleuze, G., & Guattari, F. (1994). *What is philosophy?* London; New York, NY: Verso.
Gad, C., & Jensen, C. B. (2014). The promises of practice. *The Sociological Review*, *62*(4), 698–718.
Garfinkel, H. (1967). *Studies in ethnomethodology*. Cambridge: Polity, 1984.
Horst, M., & Michael, M. (2011). On the shoulders of idiots: Re-thinking science communication as 'event'. *Science as Culture*, *20*(3), 283–306.
Law, J. 2004. *After method: Mess in social science research*. Abingdon; New York, NY: Routledge.
Lury, C., & Wakeford, N. (Eds.). 2012. *Inventive methods: The happening of the social*. Abingdon; New York, NY: Routledge.
Michael, M. (2012). 'What are we busy doing?'': Engaging the idiot. *Science, Technology & Human Values*, *37*(5), 528–554.
Parisi, L. (2012). Speculation: A method for the unattainable. In C. Lury, & N. Wakeford (Eds), *Inventive methods: the happening of the social* (pp. 232–244). London; New York, NY: Routledge.
Savage, M. (2013). The 'social life of methods': A critical introduction. *Theory, Culture & Society*, *30*(4), 3–21.
Stengers, I. (2005). The cosmopolitical proposal. In B. Latour, & P. Weibel (Eds.), *Making things public* (pp. 994–1003). Cambridge, MA: MIT Press.
Stengers, I. (2008). A constructivist reading of process and reality. *Theory, Culture & Society*, *25*(4), 91–110.
Wilkie, A., Michael, M., & Plummer-Fernandez, M. (2015). Speculative method and Twitter: Bots, energy and three conceptual characters. *The Sociological Review*, *63*(1), 79–101.

8 Sociology's archive
Mass-Observation as a site of speculative research

Lisa Adkins

Introduction

This chapter takes up the call, laid out in the introduction to this volume, to develop alternative approaches and sensibilities to take futures seriously – 'as possibilities that demand new habits and practices of attention, invention and experimentation'. Perhaps paradoxically, it does so in relation to the past and more specifically in regard to recordings of the past. It suggests that for sociologists, the past as much as the present must be understood to stand as a site for the development of alternative approaches to the future, and this is especially the case for the data sources or recordings of social life on which sociologists regularly rely to mobilize and activate the past. This chapter amounts to a call for adopting a set of alternative practices and sensibilities to such recordings which are attuned not to the 'pastness' of the data – an orientation which inevitably produces diachronic sociological accounts – but instead are attuned to the capacities of recorded data itself. Such attention, this chapter will maintain, will produce not a 'better' historical sociology, or a synchronic account designed to trump or outplay diachronic accounts, but instead an account which allows time itself to emerge as a key object of investigation. That is, such a sensibility will allow time to emerge not as a backdrop or setting for recorded data, but as part of the very data that is recorded. In as much as speculative research demands that attentiveness be paid to the relations of time, and especially to the question of futures, this chapter posits that such a sensibility contributes to the fostering of such a speculative research agenda. This is so not least because it allows a form of time to emerge which is not over or complete and stands in a chronological order or sequence ready for comparisons with the present and/or potential futures, but instead is incomplete, not-yet known, and stands in a possible or not yet relationship to the future and to the presents it inhabits.

This chapter therefore amounts to a call for the adoption of alternative stances towards sociological data, that is, to recordings of social life. It posits further that such stances might comprise one element of a speculative research agenda. To set out these interventions I focus on a specific set of archived data recorded and collected as part of the Mass-Observation project in the UK. While, as I will set out below, the discipline of sociology has not always had an easy relationship

118   L. Adkins

to the Mass-Observation project, sociologists now regularly draw on Mass-Observation data. They do so especially to craft past/present comparisons and to produce accounts of social change. That is, they do so primarily to draw what the editors of this volume term a 'modern arrow of time'. To begin to chart the interventions of this chapter I turn first, then, to the Mass-Observation project and to how present-day sociologists tend to position and locate Mass-Observation data as recordings of the past.

Mass-Observation: the science of ourselves

Conceived in 1936 in London by a poet, an amateur anthropologist and a film-maker, and launched in 1937, the Mass-Observation project (or, as it was termed at the time, movement) aimed at producing recordings of everyday life by ordinary people living in Britain. Influenced by anthropology, surrealism and psycho-analysis, and forming part of the documentary movement, the Mass-Observation project anticipated the defamiliarizing of the everyday which would later form a leitmotif of the discipline of Cultural Studies (Highmore, 2002). The Mass-Observation founders understood their project as aiming at 'an anthropology of ourselves' (Mass-Observation in Malinowski, 2009 [1938]: 100) or as a 'science of ourselves' (Madge & Harrisson, 2009 [1939]: 9). As Julian Huxley framed it, Mass-Observation was a project which aimed at the disclosure of 'ourselves to ourselves' which it set out to achieve 'by the application of scientific methods of observation and record' (Huxley, in Malinowski, 2009 [1938]: 90–91).[1]

To achieve these – for the time – highly ambitious and radical aims the project recruited volunteers (or Observers) via advertisements in newspapers and magazines to record their ordinary lives and everyday happenings. Two of the founders of the project described the beginning of Mass-Observation in the fol-lowing terms:

> On February 12th 1937, thirty people made an experiment. They had never met each other, they lived in widely scattered parts of the country and they differed greatly from each other in their surroundings, in their work and in their views about life. What they had agreed to do was to set down plainly all that happened to them on that day. That's how Mass-Observation began.
>
> (Madge & Harrisson, 2009 [1938]: 7)

Indeed, Madge and Harrison described the methods employed in the project as comprising 'experiments in social recording' (Madge & Harrisson, 2009 [1938]: 7).[2] These experiments in recording included diaries or Day Surveys in which Observers were instructed to give 'a careful and factual description of what hap-pened to them in the course of their normal routine during the whole or a part of the day' (Madge & Harrisson, 2009 [1938]: 7). They also included Directives comprising open-ended questionnaires organized around specific themes and events and/or instructions to Observers to write to respond to specific questions.[3] Examples of the latter included instructions to describe dreams and to describe what objects were on display on mantelpieces in the homes of the Observers. Via these methods Mass-Observation posed both a new set of techniques and 'a new attitude to getting facts' (Madge & Harrison, 2009 [1939]: 9). This attitude was understood by the project's founders as necessary to respond to a need for 'studying the everyday lives of and feelings of ordinary people' (Madge & Harrisson, 2009 [1939]: 9). Writing in 1939 the founders noted that this need had yet to be met – in Britain at least – by the then fledgling academic discipline of sociology and that despite spending years travelling the world 'to study remote tribes' anthropologists had 'contributed literally nothing to the anthropology of ourselves' (Madge & Harrisson, 2009 [1939]: 10).

Alongside specific studies in which Observers recorded the everyday lives of people and events in particular locations, from 1937 to 1938 the Day Survey (with Directives) took place monthly (on the 12th of each month) and formed a national panel (Goot, 2008). The data from the latter was collected and stored at the Mass-Observation headquarters in London. During the Second World War the activities of Mass-Observation continued via Directives and diary keeping on the part of Observers. In addition, during wartime Mass-Observation carried out commissioned research for the Ministry of Information.[4] This included research on the morale of the British population creating, as Mass-Observation termed it, a 'war barometer' assessing the collective mood or atmosphere (Jeffery, 1978). By the end of the war nearly 3,000 volunteers had participated in Mass-Observation activities (Goot, 2008). Indeed, even by 1939 two of the founders noted that 'through M-O you can already listen-in to the movements of popular habit and opinion' (Madge & Harrisson, 2009 [1939]: 10).

During wartime, however, divisions emerged between the project's two remaining founder members. (Humphrey Jennings had already left the project in 1938.) In 1940 one of the remaining two – Charles Madge – departed to take up a project on wartime economics which, via contact with John Maynard Keynes, he secured with the Institute of Economic and Social Research. Madge later went on to become a Professor of Sociology at the University of Birmingham (Jeffrey, 1978).[5] In 1949 the remaining member – Tom Harrisson – sold the Mass-Observation name for use in commercial market research in return for control over all of the pre-1949 material, a move resulting in Mass-Observation Limited (Goot, 2008; Jeffrey, 1978; Pollen, 2013).[6] As Pollen (2013) sets out, the early papers collected by the project from the 1930s and 1940s lay unused in the basement of Mass-Observation Limited until they were rediscovered and their potential for academic research was recognized by social historians in the 1960s (Hubble, 2006). A process of rehabilitation and revitalization of Mass-Observation then unfolded involving Harrisson deeding the pre-1949 material to the University of Sussex in the 1970s and, in turn, Sussex opening a public archive containing the papers: The Mass-Observation Archive (MOA).[7] The archive served as a resource for research into the everyday life of the late 1930s and 1940s (Casey, Courage, & Hubble 2014) and established the Mass-Observation movement papers as a critical public collection. In 1981, under the stewardship of the MOA Director – Dorothy Sheridan – Mass-Observation

120 *L. Adkins*

research was re-launched as the Mass-Observation Project (MOP). The MOP recruited a national panel of Observers to report on everyday life in contemporary Britain via themed Directives, which are issued there times a year. This panel survey is ongoing. Recent Directives have included questions on social mobility, higher education, the EU Referendum, the financial crisis, dreams and the Eurovision song contest. In addition, Mass-Observation runs a Day Survey/diary on the 12 May of each year. The MOP records, along with the original Mass-Observation materials, are now stored in a purpose built archive – The Keep – adjacent to the University of Sussex. Since its revival and re-launch Mass-Observation has achieved a celebrated status as a 'unique, extraordinarily rich and internationally significant body of material for the study of everyday life' (Pollen, 2013: 214).

Sociology and mass-observation

At its inception the Mass-Observation project aimed to establish its distinctiveness from university based social sciences and did so by locating the science of ourselves as productive of this difference. In elaborating their project the Mass-Observation founders did not hold back on what they saw as the weaknesses of university based sociology with, for example, Tom Harrisson describing academic sociologists as 'timid, bookish and unproductive' (Harrisson in Goot, 2008: 96). Indeed, the then developing (and professionalizing) discipline of sociology in Britain stood in an uneasy and ambivalent relationship to Mass-Observation. Casey, Courage and Hubble have framed this relationship in the following terms:

> Mass-Observation became known quickly to the British sociological establishment but at a time when there was only one university chair in the discipline, it was perceived as a threat and contemporary references to it in sociological literature were elliptical.
>
> (Casey, Courage, & Hubble, 2014: 1.2)

But in addition to oblique recognition, Mass-Observation came under explicit attack from sociologists and cognate social scientists (especially from anthropologists). At issue in such attacks in particular was a concern with a lack of a properly scientific attitude as well as perceived problems with the methods mobilized in the Mass-Observation research endeavours (see e.g. Firth, 1939; Jahoda, 1938; Malinowski, 2009 [1938]). Discussing the published results of a Day Survey, Marie Jahoda, for example, asked: 'Does it [Mass-Observation] give a new scientific approach?' Her response to herself was 'certainly not' (Jahoda, 1938: 208). Jahoda went on:

> It is the task of every science, and especially of the social sciences at this time, when social phenomena are so complex and difficult to understand, to represent reality in a simplifying, generalizing way. To this task mass observation contributes nothing. It is true that to abstract, one must know

Sociology's archive: Mass-Observation 121

the complex reality with all its details. But no representation of details dispenses with the necessity for abstraction

(Jahoda, 1938: 208–209)

Bogged down in details and not understanding the necessity to abstract to qualify for scientific status, Mass-Observation therefore stood accused of contributing nothing to the social-scientific project. Later, this view was to be upheld by the survey researcher Mark Abrams, who described Mass-Observation as producing 'dreary trivia' (Abrams, 1951: 107).

Nearly 80 years on from the formation of Mass-Observation, its relationship to sociology has, however, been almost entirely redrawn. Rather than as a threat to be discounted, ignored or explicitly critiqued, the early Mass-Observation material and the MOP panel data are regularly utilized by sociologists. This is particularly the case for sociologists who are interested in social change. The ongoing MOP, for example, has been recognized to 'represent a key national, qualitative, secondary data resource' (Lindsey & Bulloch, 2014: 3.1) and especially as a major repository of longitudinal qualitative data. In addition, MOP panel data is regularly drawn on by sociologists in regard to specific thematic research and is the subject and object of an ongoing debate about sociological methods. But current-day sociologists do not simply make use of MOP data and Mass-Observation materials, they are now also active in the design and crafting of MO data itself through activities such as the commissioning of Directives. Indeed, so transformed is the relationship between Mass-Observation and the discipline of sociology that sociologists now regularly locate Mass-Observation as a critical research institution. Contemporary sociologists have, for example, described Mass-Observation as 'the most studied, and arguably the most important, social research institution of the mid-twentieth century' (Savage, 2010: 57) and as of 'overwhelming' importance for the discipline (Casey, Courage, & Hubble 2014). To understand this transformed relationship between Sociology and Mass-Observation is, of course, to understand the history of the discipline, especially the history of the discipline in Britain. More particularly, it is to understand the establishment of the everyday and the ordinary as legitimate sites or scenes of sociological investigation and the establishment of the sociology of everyday as part of the core business of the sociological enterprise (Halsey, 2004; Highmore, 2002; 2011; Hubble, 2010). It is also to understand the establishment of narrative as a legitimate sociological object, especially as a site for understanding social change and in particular as a juncture between structure and agency (see e.g. Lawler, 2002; Plummer, 1995; Somers & Gibson, 1994).

Recording the past

While the relationship between Sociology and Mass-Observation has transformed, nonetheless, within this there are clear tendencies evident in the ways current-day sociologists understand and make use of Mass-Observation and MOP data. One prominent tendency is the aforementioned location of the MOP data as a

122   *L. Adkins*

longitudinal data set, that is, as a set of data which records change over time. Such an understanding is made available to sociologists because – notwithstanding inevitable attrition and the enrollment of new Observers (or Correspondents) – the MOP makes use of the same Observers over time, that is, the same cohort. Indeed, it is precisely these longitudinal or panel-like qualities of the MOP data which attracts many sociologists to it and leads to its use or, more precisely, its reuse to achieve particular sociological ends. To give just one example of such an understanding, Lindsey and Bulloch (2014) have argued that 'the MOP represents a unique source of longitudinal data, offering potential insight into changes and continuities in individual writers' lives' (Lindsey & Bulloch, 2014: 3.1). Indeed, these contemporary sociologists not only understand the MOP materials as a source of such longitudinal data but also compel other sociologists to take up this stance. They 'seek to enable potential users of the MOP to see the value of MOP as a source of longitudinal qualitative secondary data' (Lindsey & Bulloch, 2014: 1.0).

One sub-field of the discipline in which sociologists have actively taken up such an attitude is in the sociology of ageing, a take-up which is not surprising given that the MOP tracks a particular cohort in time, that is, as they age. Bazalgette, Holden, Tew, Hubble, and Morrison (2011), for example, have made use of MOP data to analyse the 'lived experience of growing old' (Bazalgette et al., 2011: 147). Collaborating with Mass-Observation to craft a Directive in 2009, and drawing on existing materials from Directives in 1992 and 2006 on the theme of ageing, Bazalgette et al. were able to extract 'a number of longitudinal case studies – comprising those who had responded to all three of the relevant directives from 1992 to 2009' (Bazalgette et al., 2011: 150). The researchers argue that these cases 'collectively narrated a hitherto concealed sea change in the experience of ageing over the past 20 years that … showed … ageing in the real world to be in a process of radical transition' (Bazalgette et al., 2011: 150). Here, then, positioned and treated as longitudinal data, Mass-Observation yields an account of change through time. Indeed, here, Mass-Observation data is positioned as precisely tracking change in time and to act as a measure of such change.

But it is not only the MOP data with its panel-like qualities which is used by contemporary sociologists to forge accounts of change in and through time but also earlier Mass-Observation materials. In their project *Families and Food in Hard Times*, O'Connell, Knight, & Brannen (2015), for example, have made use of Mass-Observation Limited materials from the 1950s, including diaries, Directives and a published survey ('The Housewife's Day'), to consider food practices in post-war austerity Britain. From analysis of these materials, and as part of their broader project, O'Connell et al. have sought to elaborate 'some key differences between food practices during the period of immediate post war austerity and the current context [of austerity in Britain]' (O'Connell et al., 2015: 1). Via this procedure, they have suggested that one major difference between the two periods:

> concerns the high level of female employment today compared with the early 1950s, alongside the reduction of time spent by women (and the smaller increase by men) on food and cooking. Foodwork overwhelmingly

Sociology's archive: Mass-Observation 123

remains women's work in the contemporary era, despite a discourse of equality.... In the 1950s' women's diaries and the survey, however, food preparation appears as a very much more taken for granted and time-consuming part of a woman's day.

(O'Connell et al., 2015: 2)

What is of interest here are not so much the substantive claims made about social change, but rather the positioning of the Mass-Observation materials (as well as the Mass-Observation archive) as a store of history, and in particular as a set of recordings of events in time which, when placed in proximity with the present, will disclose social change (and allow now/then narratives to emerge).[8] Indeed, what is of interest are the ways in which both sociologists who treat the MOP data as longitudinal and sociologists who mobilize earlier Mass-Observation materials to produce now/then accounts share in common an understanding of Mass-Observation data as recordings of events in time, and especially as recordings of the past. And it is important to make clear here that in so doing such understandings also make certain claims in regard to time itself, namely that time flows sequentially and chronologically with the past preceding the present and the future existing after the now. As such, such accounts must be understood to draw a quintessentially modern arrow of time.

While contemporary sociologists continue to position Mass-Observation data in this fashion we might, however, ask if this data should simply be understood as recordings of the past which can be called on to produce then/now narratives and accounts of social change. Are alternative stances towards this data possible? And if so what might such alternatives look like? Moreover, what might be at stake in considering the possibility of such alternative stances? In the section that follows I begin to address these questions by paying attention to the capacities of Mass-Observation data, and especially the capacities of Day Survey or diary data, a focus which necessarily requires a brief discussion of the diary as a methodological device.

Proximity, time and events

As set out above, from its inception Mass-Observation made use of Day Surveys or diaries as devices to conduct the science of ourselves, and diaries continue to be used by the MOP today. In certain methodological discussions within sociology and cognate disciplines, diaries and kindred methodological tools such as time diaries, blogs and logs are understood to record events in time, that is, are understood as devices which provide a temporal dimension to data via providing 'accounts of phenomena over time' (Symon, 2004: 98). On this understanding of diaries as a methodological device, the data generated by Mass-Observation via this method would, then, precisely allow for the generation of accounts of change over time, that is, would shore up the dominant sociological understanding of Mass-Observation data outlined above, especially the view that Mass-Observation contains recordings of the past and hence enables the drawing of a modern arrow of time.

124   *L. Adkins*

What an understanding of diaries as a method to record events in time side-lines, however, is that as devices they place time and events in close proximity or contact and, moreover, are often put to work to precisely achieve such ends. This is the case because as devices they are attuned to record events *as they happen*. Thus, typically respondents involved in diary research will be asked to record events and experiences not retrospectively but as close as possible to those events and/or experiences taking place. Indeed, in certain methodological discussion of diaries as a technique of recording it is this quality or capacity to record events as they happen which is emphasized as a key strength of this method, one which differentiates diaries from other methods such as the in-depth interview. In the latter, events tend to be narrated retrospectively (that is, events are retold) and hence the distance between time and events is stretched out and extended. In the latter, time and events tend, therefore, to be separated out. In contrast, diaries track the 'contemporaneous flow of ... events' (Plummer, 1983: 170). As Elliot (1997) has framed it, diaries 'document the present' by operating 'in proximity to the present' (Elliot, 1997: 2.4). Critically, diaries do so by closing the gap between 'experience and the record of experience' (Elliot, 1997: 2.4) since they ask respondents (or, for the case of Mass-Observation, Observers or Correspondents) to record events as they take place. It is, then, the proximity between event and record or event and time which marks the particular quality of the diary as a methodological device. Indeed, the modern-day diary, namely the personal blog, also concerns this proximity between event and record, and as such blogs have been located as important devices for sociologists to come to grips with the ever-changing present (Hookway, 2008).

This proximity between event and record (or event and time) which the method of diary keeping affords, is clearly on view in the following transcribed extract from a Day Survey (see also Figure 8.1) – Day Survey 216 – written by a Mass-Observer in 1937.[9] While this particular Mass-Observation record (along with others) was encountered as part of a broader project on the temporality of unemployment, for the purposes of this chapter what is of interest is the unambiguous proximity between events (including temperature recorded by this Observer in Fahrenheit) and time it displays.[10]

Day Survey 216

Wednesday 18 August 1937.

Sex M

DOB 1909 [28 years old]

Household Status Single

Occupation Unemployed and Forces; ex Indian Army

Place of residence New Maldon, Surrey

Played gramophone records while helping servant wash-up breakfast: 'Here Comes the Sun' and 'Sing a Happy Little Thing'. In an old copy of 'The

Times' 7th October 1932, noticed extraordinary coincidence in deaths column, where David Govie, faithful servant and friend for 32 years to Colonel Rowland Burdon, died 1st September, and Mary Govie (presumably wife) also faithful servant and friend for 32 years, died 4th October. Seeing the name Govie repeated has attracted my attention.

62.5 at 10. Bicycle tyre unfortunately was slowly deflating.

68.5 at 1.30.

Eating 'beauty of bath' apple to finish lunch I discovered maggots' eggs inside and a maggot himself I saw right in the core.

70.5 at 2.

About 3 pm pumped up cycle preparatory to going off to the dole, which I attend 3.15 Wed among other days, 2.6 miles away by cyclometer, feeling the tyre would last me there, but there was a bump, bump every time valve came near ground and it was down almost at once. Tried pumping up again but the same happened a little way on. Finally, went back and got my brother's 3 speed (having ridden flat tyre) and am at dole office 3.25. Apologized for being late – no complaints made. To library for a short while afterwards. Home by 4.10 – noticed it had been up to 71 the maximum for the day.

Tea 5 o'clock.

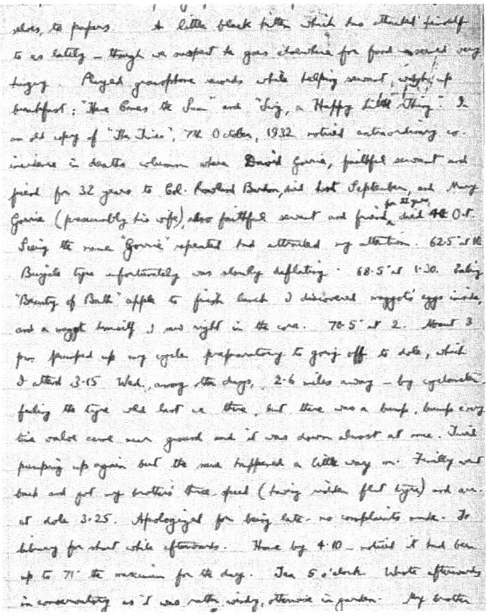

Figure 8.1 Day Survey 216 written by a Mass-Observer in 1937.

Source: reproduced with permission of Curtis Brown Group Ltd, London, on behalf of the Trustees of the Mass Observation Archive.

Mass-Observation and the unrealized potential of the present

But there is something more at stake in regard to the use of diaries as a methodological device than the observation that diaries record events as they happen and place event and record in close proximity. And this is that in so doing, that is, in recording events as they take place, diaries are attuned to – indeed record – eventful temporality. As I have elaborated elsewhere (Adkins, 2009), this is a form of time in which time and events proceed and unfold together. As an intensive form of time eventful temporality stands in contrast to externalist or extensive forms in which time acts as an external container or vessel for events. In externalist forms of time events therefore take place in time. In collapsing the distance between time and events and recording events as they take place, diaries as devices are, then, necessarily recording eventful temporality. Recognising that diaries record such time has a number of implications, not the least of which is that the diary data recorded by Mass-Observation should be understood not as a set of recordings of events ordered and arranged by a chronological, sequential or linear history but as a stock of recordings of eventful temporality.[11]

There is, however, a further issue that is important to register about eventful temporality. This is that the events it may entail are not necessarily predictable or knowable in advance, and this is precisely the case because in eventful temporality time and events unfold together. Indeed, eventful temporality exactly concerns the contingent, the unpredictable and the unexpected (Savransky, 2016; Sewell, 2005), that is, events which cannot necessarily be classified, understood or mapped via the movement of the modern arrow of time. What is vital about such contingent and unpredictable events is, however, not that they cannot be mapped, tracked or measured by the modern arrow of time, but that they are the very ground of speculative research. This is so because it is such contingent and unpredictable events which speculative research seeks to open out in its exploration of what the editors of this volume term the 'unrealised potential of the present', a present in which unexpected events may erupt and 'alternative futures may be forged'. It is, then, in the unrealised potential of the present that the resources can be found for speculative research. And it is such potential that sociologists must confront if they are to speculate, that is, to engage possible futures.

To recognize that Mass-Observation diaries are records of eventful temporality is, then, also to recognise that they are records of the unrealised potential of the present. Indeed, if it is understood that Mass-Observation data and specifically diary data are recordings of eventful temporality rather than recordings of the past, this data surfaces as recordings of such presents. These, however, are not presents which are pre-determined by pasts or by futures which have not yet arrived, but presents in which alternative futures might subsist. Mass-Observation diary data offers, then, not a resource to compare past and present or to treat as a store of the past, but an opening for sociologists to explore the as yet unrealised potentials of the present, that is, to forge alternative stances towards the future.[12] In this sense Mass-Observation data might be understood as a site for speculative research. Understanding Mass-Observation as such a site, moreover, necessarily swerves its relationship to the sociological enterprise. Rather than as an external threat or as a resource to be used, a speculative approach locates Mass-Observation's relationship to sociology as always being one concerning its unrealized (and incalculable) potential. Locating Mass-Observation data as recordings of eventful temporality therefore not only opens out possibilities to explore alternative futures, but also an alternative relationship between Mass-Observation and sociology as a discipline.

Conclusion

The purpose of this chapter has not been to claim that diaries are a method available to sociologists to explore the unrealized potential of the present and to open out and engage futures. The purpose of this chapter has therefore not been to argue that if armed with the correct methods sociologists can access alternative futures. My argument has also not been that a procedure of placing the past in proximity with the present will activate such alternatives. On the contrary, my argument has been that opening out the unrealized potentials of the present requires new stances or attitudes on the part of sociologists in regard to the social world, including towards recordings of social life. Instead, for example, of relying on the modern arrow of the time to classify and understand recordings of social life – a procedure which will always close down the possibilities of presents and of the futures which such possibilities might contain – I have suggested that such recordings might be understood as recordings of time. Via such a stance the possibility emerges of understanding recordings of social life which have been dated via the calendar not as records of the past which are already over and complete but as recordings of active presents in which potential or possible futures might subsist. In pointing to Mass-Observation data as a site for the cultivation of such a stance, that is, in pointing to a data set on which sociologists regularly rely to draw the modern arrow of time, I also hope to have made clear that the cultivation of such a stance does not necessarily require the invention of new methods or the production of new forms of data. Instead, at stake is the cultivation of a new set of sensibilities and habits in regard to time, including the recognition that presents are not coterminous with the now.

Notes

1 In this sense the Mass-Observation project should be understood to have contributed to the then emergent post-colonial critique of anthropology.
2 More broadly, the Mass-Observation project has been described as a social experiment (Pollen, 2013).
3 Observers were understood to stand as cameras 'to photograph contemporary life' (Madge & Harrison, 2009 [1938]: 7).
4 On how the techniques of Mass-Observation became implicated in modern governance see Harrison (2014).
5 On the traffic in personnel between Mass-Observation and university based sociology see Stanley (2007).

128 *L. Adkins*

6 On the relationship between Mass-Observation and market research see Goot (2008) and Jeffery (1978).
7 The historian Asa Briggs, then Vice Chancellor of the University of Sussex, was central to this move.
8 Critical archive scholars have outlined a range of problems associated with locating archives as a store or storehouse of materials or documents, not least because this understanding bypasses the productivity of the archive itself (see e.g. Dever, 2014; Eichhorn, 2013). As Dever (2014: 70) has argued archives 'do not so much preserve as produce meaning'.
9 This Day Survey is stored at the Keep as part of the Mass-Observation collection and a digitized version is available via Adam Matthew Digital.
10 My current research on the temporality of unemployment is funded by the Academy of Finland (Academy of Finland Distinguished Professorship 'Social Science for the Twenty-First Century: The Changing Economy–Society Relation' 2015–2019) and the Australian Research Council (Discovery Project 150101772 'Employment Activation and the Changing Economy-Society Relation' 2015–2017).
11 Adding fuel to this view, Highmore (2011: 92) has suggested that Mass-Observation documents might be understood as recordings of temporal atmospheres.
12 See also Ketelaar (2012: 29) who suggests that archives should be understood in terms of 'activation and openness'.

References

Adkins, L. (2009). Sociological futures: From clock time to event time. *Sociological Research Online, 14*(4): www.socresonline.org.uk/14/4/8.html.
Abrams, M. (1951). *Social surveys and social action*, London: William Heinemann.
Bazalgette, L., Holden, J., Tew, P., Hubble, N., & Morrison, J. (2011). *Coming of age*. London: Demos.
Casey, E., Courage, F,. & Hubble, N. (2014). Introduction: Mass-Observation as method. *Sociological Research Online, 19*(3): www.socresonline.org.uk/19/3/22.html.
Dever, M. (2014). Archiving feminism: Papers, politics, posterity. *Archivaria*, 77: 25–42.
Eichhorn, K. (2013). *The archival turn in feminism: Outrage in order*. Temple University Press. Philadelphia, PA.
Elliot, H. (1997). The use-of time diaries in sociological research on health experience. *Sociological Research Online, 2*(2): www.socresonline.org.uk/2/2/7.html.
Firth, R. (1939). An anthropologist's view of Mass Observation. *Sociological Review, 31*(2), 166–193.
Goot, M. (2008). Mass-Observation and modern public opinion research. In W. Donsbach, & M. W. Traugott, (Eds), *The Sage handbook of public opinion research*. London: Sage.
Halsey, A. H. (2004). *A history of sociology in Britain*. Oxford: Oxford University Press.
Harrison, R. (2014). Observing, collecting and governing 'ourselves' and 'others': Mass-Observation's fieldwork agencements. *History and Anthropology, 25*(2), 227–245.
Highmore, B. (2002). *Everyday life and cultural theory*. London: Routledge.
Highmore, B. (2011). *Ordinary lives: Studies in the everyday*. London: Routledge.
Hookway, N. (2008). 'Entering the blogosphere': Some strategies for using blogs in social research. *Qualitative Research, 8*(1) 91–113.
Hubble, N. (2010). *Mass observation and everyday life: Culture, history, theory*. Basingstoke: Palgrave Macmillan.

Jahoda, M. (1938). Review of Mass-Observation and of May 12. *Sociological Review*, *30*(2): 208–9.

Jeffery, T. (1978). *Mass Observation – A short history* (Stenciled Occasional Paper No. 55), Birmingham: Centre for Contemporary Cultural Studies.

Ketelaar, E. (2012). Cultivating archives: Meanings and identities. *Archival Science*, *12*(1): 19–33.

Lawler, S. (2002). Narrative in social research. In T. May (Ed.), *Qualitative research in action*. London: Sage.

Lindsey, R., & Bulloch, S. (2014). A sociologist's field notes to the Mass Observation Archive: A consideration of the challenges of 're-using' mass observation data in a longitudinal mixed-methods study. *Sociological Research Online*, *19*(3): www.socresonline.org.uk/19/3/8.html.

Madge, C., & Harrisson, T. (Eds). (2009 [1938]), *First year's work 1937–1938 by Mass Observation*. London: Faber and Faber.

Madge, C., & Harrisson, T. (2009 [1939]). *Britain by Mass Observation*. London: Faber and Faber.

Malinowski, B. [1938] 2009. A nation-wide intelligence service. In C. Madge, & T. Harrisson (Eds), *First year's work 1937–1938 by Mass Observation*. London: Faber and Faber, 83–121.

O'Connell, R., Knight, A., & Brannen, J. (2015). Food austerity from an historical perspective: Making sense of 1950s Mass Observation data in the contemporary era. *Discover Society*, *16*, 1–3.

Plummer, K. (1983). *Documents of life*. London: George Allen and Unwin.

Plummer, K. (1995). *Telling sexual stories*. London: Routledge.

Pollen, A. (2013). Research methodology in Mass-Observation, past and present: 'Scientifically, about as valuable as a chimpanzee's tea party at the zoo'? *History Workshop Journal*, *75*(1), 213–235.

Savage, M. (2010). *Identities and social change in Britain since 1940*. Oxford: Oxford University Press.

Savransky, M. (2016). *The adventure of relevance: An ethics of social inquiry*. Basingstoke: Palgrave Macmillan.

Sewell, W. (2005). *Logics of history: Social theory and social transformation*. Chicago: Chicago University Press.

Somers, M. R., & Gibson, G. D. (1994). Reclaiming the epistemological 'other': Narrative and the social constitution of identity. In Craig Calhoun (Ed.), *Social theory and the politics of identity* (pp. 37–99). Oxford: Blackwell.

Stanley, L. (2007). Mass-Observations fieldwork methods. In P. Atkinson, A. Coffey, S. Delamont, J. Lofland, & L. Lofland (Eds), *Handbook of ethnography* (pp. 92–108). London: Sage.

Symon, G. (2004). Qualitative research diaries. In Catherine Cassell, & Gillian Symon (Eds), *Essential guide to qualitative methods in organizational research* (pp. 98–113). London: Sage.

9 Developing speculative methods to explore speculative shipping
Mail art, futurity and empiricism

Rebecca Coleman

This chapter discusses one iteration of a visual sociology project to draw out and put into play different approaches to and practices of speculation.[1] The project focuses on the business practice of 'speculative shipping' recently patented by Amazon, where goods are shipped, and perhaps delivered, without orders having been placed to minimise the time between order and delivery. It develops a speculative methodology, inspired by approaches developed in design, art, sociology and Science and Technology Studies (STS) that aim in assorted ways to create and engage potentiality and futurity. In particular, I examine the shifting relationships between speculation, futurity and potentiality through a focus on a Deleuzian understanding of empiricism, that is, an approach that seeks novelty and creativity. The project examines how speculative methodologies might be a means to explore, and perhaps intervene in, the ways in which speculative shipping can be seen as closing down the uncertainty and potentiality of the future through commercialisation. It experiments with a mode of exchange intended to elicit surprise and delight, which I suggest might create an alternative reality by opening up (to) futurity. Drawing on the principles and practices of mail art, where artists exchange their art works through the post, I made postcards that I sent to unsuspecting recipients as an attempt to produce a non-commercial form of exchange. Here, I tease out some connections and tensions in how speculation is understood and deployed in the business practice of Amazon's speculative shipping and in speculative methodologies, and reflect on the testing out of a speculative method.

Speculation, futurity, potentiality

As this collection makes clear, speculation has been taken up in a range of philosophical and theoretical traditions, and across different commercial, medical, environmental, scientific and cultural settings. One important feature of speculation is its attention to futurity, where, as Martin Savransky (this volume) explains "speculation can be conceived as wager on an unfinished present, whose potential is none other than the production of instruments and operations, or ideas, capable of vectorising a transition into future and thus into novel situations". In this chapter, I argue that while both Amazon's speculative shipping

Mail art, futurity and empiricism 131

and speculative methods are interested in "vectorising a transition into the future and thus into novel situations", the potentiality of the future is understood and put to work differently. For example, while Amazon's speculative business practices can be understood as making predictions about the future, turning it into something knowable and "firm" (Uncertain Commons, 2013), speculative methodologies are interested in engaging and participating in the uncertainty of the future.

In attending to these different, and contradictory, senses of speculation, one aim of the project at stake in this chapter is thus to examine the possibilities of developing speculative methods to explore speculative shipping. If the speculative shipping patented by Amazon closes down the potentiality of the future, is it possible to develop speculative methods to engage this potentiality, to open up a different future? If Amazon's speculative shipping works via a mode of exchange between brand and customer (actual or prospective), is it possible to put to work an artistic practice such as mail art to facilitate an alternative style of exchange, which functions through surprise, delight and uncertainty?

A second aim of the project is to contribute to the growing field of work of social science methods that are termed variously, inventive (Coleman & Ringrose, 2013; Lury & Wakeford, 2012), performative (Law & Urry, 2004), and/or speculative (Michael, 2016; Wilkie, Michael, & Plummer-Fernandez, 2014). While these methods cannot be collapsed into each other, what they have in common is a concern with: (1) the changing character and co-ordination of the social, and the need for methods to change with them; (2) the entanglement of methods with the worlds they study – methods are not neutral observers of but active participants in the world; and (3) what Wilkie et al. call an "open[ing] up [of] the prospective" (2014: 20), that is, an interest in and engagement with potentiality, novelty and transformation. In these senses, the social is seen as capable of being made and re-made differently – and methods play a part in this (re)creation of the social.

As I develop them here, methods also have a foothold in Deleuze and Parnet's (2002) conception of empiricism, whereby the aim is "to find the conditions under which something new is produced (*creativeness*)" (vii). Empiricism here refers to a conception of the world as multiple, relational and processual, or becoming; the social is in the making, through the relations between methods and realities for example. Furthermore, for Deleuze more generally, empiricism can be seen to refer to a particular methodological approach to the world (see Coleman & Ringrose, 2013). Empiricism demands both a confusion of the conventional border between theory and practice (Deleuze 2001: 36), and a recognition of, and attempt to coincide with, that which is immanent to the thing at stake (Coleman, 2008; Deleuze & Parnet, 2002: vii). Also important here is that creativity necessarily emerges through particular ontological, social, practical conditions (see Wilkie and Michael, this volume). What this project is interested in, then, is making speculate methods coincide with speculative shipping in order to find the conditions under which it might be possible to produce novelty or creativity.

Speculative shipping

In August 2012, amazon.com filed for a United States patent for a "Method and system for anticipatory package shipping". The patent was granted on 24 December 2013. Amazon describes the patent as a response to its online business operation, noting a "substantial disadvantage" of existing online only as the delay between order and delivery, or the additional costs involved in expedited shipping methods.[2] They worry these issues "may dissuade customers from buying items from online merchants, particularly if those items are more readily available locally". Anticipatory package shipping – or what is more commonly referred to in the patent as speculative shipping[3] – is intended to deal with this problem by shipping products to different geographical hubs in advance of specific orders.

The patent includes much technical detail on speculative shipping, and covers a range of scenarios whereby a product may be moved from fulfillment centre to consumer via physical hubs, different modes of transport and computer systems. These scenarios include a package being "shipped to a destination geographical area without completely specifying a delivery address", the specification of a "partial street address", or a "complete street address or other physical address may be provided, but the addressee [...] may be omitted". The latter cases might involve a product being shipped to an address with a large number of residents or tenants, and/or would cover situations where a consumer has a number of addresses attached to their account, or is moving between addresses at the time of the speculative shipment.

The situation of a product being speculatively shipped and then not ordered is also covered in the patent, with Amazon outlining at least two cost-effective alternatives to returning a product to the fulfillment centre without a sale: (1) where "some or all of the potential cost may be offered as a discount to a potentially interested customer"; and (2) where "if a given customer is particularly valued (e.g. according to past ordering history, appealing demographic profile, etc.), delivering the package [...] to the given customer as a promotional gift may be used to build goodwill".

Firmitive and affirmative speculation

The forecasting and prediction models that Amazon and other businesses work through have recently been subject to critique. For example, in *Speculate This!* the anonymous collection of academics and activists called the Uncertain Commons describe the kind of business speculation patented by Amazon as "firmative speculation": "a firming [...] or solidifying of the possibilities of the future. It is a speculative mode that seeks to pin down, delimit, constrain, and enclose – to make things definitive, firm" (2013: 12). The manifesto is interested in how firmative speculation is a central orientation of contemporary capitalism, which "operates as if everything in the future were representable, knowable, and calculable in principle, as if the future could possibly escape valorisation through either thought or money" (2013: 10).

Mail art, futurity and empiricism   133

Amazon's speculative shipping can be understood as a technique of firmative speculation. It projects into the future – what might a customer not yet have purchased but potentially be interested in? – and brings that future potentiality into the present. As outlined above, if a product is speculatively shipped but then not ordered, the product may be delivered to a customer who has shown interest in it as "an inducement to convert the potential interest into an order". Or on other occasions, the un-ordered product "may be delivered to a potentially-interested customer as a gift" in order to "build goodwill". Understood in this way, Amazon "*produces* potentialities and then *exploits* and thus *forecloses* them" (Uncertain Commons, 2013: 27). The future is predicted and "engaged" in order to create potential that can then be utilised (Adkins, 2008: 194). The future is thus made firm.

In contrast to firmative speculation, the Uncertain Commons posit "affirmative speculation"; a mode of speculation concerned "to hold on to the spectrum of possibilities while remaining open to multiple futures whose context of actualisation can never be fully anticipated" (2013: 13). Affirmative speculation:

> functions and thrives by concerning itself with an uncertainty that must not be reduced to manageable certainties. By definition, affirmative speculation lives by thinking in the vicinity of the unthinkable (rather than by asserting that the unthinkable is in principle always thinkable, knowable, calculable, and so on).
>
> (2013: 72)

The Uncertain Commons are keen to stress that the manifesto is not only concerned with critiquing firmative speculation. Rather, the aim is to "unsettle familiar analytical habits [...] and instead attend to vernacular practices of speculation" (2013: 21). Affirmative speculation is not only developed as a theoretical device – as that which is in contrast to firmative speculation – but to attune to and be(come) alternative ways of living.

Speculative methods

The manifesto shares some similarities with speculative methods currently being developed across the social sciences. Discussing the development of speculative methods, Mike Michael (2012) draws attention to the tradition of the speculative in design. He explains that design is "routinely represented as oriented towards both objects and the future": design makes stuff that is intended to make the future better (2012: 171). Speculative design is less interested in the production of objects that accomplish a specific goal or achieve a specific purpose, and more in creating particular engagements with possible futures.

For example, Michael discusses how in interaction designers Anthony Dunne and Fiona Raby's 2009 exhibition in Dublin, titled "What if ...", the aim was to:

> probe our beliefs and values, challenge our assumptions and encourage us to imagine how what we call "reality" could be different. They help us see that the way things are now is just one possibility, and not necessarily the best one.
>
> (Dunne & Raby in Michael, 2012: 172)

134   *R. Coleman*

While Dunne and Raby's version of speculation may be understood as the probing and incitement of imagination, for Wilkie et al., the meaning of speculation is also drawn from the speculative philosophy of Whitehead and Whitehead inspired theorists. In the context of a broader project on how individuals and communities use, understand and manage energy, Wilkie et al. focused on exchanges on energy on Twitter. They created software research robots – or Twitter bots (automated software programmes that automatically follow accounts and/or respond to tweets) – which respond to tweets about energy in ways that disrupt "the normal flow of exchange" on Twitter (2014: 2). For example, one bot, @ErtBot, detects tweets about technological practices and replies to them framing the practice in terms of energy consumption, whether or not the initial tweet was concerned with energy.

In their project, Twitter is understood as a social space that might be performed in particular ways, and that might be performed differently: @ErtBot doesn't simply observe interactions on Twitter, but actively engages in them, making or performing Twitter in the process. This speculative design method therefore intervenes[4] in the social space of Twitter: the method, at least in part, makes the reality it studies. In such a project:

> methodology becomes less a case of answering a pre-known research question (why do people fail to engage energy-demand reduction) than a process of asking inventive, that is, more provocative questions where intervention stimulates latent social realities, and thus facilitates the emergence of different questions.
>
> (Wilkie et al., 2014: 4)

Putting to work the speculative design practice of bots as a research method therefore highlights both research and the social as processual; the social is not settled but is always in the process of being made or performed, and methodology is a means of posing rather than necessarily answering a question. As well as studying what is "already there", social research might also "stimulate [...] latent social realities". Indeed, Wilkie et al. explain that:

> Speculative methodology, of course, is not descriptive: it is performative. Its interventions are designed to "prompt" [...] emergent enactments that can problematize existing practices (in our case, the neat conceptualization of community and the practices of energy-demand reduction) and open up the prospective.
>
> (2014: 20, reference omitted)

As I have noted, there are distinctions between what speculation refers to for Wilkie et al. and Dunne and Raby. Nevertheless, in prompting and opening up the prospective, we might see the speculative methodology developed by Wilkie et al. in terms of Dunne and Raby's definition of speculative design; in drawing attention to energy and energy reduction, the bots "help us see that the way

Mail art, futurity and empiricism   135

things are now is just one possibility, and not necessarily the best one", and encourage a speculation on "how things could be".

Such an approach clearly resonates with the understanding of empiricism that I introduced above; speculative methodologies are involved in finding the conditions under which creativity and novelty might emerge. However, as Wilkie et al. go on to caution, "there is no guarantee that speculative interventions and devices will 'affirm the possible'. [...] There is, therefore, no guarantee that speculative devices and their provocations will work – experiments can and do fail" (2014: 20–21). In the next section I return to the experimental character of speculative methods. And I will come back to two other points that Wilkie et al's speculative methods highlight: one, the significance of *exchange*, and, two, the engagement of the prospective, or what might also be called *the future*.

Reflections on a visual sociology project

Both the Uncertain Commons' manifesto and the speculative methods developed by Wilkie et al. are concerned with not only understanding the world, but also intervening in it. Furthermore, they both take up the proposition of performative methodologies, where, as Law and Urry argue, methods are involved in enacting – and thus intervening in – social worlds. From the perspective of speculative methods then, in taking an interest in the method and system of speculative shipping patented by Amazon, the point is not only to understand Amazon's plans but to engage them, to intervene in them.[5] This point matters insofar as social scientific research might want to be involved in dislodging a capitalist project of instrumentalising and firming the future, and instead try to open up the prospective. To develop a project drawing together these themes, my question was therefore: how might I develop speculative methods to explore speculative shipping? Or, put another way, if the speculative shipping patented by Amazon is a form of firmative speculation, closing down reality by producing potentiality to exploit and foreclose it, how might I develop affirmative speculative methods to explore and intervene in the practice of speculative shipping?

To address these questions, I returned to Amazon's plans to deliver a speculatively shipped but un-ordered product to a potentially interested customer as a gift.[6] This cost-effective solution from Amazon was interesting to me for a number of reasons, including because it is framed as a means of building "goodwill", enabling Amazon to further foster their relationships with "particularly valuable" customers (and presumably gain more data and knowledge on them). It also interested me because it seemed to tap into the affective experience of receiving goods in the post – an experience that many journalists and marketing experts picked up on when reporting the speculative shipping patent. For example, Parveen Kopalle (2014), a professor of marketing writing in *Forbes* magazine, described Amazon as "widely popular" in part because it is:

> the purveyor of the three-Ds of consumer psychology: delight, discounts and deals. Anticipatory shipping adds to these. Think of the feelings you get

136   R. Coleman

when you see that an Amazon package has arrived at your door – it's delightful and exciting, even though you know what it is. I bet those feelings amplify when you don't know what's in the box. [...] We like getting things in the mail, even if we didn't ask for them.[7]

While Amazon's speculative shipping operates via prediction, a gift might be sent when their forecasting model has failed: the product hasn't been ordered, despite being speculatively shipped. However, through this failing, the feelings of delight and excitement that a customer might experience when a product they have ordered arrives might be amplified, because they don't know what's in the package.

My question about how I might develop speculative methods to explore speculative shipping therefore became more focused around how sending "gifts" in the post might be a means of exploring speculative shipping. Might sending gifts in the post be a means of creating a mode of exchange not based on firmative speculation? Would an "affirmative" mode of exchange be capable of engaging an uncertain future and creating a reality different to Amazon's, so that the potentiality of the future is engaged rather than made firm? Working with the constraints of my project (which is unfunded and does not possess the technical or financial infrastructure of an organisation like Amazon), I needed to further hone this question by settling on a relatively inexpensive and accessible way of sending gifts in the post. Mail art, a movement whereby artists send each other art in the post, seemed a good starting point.

Mail art – or post art, postal art and correspondence art – is a varied practice, and includes relatively simple doodles or sketches, collaged postcards, decorated or stamped envelopes, and more collaborative work where there may be many recipients of one piece of art. One of its main features is that it involves an exchange of art through the post, and the formation of a network of communication and exchange (see Bleus, 1995). Mail art is commonly seen to have been established by US based artist Ray Johnson in the 1950s (Gangadharan, 2009). Johnson began mailing pieces of his art to fellow artist friends and acquaintances and an international network became what Johnson called the New York Correspondance *[sic]* School. This network was largely private, although exhibitions in the early 1970s did publicise some of the art produced. Also in the 1970s, mail art was used to circulate alternative ideas in countries where state censorship was dominant (Petasz, 1995). Mail art has remained popular since then, and contemporary communication technologies such as the internet are exploring the boundaries of the practice.

Although Johnson is seen as initiating mail art, its roots are also in avant-garde or alternative art practices, including Fluxus, an international network which from the 1960s mixed different methods and media (often taken from popular or 'low' culture), developing an aesthetics challenging the increasing commercialisation of art and culture (Friedman, 1995). Fluxus was influential in the early days of mail art (Friedman, 1995), and the contestation of commercialism remains central to mail art. Indeed, mail artist Clive Phillpot (1995) argues that:

Mail art, futurity and empiricism 137

When one receives mail art from Ray Johnson, one is receiving a gift of art. An ongoing practice based on gifts, or gift exchange, is rather extraordinary in developed countries in the late twentieth century. The current convention that the value of art depends upon public exposure and a price tag is dented by this practice.

(1995: 26)

I noted the connections between mail art as a mode of exchange based on gift-giving and a challenge to growing commercialism, and speculative shipping as a system that might result in the sending of gifts. Furthermore, I noted the ways in which mail art might be put to work as a speculative method; a performative intervention in a sociality that might "problematise existing practices and open up the prospective" (Wilkie et al., 2014: 20). In this case, the existing practice that might be problematised is the firming of the potentiality of the future through forms of probabilistic business speculation, and the prospective might be the opening up of a non-commercial mode of exchange, and a different relation to potentiality. Sending "art" in the post as "gifts" is a means of studying a social world in which gifts become commodified products intended to lock us into ongoing commercial relationships with particular brands – and it is a mode of studying this world by intervening in or unsettling it. Put another way, speculative methods are a means of exploring speculative shipping through making stuff and prompting particular engagements with potential futures.

To examine these ideas through intervening in the social world, I designed a postcard, or rather two postcards joined together along a perforated line. I decorated one postcard in the rough and ready style of much mail art. Picking up on the theme of gifts and speculative business, I decorated the postcards with parcels and bows from materials bought from and delivered by Amazon (Figure 9.1). This postcard included the recipient's name and address on one side, and instructions on what to do with the other postcard on the back. These instructions also included brief project information, and a link to a webpage with further details (Figure 9.2).[8] One side of the other postcard had my name and work address on it, and was stamped for return. The other side was left blank for recipients to write on or decorate, saying something about what they imagined their future to be (Figure 9.3). Recipients were invited to tear along the perforated line, keeping the postcard I had decorated as a gift and posting the second postcard back to me.

The aim of the postcards was to facilitate a mode of exchange outside of commercial interests. Amazon's gifts are carefully targeted, and involve the collection of data on customers that is then used to calculate further opportunities to induce purchases. In contrast, this project utilised a more haphazard process of selecting potential receivers of gifts than Amazon's, in part to unsettle how "value" is attributed to particular customers. I researched the most popular surnames in the UK, and then searched the online British Telecom Phone Book for people with these names living within the postcodes surrounding Goldsmiths. I was hoping that by sending the postcards to residents who lived near

138 R. Coleman

Figure 9.1 Selected postcards: front.

Goldsmiths, some kind of relationship with the project might be established. I sent a postcard to one recipient with a surname beginning with each letter of the alphabet.

In keeping with what are described as the ethical and democratic principles of mail art – where, for example, calls for exhibitions of mail art are made public, all work submitted is shown, and the making and exchange of art was designed (at least initially) to take place outside of the art market (see Friedman, 1995) – I promised each resident who returned their postcard to me a booklet including all of the returned postcards, and to let them know about any further use of the postcards in academic publications or public exhibitions. In keeping with sociological ethical guidelines (IVSA, 2009), I also guaranteed their anonymity.

From the 26 postcards I sent out, one was returned to me. This postcard was blank – the recipient had not written or drawn anything about their future. Remembering Wilkie et al's caution that there is "no guarantee that speculative

Mail art, futurity and empiricism 139

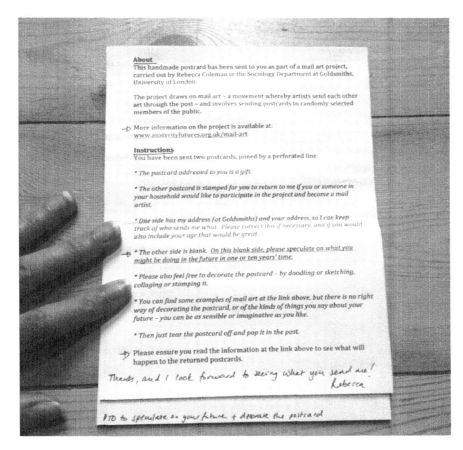

Figure 9.2 Postcard: instructions.

methods and their provocations will work – experiments can and do fail", I want to acknowledge this project as in some ways a failure.

One reason for this failure might be that in selecting recipients from an online phone book, I narrowed down recipients too far: anyone ex-directory or who only has a mobile phone was excluded. Another might be that I was misguided in selecting postcodes around Goldsmiths; residents in these areas may have no relation, or even a hostile relation, to the institution. A further constraint of the project might be that the design of the postcard was unappealing; I am not an artist or designer.[9] Rather than prompting an engagement with the possible, the postcards might have been indecipherable, or uninteresting.

I do not want to downplay these reasons. But it is also worth asking questions of the failure to encourage unsuspecting recipients to return the postcard in light of the description of Amazon's speculative shipping as provoking feelings of delight and excitement:

Figure 9.3 Postcard: back.

- Might a handmade postcard not be recognised/recognisable as a gift? Perhaps especially when it is associated with a sociological research project and/or an educational institution?
- Might receiving unexpected packages in the post be unwelcome or create feelings of ambivalence rather than delight and excitement?
- Might positive feelings only be produced when the package is from someone known? Or, indeed, might speculative business have become so successful and pervasive that positive feelings might only be produced when the package (or gift) is from a brand?
- Might the postcard have elicited positive feelings, but not have the capacity to convert these feelings into the action of sending the postcard back to me?

I am clearly not able to fully answer these questions. But posing them does help me to think about what the failure of the project might make apparent about speculative shipping and speculative methods.

Mail art, futurity and empiricism 141

For example, sending recipients unexpected "gifts" in the post was a means to put into practice the method through which both Amazon's speculative shipping and mail art function. This iteration of the project focused on the development of a speculative methodology capable of putting into play an alternative mode of exchange that might – or indeed might not – be taken up. In response to the questions raised above, what the failure of the project illuminates is the difficulty of establishing a mode of exchange, through the postal system, with unknown people. While this may be a mundane point to make, it enables a further series of questions to be posed regarding the technologies via which items are sent and received, how the post might now be a system that is routinely solicited by junk mail, how research, artistic and commercial relationships might be forged and maintained, and positive feelings elicited. Posing these further questions, then, recalls one of Wilkie et al.'s formulations of speculative methods as a process of asking questions, which in themselves "facilitates the emergence of different questions" (2012: 4). It is also consistent with speculative thought itself, which in its orientation to "novel situations" (Savransky, this volume) and the uncertainty of the future, is necessarily open-ended, unsettled, changing.

Coda

In designing, doing and reflecting on this project, what I have tried to do is pose, rather than necessarily answer, questions. These questions concern "the common byways" along which speculative design and sociology travel, and how "the engagements between these [can] be rendered open, multiple, uncertain, playful" (Michael, 2012: 177). In this project, I have tried to extend the "common byways" from speculative design and sociology to the Uncertain Commons manifesto and Amazon's patent for speculative shipping, examining through practice how speculative methods may – still – be a means of exploring speculative shipping.

At this point, though, a further question is raised: Why might social researchers want to do this? To begin to address this question, it is helpful to return to the notions of the empirical and empiricism that I introduced above. One response is that methods need to be open, multiple, uncertain, and also affective or playful, because of the nature of the social world itself. As I noted in the introduction, this is a world that is changing; in Lisa Adkins and Celia Lury's (2009: 18) terms, "a newly co-ordinated reality, one that is open, processual, non-linear and constantly on the move". Speculative shipping is part of such a reality, in that it is a practice that is open-ended, process-based and "on the move". In order to grasp and account for this "newly co-ordinated reality", methods themselves need to be re-co-ordinated. In particular I have taken up and attempted to (re) create the affective feelings of delight and excitement that Amazon's patent has been described in terms of, and to re-adjust – or lure – these feelings away from a firmative speculation and towards an affirmative one. These attempts failed, and instead a broader register of feelings may be identified.

142 *R. Coleman*

To (attempt to) be affirmative, then, does not necessarily collapse openness, multiplicity, uncertainty and playfulness into positivity, just as to (attempt to) be speculative is not necessarily to be affirmative. However, in developing speculative methods to explore speculative shipping, what this project has also been interested in is what Law and Urry propose in their (re)formulation of the empirical. Methods help to bring realities into being, even if such realities cannot be reduced to that which the method provokes, or do not proceed in the ways that they are imagined or designed to. Amazon's patent seeks to bring the world into being in a particular way: through firmative speculation. Law and Urry note that "it is much easier to produce some realities than others" (395–396). Amazon's reality might therefore be one that is pretty easy to make. The system via which particular goods can be shipped in advance of orders to particular geographical areas is based on the collection of data on and predictions about customers (actual and envisioned), is highly probabilistic, and is achieved through various sociotechnical arrangements (computer and algorithmic systems, various modes of transportation, affective relationships between Amazon and real or potential customers, for example). It is intended to keep the transition from the present to the future smooth and certain.

However, drawing on Donna Haraway's work, Law and Urry go on to ask, "Is it possible to imagine social science method as a *system of interference* [...] for working towards and making particular forms of the social real while eroding others?" (397). Such a question has animated my project. How might (affirmative) speculative methods be a system of interference, working towards making a social based on modes of exchange that are not about exploiting and foreclosing potentiality, but rather opening it up? How might mail art be a part of such a project, encouraging speculation on "how things could be"? In these ways, the project has also engaged with the empirical in a third sense, in terms of how Deleuze and Parnet lay out their understanding of empiricism as finding the conditions through which novelty and creativity emerge. In experimenting with mail art as a speculative method, the project has attempted to "vectoris[e] a transition" into a future that is uncertain rather than known, and to see potentiality not as that which can necessarily be converted into financial value, but as that which might lead to "novel situations". The project discussed here, then, explores and poses questions about the creative capacity of methods to interfere with worlds organised around firmative speculation, by opening up (to) potentiality, and by seeing the future as that which is decidedly unsettled.

Notes

1 I call this a visual sociology project because it seeks to develop the methodological shifts, outlined below, via arts-based methodologies. While these shifts may not be specific to *visual* sociology, they are one key way in which they have been taken up; see for example, the MA in Visual Sociology, Goldsmiths.
2 All references to the patent are from Spiegel, Mackenna, Lakshman, and Nordstrom (2013). Thanks to Anja Kanngieser for alerting me to this patent.

Mail art, futurity and empiricism 143

3 I do not have space here to consider the different logics of anticipation and speculation, but worth noting is that anticipation is sometimes argued to be a mode where the future is, or should be, a time separate to the present; (see Adkins 2011), and/or that closes down the possibilities of the future (see Adams, Murphy, & Clarke, 2009). Although Amazon describe the patent in terms of "anticipatory shipping" in its title, "anticipatory" appears infrequently in the patent itself (five times compared to 152 times for terms pertaining to speculative shipping).

4 I use "intervene" to suggest a method that understands itself as (re)making reality, rather than neutrally observing it. Another term might be "interference" (see Law & Urry, below).

5 Thanks to Michael Guggenheim for making this point sharper and pointing me in the direction of mail art.

6 I am not able to address the large anthropological literature on gift-exchange, but it is worth noting that much of this remarks on how the giving of gifts creates certain obligations, which intertwine people, objects and organisations into particular social relations (Mauss, 1950), and that increasingly commodities are invested with the qualities of gifts, through advertising (Carrier, 1990) – and in the case of Amazon, branding and speculative shipping.

7 See Deville (2015) on debt collection for occasions where receiving things in the post might elicit negative feelings.

8 See: www.austerityfutures.org.uk/mail-art/

9 A point that has been remarked upon when presenting the project to some arts and design audiences. The diametrically opposed point has also been raised when presenting in more sociological contexts; what is sociological about this project? Although I do not have space to address these points here, it is worth noting that the interdisciplinarity of speculative methods may raise concerns about the boundaries of disciplines and what are appropriate disciplinary practices and forms of expertise.

References

Adams, V., Murphy, M., & Clarke, A. E. (2009). Anticipation: Technoscience, life, affect, temporality. *Subjectivity*, *28*(1): 246–265.

Adkins, L. (2008). From retroactivation to futurity: The end of the sexual contract? *Nordic Journal of Feminist and Gender Research*, *16*(3): 182–201.

Adkins, L. (2011). Practice as demoralization: Bourdieu and economic crisis. In S. Susen, & B. S Turner (Eds), *The legacy of Pierre Bourdieu: Critical essays* (pp. 347–365). London: Anthem Press.

Adkins, L., & Lury, C. (2009). What is the empirical? *European Journal of Social Theory*, *12*(1): 5–20.

Bleus, G. (1995). Communication: 44 Statements. In C. Welch (Ed.), *Eternal network: A mail art anthology* (pp. 85–87). Calgary: University of Calgary Press.

Carrier, J. (1990). Gifts in a world of commodities: The ideology of the perfect gift in American society. *Social Analysis*, *29*, 19–37.

Coleman, R. (2008). A method of intuition: Becoming, relationality, ethics, *History of the Human Sciences*, *21*(4), 104–123.

Coleman, R, & Ringrose, J. (Eds). 2013. *Deleuze and research methodologies*, Edinburgh: Edinburgh University Press.

Deleuze, G. (2001). Immanence: A life. In *Pure immanence: Essays on a life* (pp. 25–33). (A. Boyman, Trans.). New York, NY: Zone.

Deleuze, G., & Parnet, C. (2002). *Dialogues II.* (H. Tomlinson, & B. Habberjam, Trans.). London: Continuum.

144 *R. Coleman*

Deville, J. (2015). *Lived economies of default: Consumer credit, debt collection and the capture of affect.* London; New York, NY: Routledge.

Friedman, K. (1995). The early days of mail art. In C. Welch (Ed.), *Eternal network: A mail art anthology* (pp. 3–16). Calgary: University of Calgary Press.

Gangadharan, S. P. (2009). Mail art: Networking without technology. *New Media and Society, 11*(1–2), 279–298.

International Visual Sociology Association. (2009). IVSA Code of Research Ethics and Guidelines: http://visualsociology.org/about/ethics-and-guidelines.html, last accessed 16 February 2015.

Kopalle, P. (2014). Why Amazon's anticipatory shipping is pure genius. *Forbes*, 28 January 2014: www.forbes.com/sites/onmarketing/2014/01/28/why-amazons-anticipatory-shipping-is-pure-genius/, last accessed 16 February 2015.

Law, J., & Urry, J. (2004). Enacting the social. *Economy and Society*, 33(3): 390–410.

Lury, C., & Wakeford, N. (Eds). (2012). *Inventive methods: The happening of the social.* London; New York, NY: Routledge.

Mauss, M. (2002[1950]). *The gift: The form and reason for exchange in archaic societies.* London; New York, NY: Routledge.

Michael, M. (2012). De-signing the object of sociology: Toward an "idiotic" methodology. *The Sociological Review, 60*(S1), 166–183.

Michael, M. (2016). Notes toward a speculative methodology of everyday life. *Qualitative Research*, online first, 21 January 2016, 1–15.

Petasz, P. (1995). Mailed art in Poland. In C. Welch (Ed.), *Eternal network: A mail art anthology* (pp. 89–93). Calgary: University of Calgary Press.

Phillpot, C. (1995). The mailed art of Ray Johnson. In In C. Welch (Ed.), *Eternal network: A mail art anthology* (pp. 25–32). Calgary: University of Calgary Press.

Spiegel, J., Mackenna, M., Lakshman, G., & Nordstrom, P. (2013). Method and system for anticipatory package shipping, United States Patent, 24 December 2013: http://patft.uspto.gov/netacgi/nph-Parser?Sect1=PTO1&Sect2=HITOFF&d=PALL&p=1&u=/netahtml/PTO/srchnum.htm&r=1&f=G&l=50&s1=8615473.PN.&OS=PN/8615473&RS=PN/8615473, last accessed 16 February 2015.

Uncertain Commons (2013) *Speculate this!* Durham and London: Duke University Press.

Wilkie, A. Michael, M., & Plummer-Fernandez, M. (2014). Speculative method and Twitter: Bots, energy and three conceptual characters. *The Sociological Review*, online first, 14 August 2014, 1–23.

10 Creating idiotic speculators

Disaster cosmopolitics in the sandbox

Michael Guggenheim, Bernd Kräftner and Judith Kröll

1 From speculation as thinking to creating speculative situations

How can we create speculators and make the world speculate? Posing this question moves speculation away from the assumptions that speculation is the province of philosophers and is merely a mode of thinking. Producing speculations is also a mode of doing and making. Objects take part in the constitution of the world. By focusing on the role of objects, speculative design has focused on the complex role precisely designed objects can play to complicate the world (Wilkie, Michael, & Plummer-Fernandez, 2015). But both philosophy and speculative design share the idea that speculation remains with the expert.

In this chapter, we would like to show that such a reduction of speculation to expert practice reduces speculation to an epistemic practice, rather than a situated and material practice. To allow anyone to speculate, we thus suggest to create a device that triggers a speculative practice that brings into existence immediate actions of anyone, expert or non-expert, and granting those actions, to paraphrase Whitehead (Whitehead, 1978: 351), "unfading importance" without any limitations. Such a device would produce a speculative coherence, that allows "to escape the norms to which experiences, isolated by the logical, moral, empiricist, religious, and other stakes that privilege them, are subject" (Stengers, 2011, 239).

Such a device we contend, is first and foremost a device of rupture and follows recent shifts in social sciences from describing the world as stable and ordered to one that focuses on ruptures (Callon, 1998: 252). Such a device conceives of speculative design as the participatory art of staging and as a matter of distributing roles. A design that aims at "imbuing political voices with the feeling that (...) the political arena is peopled with shadows of that which does not have a political voice, cannot have or does not want to have one" (Stengers, 2005: 996).

The initial inventor of speculative methodologies and practice of disruption, although rarely acknowledged in the literature on speculation, was probably Harold Garfinkel with his breaching experiments (Garfinkel, 1967). For example, he would ask his students to return home to their parents and pretend not to

146 *M. Guggenheim* et al.

know them. The confused parents would then try to repair the situation by first being puzzled, then asking what is wrong and stop acting silly etc. Garfinkel's methods are radical for two reasons: first he shifts the territory of social science from observation to intervention. Rather than looking at orderly social reality, he disturbs it, to observe the consequences of his intervention. In short, he creates the very phenomena he is interested in. But, second, he does not avoid situations, which he cannot control and which, differently from similar social–psychological experiments (see Lezaun, Muniesa, & Vikkelsø, 2013), unleash the creativity of the actors involved. What emerges from his experiments are new social forms, or, speculative practices.

For, speculation is precisely what emerges from confusion and rupture. This is why Isabelle Stengers borrows from Deleuze and Guattari the figure of the idiot (Stengers, 2005). Their idiot, Stengers maintains, "is the one who always slows the others down, who resists the consensual way in which the situation is presented and in which emergencies mobilize thought or action" (Stengers, 2005: 994). Or as Deleuze and Guattari themselves put it, "the idiot wants the lost, the incomprehensible, and the absurd to be restored to him" (Deleuze & Guattari, 1994: 63).

Halewood (in this volume: 53) worries that speculation can be problematic, when it "offers anyone the chance to think whatever they want" or what he terms "imagination". But this is an anti-sociological view, which ignores the problem of the cultural situatedness of thinking. On the contrary, we suggest that it is very difficult to imagine alternatives and to restore the absurd. Deleuze and Guattari do not tell us how to become an idiot. The idiot remains a celebration of a figure, in the same way as other figures, such as Simmel's stranger, are celebrated in social science. But how do we become such figures?

The main problem here is to not commit the intellectualist fallacy that becoming an idiot is a matter of thinking. Rather we suggest that to become an idiot, it is far easier to create devices and situations that help people to become idiots.

To understand this point, let us turn to the financial speculator for a moment. Rather than slowing things down, he is a figure obsessed with speedy actions of buying and selling. But how is it possible that people without special training become financial speculators and buy and sell stocks? This does not happen by reading financial literature or philosophy. A person becomes a speculator through the mediation of a technical infrastructure that allows her to speculate. In the case of speculation, this infrastructure consists of standardized financial data and computer terminals that allow for fast buying and selling of stocks (Stäheli, 2013). The figure of the speculator is not just a self-description, it is not so much a cognitive process, but it emerges from the speculative infrastructure.

Similarly, to create idiotic speculators, we suggest the building of speculative machines that encourage idiotic speculation. Such machines, designed properly, are like a computer terminal for financial speculators, but for idiotic speculators. It is a mediator for the precise nature of what a particular kind of speculation should entail. The problem with financial speculation is not that the computer terminal lures unsuspecting people into risky behaviour. The problem is that it

Disaster cosmopolitics in the sandbox 147

reduces the world to a selection of buy and sell, which is a rather impoverished form of making sense of the world. To undertake cosmopolitical speculation, to engage in idiotic thoughts about the future of us, our planet, civilization, Gaia and ecology we need a far more refined machine that can mediate the world in all its complexity. We need to create a machine, which is "potentially capable of allowing us to creatively resist the mere extension of the present into a likely future", as Savransky puts it (in this volume: 25). We need to create a machine that can engage with what Halewood (in this volume) calls "situated speculation". It is a form of speculation, which is both situative and risky. It creates new worlds, it is "performative" (Wilkie et al., 2015), which in turn creates constraints on what can happen and which encourages us to take risks to engage with these constraints. In the remainder of this chapter, we report on an attempt to build such a machine and on some results derived from its operation.

2 The sandbox

The machine we built emerged from a research project entitled, "In the Event of … Anticipatory and Participatory Forms of Emergency Provision."[1] The project aimed to create new disaster scenarios and new forms of emergency provisions. For our project we wanted to create a speculation device that would allow us, as a society, to open up the business of thinking about future disasters and to move it away from disaster experts. We needed to create a machine that would slow people down (to avoid creating the ever same stories of earthquakes and terror strikes), to think in unusual ways what, if anything, might endanger us?

After many trials, we ended up with a sandbox that is a rectangular wooden table with a surface of $c.$ 180 cm × 150 cm that provides enough space to allow for the creation of "worlds" where props can be comfortably arranged.

We structured the sandplay into three steps. First, we asked subjects to "create your world". They could create any world in which they live or which they can imagine, and it could include anything, from humans to animals and objects as well as non-tangible things such as emotions and concepts. The players had to represent each entity with a prop and explain and comment on it.

Second, we asked subjects to imagine something that could unhinge their world. We pointed out that this could be any kind of event that turns this world upside down, in which nothing is as it was before. We asked them to randomly select two cards with I-Ching terms written on them and let these terms inspire (in the sense of Garfinkel's breaching) their disaster. Again we asked them to represent the unhinging event by adding and (re-) moving already placed props.

For the third step, we asked the subjects to come up with an emergency provision that, if it were available before the world was unhinged, would have changed the course of events in a positive way. We recorded 93 speculations in three different locations.[2]

What are the signs of successful speculation? How can we describe speculation? The literature on speculation so far has been very good in discussing what speculative methods are (Parisi, 2012) and what proper speculation could be (see

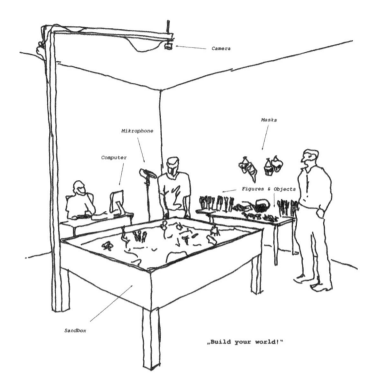

Figure 10.1 The sandbox.

the contributions of Halewood, Savransky, Thomas and Bell in this volume). But it has been almost silent about how speculation *works*. With our sandbox, we do not only produce speculation, but we can make its processes visible and create a catalogue of speculative practices.

3 Turning people into speculators: how to begin

Starting to speculate is easy, and it is easy because our speculator makes people speculate quickly, without too much ado:

PLAYER: But how can I build a world when I do not know the script?
G. (A TEAM MEMBER): You could orient yourself on your own world or just have a look at the props and get inspired by them.
PLAYER: Hm. One world. Only one world?
G.: You can also create several.
PLAYER: Difficult, difficult. These are all animals.
G.: Do the animals remind you of someone?
PLAYER: Yes, Yes. (pause) Hmhmhm (humming)

Disaster cosmopolitics in the sandbox 149

Figure 10.2 A start.

PLAYER: This is a German Shepherd with a black face. Number 92 is a jumping dolphin. (Note: each figure has a number, and players are asked to tell the number for recording purposes.) A monkey. Tortoise. Let's go on, doodel-doodeldoo (singing).

It all starts with a confusion about the task at hand: the player stumbles about what appears to be an insurmountable task, namely to build a whole world without using a script. But she then quickly moves from pondering the problem and questioning us to a speculatory groove in which she hums, collects props, ignoring us altogether. What is striking in this instance is how quickly the conversion from questioning the setup to free-flowing play happens. By contrast, let us turn to a second example:

PLAYER: Ready
M. (A TEAM MEMBER): Lets go, start (*c.*10 seconds pause).
PLAYER: (Moves two figures into the sandbox) 88. 28.
G.: Can you give it a name or a description?
PLAYER: Ah, the third. So these are three … (…). Those are three colleagues, friends, who, uhm, regularly commute together for work. They work quite far away from where their partners, uhm, families live. So, uhm, this is the starting point. I am hesitating whether to put them in the workplace, but it could be nice if we could have the home separated. Is this OK from your point of view?

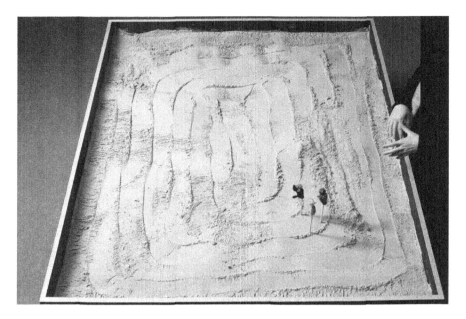

Figure 10.3 Another start.

In this example, there is no hesitation. Her first step, after declaring herself "ready", is to move two figures into the sandbox, announcing the numbers. This is followed by the declaration: "this is the starting point", both an assertion that her previous move feels right, but at the same time an indication that she did not think ahead and does not know what is going to happen next. There is no indication here of the complexity of the world she is going to build or any kind of story that is going to unfold. This openness about the scope of the world is further elaborated in the next step, when she puts her doubts to us about whether "home" should be separated from "workplace". Contrary to the first, this speculation started without any hesitation, but, once a first step is made, the constraints of speculation become apparent to the player and hesitation sets in. Once a player gets started, how does speculation take place?

4 A catalogue of speculative techniques

Of dices and dikes: the on-going production of risks and constraints

Once speculation has begun, its most central feature is its openness and continual risk taking. Speculation by definition is not about telling a story with a predefined narrative arc. The players themselves develop the play *while playing*. Each step is risky, as it establishes a new and unknown situation, while at the same time it constrains what can happen next. This cannot only be observed as a

Disaster cosmopolitics in the sandbox 151

constituent part of the game, but it is a feature that is very often reflexively accounted for during play. Consider for example the following sequence:

PLAYER: Somewhere there must be an origin. I don't know where this leads. This is first of all a meandering dike. It still has to develop.

The player starts by making an observation about her world, "there must be an origin", as if this were a fundamental feature of this world. This origin is a dike, built with sand. But the dike, already while digging it into the sand is not just an assertion but also a constraint: "It still has to develop."

The openness also highlights the problem that it is impossible for the players to develop a storyline merely by thinking without creating it with objects in the sandbox.

PLAYER: A dice is a good start. The throw and the chance (player throws a crystal ball into the sand). This opens up possibilities. It doesn't even result in an obvious situation, which is nice. (The player considers adding a ship and creating turbulences in the sand.) From my perspective, this would allow non-directedness, mobility, to leave a place, and the waves connect to the dice, chance, to drift but you also know you are quite safe on the ship.

In this second example, rather than simply declaring some step to be open-ended, a particular element is introduced to *add* an element of contingency to the scenario. For the player, the dice allows to "open up possibilities",

Figure 10.4 Origins.

Figure 10.5 Dice and ship.

circumventing the problem that any element constrains options. It is the ship, which comes to play the role of both adding an element of "non-directedness" but also the knowledge that he is not simply adrift, but also "quite safe".

Why did the pigs throw an object into the hole? Speculation as puzzle

While the openness of the story is a precondition of speculation, it also is a permanent puzzle for the players. With every move emerges a new situation. This new situation is *not* a result of some change within the game, such as in computer games. The sandbox does not change unless the player speculates. Each and every step of speculation is a cooperation between the player, the sandbox and the props, yet each and every step is a surprise, a puzzle and a trigger for new speculation. As such, the world contains the elements of the story, but it does not tell about its dynamics. It is like structuralism, except that "structure" here has potentially endless dimensions. It is a structure that emerges from the sand, and that dissolves in the sand again.

PLAYER: I would say, the world is now built. The pigs deliberate and aim to get to that hole, where they should throw something in. What is now missing is the story, the why and what they actually throw in there.

To build the world is a cumulative and additive practice in which the speculators usually pile up entities. The end of the first step usually comes slowly, when the players do not see the need to have even more props in the sand.

Disaster cosmopolitics in the sandbox 153

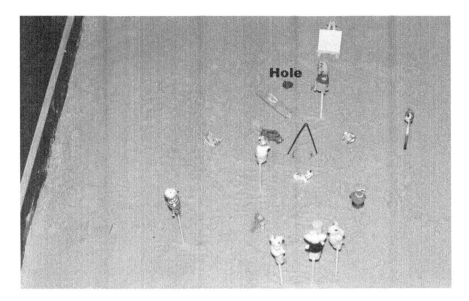

Figure 10.6 Pigs deliberate.

But the world then also moves from being static to being dynamic, from answering questions of "who?" and "what?" to "why?" to a story and interactions. This need for answers is imposed on the players by their worlds:

PLAYER: OK, now I need to bring the figures together to a good ending. That's not easy. The elephant as a wise animal is a means to propel the story.

For this player, the world itself demands a "bringing together". The building of a world was an exercise in atomism, in building a world without connections and thus without a story. To bring the figures "together" is a problem of interactions. As in the examples before, this question is answered by introducing a further element that provides the narrative.

The black penguin: how props acquire agency

Beside the processes of speculation, conceived as an interaction between the rules of the game, the sandbox and the players, it is important to understand in more detail the micro-techniques of speculation. At the heart of our speculator are the props. The starting point for speculation, the possibility to enact alternatives, is to have props to *acquire* qualities during play. Rather than *resembling* what they represent, they would have to acquire qualities that either come from the player, the plot or from within the props, rather than from any resemblance to the world outside.

Figure 10.7 A wise elephant.

Figure 10.8 Props.

Disaster cosmopolitics in the sandbox 155

The props should be able to represent whatever the speculation afforded and they should be able to adopt any capacity needed. Thus we had to find props that were radically different from entities outside the sandbox. We settled on two different kinds of props: knitted figures of animals and superheroes and abstract found objects. We can identify from our plays at least the following ways of acquiring meaning and capacities: naming, representing, identifying, mediation and blank.

A straightforward option, naming, is to take an object and give it a *name*. The propensities of the prop are simply named and not specified. We do not know at the moment of naming what the features of the shepherd are (see Figure 10.2). A slightly different version is to qualify the object, as in the case of the elephant (see Figure 10.7), where the figure of the elephant represents an elephant, but then the player attaches some qualities, such as in this case "wise".

Another option, which involves *representing*, is that some feature of a prop is taken to represent a capacity, such as in the example of the crystal ball (see Figure 10.5) that represents chance.

While these options all indicate how props mediate between the player, the sandbox and the story, we can also observe radical versions in which the objects are purely defined by the player, but not with respect to what is happening in the sandbox. We can call this also *identifying*.

PLAYER: By the way, I have my grave in Vienna with my name. Have you got a black animal? At the central cemetery my story ends, maybe. My favourite animals are part of my world. Have you got a Teddy bear? No.... This is another favourite animal of mine. A penguin.

She ends her story by talking about her grave. And at this point, talking about her pre-planned death, she invokes her "favourite animals". These do not represent some known feature of her world, but themselves.

The radical alternative to identification is what we could call *blank*, in which case a prop is used without giving it any kind of meaning or agency:

PLAYER: (selecting a metal cage) Can I open this? I don't know what this is going to be, this object. I will have to think about it.

The object is precisely selected for its capacity of being non-specific, and its quality to make the player think about it. Blank objects can be selected both, because as props they have aesthetic or haptic qualities to which the player gravitates, or because the player wants to fill certain positions in the story but doesn't know how.

Some props are also instrumental for world building. While all the props discussed so far have agency only within the sandbox, some props also *mediate* between the player and world. Props can be used as "shovels", "trains" or "bulldozers" for the player to move other props around and particularly to create structures in the sand. But props that are used to create structures in the sand

156 *M. Guggenheim et al.*

disappear from what they created. They are media in Fritz Heider's sense and resemble the modern tools of science in creating truth (Heider, 1926): once a new state of the world is created, these objects disappear and are unaccounted for in their help to create the world.

These various versions of agency show that the sandbox as speculator has no inbuilt theory about how props relate to the sandbox and players. Such a theory has neither been inbuilt by us, nor is it possible to deduce a general theory from what happened in the various speculations. Indeed, we built the sandbox to allow and even produce the widest possible range of relationships.

Two hectares for every average human: the sandbox as diagrammatic space

The props do not simply acquire agency from the relationship between themselves and the player. The world that the players build, the speculation itself, emerges from the interaction with a third element, namely, the sandbox. The sandbox, other than the props, cannot be selected. It is already there as the space in which the world will be built. The sandbox acts as a diagrammatic space in the sense that the sandbox endows meaning and agency to the entities within it through its form. Let us demonstrate this with one particularly complex example.

The player began building a world by explaining that the world is covered by two thirds with water and only one third by land. He thus wrote the number "⅓" to indicate that the whole sandbox would represent the liveable land. Next, he

Figure 10.9 Diagrammatic space.

Disaster cosmopolitics in the sandbox 157

added a knitted green pig, "a creature that reminds me of nothing", as the average person. If the world were divided evenly among humans, he had calculated that every person would get two hectares of land. He drew a square into the centre of the table to indicate these two hectares.

PLAYER: I have located the prototype in the centre. I am a hierarchist. I believe in order. So when I demarcated the centre, I probably feel inclined to define the margin, the periphery. There will be much more on the periphery than in the centre.

What we can observe here is that the sandbox assumes a very complex role: First, in its entirety it represents the world. Through writing a number it shrinks to land. Then, this land is divided, but indicated through a pars-pro-toto relationship, in which a "prototype" person stands for the average human being. By putting that prototype in the centre of the sandbox the player turned the sandbox into a force field, in which their distance from the centre-average would define positions of entities. Note that the centre here is not a centre of power, but a centre of the average or the normal, in which average is imagined as "order".

This basic force field of "normal", centre and periphery serves to position various figures. The positioning of the figures opens up another level, namely the positioning of figures vis-à-vis each other. After having positioned some figures, the player realizes that by being closely positioned to each other they are now "neighbours". This reminded him of "this funny line in a Nick Cave song: I look at my neighbour and my neighbour looks at me but my neighbour is my enemy."

Figure 10.10 Neighbours.

158   *M. Guggenheim* et al.

It prompted him to turn a figure away from facing its neighbour. The sandbox had shifted from a force field, which defines positions, into a space ruled by Goffmanian face-to-face interaction. In the next step he quoted a line by Robert Frost "good fences make for good neighbours" and thus added a further possibility, namely the option of separating entities by physical means, thereby negating both the force field of the centre and periphery and the logic of Goffmanian interaction through physical proximity.

The sandbox as a diagrammatic space opens up a multiplicity of possible relationships that can be enacted within it, precisely because it offers a physically stable space with no predefined internal form.

5 A catalogue of forms: of speculatory attractors

We focus here on one particular way to understand the scenarios, by looking at different attractors. By attractors we mean specific forces that influence how a scenario develops. These attractors also show that the speculator, as the assemblage of player-sandbox-sand-props, acts on different levels of medium specificity. The speculator can operate mainly as a machine to process the culture knowledge or background of the human player that operates it. But the speculator can also highlight other elements, such as the sandbox, the sand or various props. In short, the speculator can produce various scenarios in which either of these elements acts as an attractor or conduit, which channels all the other elements.

In the first type, the main attractor is the *player*, and not the sandbox. As attractor, the player can have several layers, from her biography, psychology or profession, to the actual situative context in which the play takes place. An example for a very biographic version can be seen in the case of the player with the black penguin mentioned above, who creates a world and a scenario largely defined by her life, and her anticipated death in Vienna.

The context, place and time where we installed our sandbox was one possible attractor for speculations. Thus a player who is an academic and works on forced migration and who is invited to speculate with our sandbox at the centre for interdisciplinary studies (ZiF) in Bielefeld played a scenario, which was heavily influenced by both of these circumstances. The sandbox, or the props, play very minor roles in shaping the scenario. They are completely transparent and only help to stage the respective play.

The second type is radically different. Here, the speculatory *apparatus* defines everything, and the background of the player very much disappears. The interplay of sandbox and props works as a decisive attractor in the speculation of the player. In one example, the player bypassed all the rules we set. She was not happy with the hierarchic positioning of the props on the device that displayed them. She decided that in her world, there should not be any inequality. She proceeded to move one prop after the other into the sandbox until the sandbox was filled with props and not a single prop remained outside the sandbox.

Within the sandbox, all figures were equal, and had no particular agency. In radically making the props the same, the player also managed to shed light on

Disaster cosmopolitics in the sandbox 159

Figure 10.11 Everything in the sandbox.

the differentialist ideas behind our setup and the role of the sandbox. The sandbox as attractor in this extreme case then not only defined the props; it even eradicated the agency of the props by making them alike and putting instead the sandbox as a main actor centre stage.

The third type is defined by the materiality of the sand as attractor. In one case, the player started by putting various props into the sand, but then became wary as to what these props should do in the world, and continued to bury them all in the sand. When the world was finally built, all objects were buried and the world looked like at the beginning: a plane of sand, or in her words: "a cosmic unitary mass".

The disaster then consisted in excavating all these objects, with the sand flowing "like a reverse deluge into one corner", leaving the stranded props "out of context". The difference between the world and the disaster did not imply a movement of the figures, but a movement of the sand, which altered the situation of the objects completely.

The fourth version is *attractive props*. In this case, it is individual entities that command the energy to drive a scenario forward. These entities work like heroes or protagonists in stories. The sandbox shrinks to serving as foil for what happens to the protagonist. But the protagonist is not an extension of the context of the play or the biography of the player, but rather has its very own capacities that interact in various ways with the world in the sandbox.

In this example the player first introduced apes in the world, immediately followed by a figure that represented Dominique Strauss Kahn (DSK) who quickly

Figure 10.12 A cosmic unitary mass.

Figure 10.13 Attractive props.

Disaster cosmopolitics in the sandbox 161

became the main actor, who languished in Rikers island prison, while some primatologists were fighting for human rights for apes and their release from the zoo. The disaster consisted of DSK jailbreaking and hiding in the jungle with the primates. The primatologist, who observed the apes, gets very irritated. Meanwhile the apes get arrested because they hid a jail breaker. The emergency provision in this case consisted in a massive Chinese wall that would have separated the apes from DSK and humanity in general. Here, everything revolves around DSK as main actor.

The world is not so much an assemblage of actants that have to be brought together through some kind of narration, but rather a main protagonist connects the various actors and brings meaning to the world. Moreover, differently from most other scenarios, the disaster is not a further actant, but the main protagonist himself.

Conclusion

We have discussed a number of techniques of how to make the world speculate and we have introduced you to some of the forms speculation with our sandbox can take. This is but one example for creating idiotic speculators. Behind our speculator stood a research project aimed at creating disaster and emergency provision scenarios. But it should have become clear that our speculator does not need to be confined to this theme. We can easily imagine that the sandbox could be used to speculate about environmental politics or recent issues in metaphysics. But we may also think about the limitations of this form of speculation and we may want to think about how to build speculators for other contexts. Among the limitations, we can easily see that this speculator, as assemblage of player, sandbox and props, is limited in its mediality. It is first and foremost a visual, haptic and narrative device. Thus, this sandbox is less well suited to create atmospheres, sounds, taste and smells. To achieve these, it needs to translate these things into props first. The sandbox allows primarily creating very nuanced and complex qualitative relationships. But it is limited in its possibilities to create complex relationships that are based on numbers. There are necessarily a limited number of props and these cannot really be used to create quantitative relationships, let alone produce calculations based on such relationships. The speculator cannot be used to test ideas, say about the relationship between population growth and pollution.

But we can also think about what we can learn from the sandbox to build other speculators. First – and herein lies probably its most unusual quality as a method in social science – it is extremely productive to combine a laboratory situation with open-ended qualitative research practices. The sandbox shows that for making the world speculate, it helps to create a heterogeneous context in which speculators are facing an assemblage of materials, ambivalent instructions and an unfamiliar setup, that all together allows creating unexpected solutions. But different from experiments in social psychology where a reductive approach aims at testing altering effects of one variable on another one, the focus of the

162 *M. Guggenheim* et al.

experiment here is not to narrow down the possible answers, but to produce an environment in which anything is possible. The sandbox is but one first option how to bring experiments back to a social science that is interested in social forms, materialities and meaning rather than replication. The sandbox also shows that to create the environment for speculation, players need to be stimulated by a speculatory apparatus that in itself has the power to capture the players and keep them speculating. To create more speculators implies to think more about how to engage people in speculatory practice, to remove them from their on-going concerns and set them to a path of speculation and to think about which devices can help us to achieve this.

Notes

1 The project was funded by an "art(s) and science(s)" grant by the Vienna Science and Technology Fund (WWTF) No.: SSH09–036.
2 At the Center for Interdisciplinary Research (ZiF) at the University of Bielefeld we played with an interdisciplinary group of disaster experts, composed of practitioners, engineers, anthropologists, sociologists and geographers. As guests of Akademie Schloss Solitude, Stuttgart, we played with artists, filmmakers, actors, composers and designers. Finally, at the Franz-von-Assisi church in Vienna, we played with visitors of the church.

References

Callon, M. (1998). An essay on framing and overflowing: economic externalities revisited by sociology. In M. Callon (Ed.), *The laws of the markets* (pp. 244–269). Oxford; Malden, MA: Blackwell Publishers/Sociological Review.
Deleuze, G., & Guattari, F. (1994). *What is philosophy?* New York: Columbia University Press.
Garfinkel, H. (1967). Studies of the routine grounds of everyday activities. In H. Garfinkel (Ed.). *Studies in ethnomethodology* (pp. 35–75). Englewood Cliffs, N.J: Prentice-Hall.
Heider, F. (1926). Ding und Medium. *Symposion. Philosophische Zeitschrift für Forschung und Aussprache, 1*(2), 109–157.
Lezaun, J., Muniesa F., & Vikkelsø, S. (2013). Provocative containment and the drift of social-scientific realism. *Journal of Cultural Economy, 6*(3), 278–293.
Parisi, L. (2012). Speculation: A method for the unattainable. *Inventive Methods: The Happening of the Social,* 232–243
Stäheli, U. (2013). *Spectacular speculation: thrills, the economy, and popular discourse.* Stanford, California: Stanford University Press.
Stengers, I. (2005). The cosmopolitical proposal. In B. Latour, & P. Weibel (Eds.), *Making things public-atmospheres of democracy* (pp. 994–1003). Cambridge, MA: MIT Press.
Stengers, I. (2011). *Thinking with Whitehead: A free and wild creation of concepts.* Cambridge, MA; London, England: Harvard University Press.
Whitehead, A. N. (1978) *Process & reality: An essay in cosmology.* New York: Free Press.
Wilkie, A., Michael, M., & Plummer-Fernandez, M. (2015). Speculative method and Twitter: Bots, energy and three conceptual characters. *The Sociological Review, 63*(1), 79–101.

11 2Sweet2Kill

Speculative research and contributory action

Michael Schillmeier and Yvonne Lee Schultz

Introduction – speculating with contrasts

The *general* question this chapter engages with is a well-known controversy in modern thought: The questionability of dualistic strategies of understanding existence along 'natural contrarities' (Tarde, 2000 [1899]: 44). Conceptually, 'opposition', as the French sociologist and philosopher Gabriel Tarde argues:

> is erroneously conceived (...) as the maximum degree of difference. In reality, it is a very special kind of repetition, namely, of two similar things that are mutually destructive by virtue of their very similarity. In other words, opposites or contraries always constitute a couple or duality, they are not opposed to each other as beings or groups of beings, for these are always dissimilar and, in some respect, sui generis; nor yet as states of a single being or of different beings, but rather as tendencies or forces.
>
> (Tarde, 2000 [1899]: 44)

Tarde identifies three major modes of oppositional human strife, which enact relations of differences and specific modes of solving them: war, competition and discussion. As Tarde stresses, all three forms of social strife are costly, exhaustive and offer more or less unstable – i.e. temporal – solutions to problems of difference. As Tarde says, 'if war and competition are discussions, one is a discussion in deeds of blood, the other a discussion in deeds of ruin' (Tarde, 2000 [1899]: 60). Thus, peace may be disrupted by war again, winners of competition may face new forms of competitive contest, discussions may produce a temporal settlement which may attract new forms of discussions, polemics etc.[1] Oppositional strive is primarily an 'auxiliary and intermediary' (ibid., 67) force in order to aim either at a settlement (politics), a gain (economics) and/or invention (science, law etc.). From within the logics of opposition, civilization may be understood as the process by which the killing fields of wars may translate into processes that effect fewer killings and atrocities and give way to ruthless competition that may be accompanied by regulated spaces of heated controversies and debates that frame verbal and written slugfest.

However, speculating with oppositions and their costly affairs is only one possibility of engaging differences. Following from this brief discussion of Tarde's

164   *M. Schillmeier and Y. L. Schultz*

understanding of oppositional strife it appears worthwhile to think about non-oppositional modes of strife, which are less violent, costly and self-exhausting. The question needs to be asked: What practices may be thought of which make a difference by multiplying and celebrating differences instead of counting on their mutual destruction? And indeed, it is precisely speculative research as understood by the authors of this chapter, which unfolds an ongoing and collective engagement in *estranging* the antagonistic carving of differences and its effects on world making. To do so we employ the idea of *contrasts*, which draws attention to differences without the need of engaging in oppositional strife.

* Employing contrasts, so our argument goes, is less violent, costly and damaging than the enactment of oppositions as set in place by the politics of war, the economies of competition and the logic of dispute. Like oppositions contrasts are not essences or substances, but tendencies and forces that relate and thus create differences by the way they relate. Unlike oppositions, though, contrasts care about the possibilities of relations of differences, which enable the process of differing (cf. Schillmeier, 2016).

Hence, with the idea of speculating with contrasts the realm of differences is no wasteland to be appropriated, occupied, invaded, colonized, utilized, sacrificed or victimized. Rather, speculating with contrasts unfolds and preserves differences. By doing so contrasts perpetuate as contrasts, they shine as such. Contrasts are *caressing differences* [*zärtliche Differenzen*] since they allow the co-habitation, the co-dwelling, co-existence and co-creation of differences. In the ways they relate they bring to the fore and keep the multiple ways they differ. Contrasts enact the sheer dis/closure of differing matters of concern. As contrasts, differences *enjoy* the neighbourhood of differences by engaging their similarity of *being different.*

The idea we propose is that the *work of art* offers a specific mode of existence/difference that evokes and preserves contrasts (cf. Schillmeier, 2016). Hence, we are concerned with the following questions: How can we insert a contrast so much so that it slows down the act of violence? How can we insert non-violent gestures that both trace and resist the violence of oppositional strife? How can we make violence at the same time absent and present such that we are able to betray the mutilating logics of oppositional strife? How can we reveal the marks, the faces, routines and practices of violence and divulge their hideous effects at the same time? How can we re-insert a form of hesitation that is not extrapolating the logics of war by other means as competition and polemics do? How can we make the out-dated 'man of war' and his/her weaponry become present in all their ambiguities? How can we 'shoot back' by bracketing and questioning the shooting? How can we create an affective contrast, i.e. affects and percepts of violence and war that alienate violence and war? How can we turn weaponry into a cause of thinking?

Following Isabelle Stengers' quest for a political ecology we will try to answer these questions by employing a contrast to 'politics "as usual"', which 'is besieged by dramatic "either ... or ... " alternatives that slice up our imaginations' (Stengers, 2005: 1002). To do so, we will advocate what can be called the *artificial staging* of a cosmopolitical scene that artfully stages the issue of war, weaponry and violence. In particular, we will draw on the work of co-author Yvonne Lee Schultz and her engagement with issues of violence in everyday life experience.[2] Her works Porcelain Pistol, Schokokids and 2Sweet2Kill (ibid.) re-assemble the famous Walther PPK pistol used by Mossad, loved by James Bond and an object of desire by many others.[3,4]

- Rather than being a wasteland for difference, the reality of contrasts as unfolded by the work of art offers a playground to bring to the fore the mediation of the rift between the affective, the sensuous, and the world of meaning and non/sense. For the work of art, the material and the immaterial require each other to become what they are, to gain from each other and to go *beyond* each other, i.e. to enable novel relations *without* being conquered or destroyed by the other (cf. Heidegger, 1971a). The material, as the 'non-quantifiable sensuous' (Mitchell, 2015: 8), is mediated by the work of art so much so that it offers a novel 'compound of percepts and affects' (Deleuze & Guattari, 1994: 164) which 'emerges into world' (Mitchell, 2010: 51). As long as the work of art lasts, it unfolds the possibility of opening novel spaces of concern, care, thought and practice.

As a compound of affects and percepts, the work of art becomes its own agentic existence through which the human is fully absent and entirely present at the same time. Created by men the work of art can stand on its own. It is the specificity of the work of art to preserve and to create. The work of art links the human and non-human by letting shine the multiplicity of non-human and human becomings. As Mitchell (ibid.) notes:

> To be open is not to be open at a point and closed off at another, it is to be open through and through, so much so that everything about oneself is destabilized, translated, emergent (...). Openness means existence in the midst of things.

Deleuze and Guattari have stressed: 'The artist is always adding new varieties to the world.' (Deleuze & Guattari, 1994: 175). Affects and percepts open spatial and temporal, material and immaterial interstices of 'creative fabulation' (Debaise, 2013; Deleuze & Guattari, 1994). The artist and his/her work invite us to dwell within these interstices of the open. It is precisely the 'beauty' of the work of art that suggests a novel cosmos by 'undoing the opposition of presence and absence' (Mitchell, 2010: 39; cf. Heidegger, 1971) as well as that between subject and object, perceiver and perceived, percept and perception (Deleuze & Guattari, 1994: 194). Thereby, the interstices of the work of art unfold hesitation and irritation. Generally speaking, the work of art politicizes the cosmos of the taken for-granted, the normal and normalized, the common and unquestioned.

Cosmopolitical collaborations – hesitation, questionability and the wellbeing of the social

Consequently, the work of art can be understood as a cosmopolitical 'composition' (ibid.: 196). By the composition of 'being[s] of sensation' (ibid.: 203) the work of art disrupts, questions and alters the taken for granted, the normal/ized or the common sense, rendered as the 'good sense' (Schillmeier, 2014). Deleuze & Guattari (1994: 196) put it like this: (Schillmeier, 2014). The composite sensation, made up of percepts and affects, deterritorializes the system of opinion that brought together dominant perceptions and affections within a natural, historical and social milieu.

The work of art and its contrasting engagement, then, appear to be excellent collaborators in speculative research, which is concerned and cares about *wellbeing of the social* in the ways it unfolds 'the belonging together of what differs, through a gathering way of the difference' (Heidegger, 1971b: 218). As the sociologist in this collaboration argues, the work of art materializes ' "counterpoints", which assemble processes of counter-effectuations, novel percepts and affects that create new worlds by betraying realities assumed as naturally given' (Schillmeier, 2016). Through the 'erection of monuments with its sensation' (Deleuze & Guattari, 1994: 199), the work of art unfolds a mode of existence that can be understood as a mode of caring about the social insofar as it: keeps the social active and contributes to the preservation of its wellbeing: It safeguards the social as an event that links the social with the nonsocial, the human and nonhuman beyond the ideologies of destruction and war, as well as it protects from the pitfalls and dangers of human exceptionalism. In collaboration with artists and their work of art a cosmopolitical perspective is enabled *to make* 'societal data' with the 'language of sensation' (Deleuze & Guattari, 1994: 176) and to make matters of concern public by composing *matters of sensations* that differ from classical means of political, economic and scientific engagement. Thus, cosmopolitical collaborations between social sciences and art contribute to an activist and speculative research agenda that engages in *differences in the making*.

Cosmopolitical research contributes to a 'radical empiricism' (James, 2003 [1912]) for which 'difference comes about by differing and that change comes about by changing' (Tarde, 2012: 37). To care about differences means to draw attention to the processes of differing and how it evokes issues that provoke hesitation and questionability. Following Tarde, a cosmopolitical research is adamant that 'difference as differing' cannot be understood in general terms, but requires close attention to the *situation* that unravels the 'fright' of hesitation and questionability.

To resist any form of violence that extinguishes the power of hesitation and questionability is the beginning of speculative thought the virtue of speculation, of caring and thus keeping active the *social possible*. Clearly, speculative thought accompanies the collaborators of this chapter in rather different ways. For the sociologist and empirical philosopher speculative thought embraces an ongoing investigation – in written and spoken words – into ways of understanding the social i.e. to investigate how differences come into being in the ways humans and nonhumans relate and how these relations can be analysed and conceptualized in a way that makes the world more diverse, more complicated, more interesting (Schillmeier, 2014, 2015). For the artist, speculative thought translates into the adventures of crafting materialities, objects and practices of all kinds that create novel percepts of how to think, imagine and intervene in world making (Dewey, 1980 [1934]). Clearly, then, the artistic work is a sociological feast for understanding as well as contributing to the *social multiple*. Moreover, the work of art not only offers novel ways of sociological intervention that go beyond the spoken and written word, but draws attention to social issues that challenge the sociologist's pre-understanding of it. The artist/sociologist collaboration can be understood as an adventurous experience of mediation, a 'conjunctive relation', as James (2003[1912]) would say, of folding and unfolding the empirical concreteness of social change and societal problems, the perceptual novelty of the work of art and the engagement with conceptual creation.

Tracing and resisting the violence of oppositional strife

In particular, we are interested in tracing as well as resisting violent engagements of dealing with the threat of differences through which the 'either-or' frames the

Figure 11.1 PP/S porcelain PPK, strewn flowers, tea cup and saucer.
Source: ©YLS Yvonne Lee Schultz.

Figure 11.2 PP/C-G golden chocolate gun.
Source: ©YLS Yvonne Lee Schultz.

problematic situation and its solutions. *Situations of war* are the most mutilating forms of oppositional strife. Situations of war unfold hideously violent and devastating expressions of living and dying in antagonistic strife. War suggests either *kill or be killed*. Shackled by the either/or of living in war enacts the ruthless power of an *in-sane (la bêtise)* option through which everyone is equally exposed to be/come victim or perpetrator (Weil, 1965). It names a traumatic experience of mobilizing adverse oppositions in which *everyone* may become a victim. Although one may argue that the wars are exceptional events and not everyday occasions, situations of war nevertheless *may* emerge every day. Or, as Deleuze and Guattari (1988: 445) put it: 'Undoubtedly, nothing is more outdated than the man of war (....) And yet men of war reappear, with many ambiguities.' As we have argued, the economies of competition and polemics (as e.g. in parliamentary debates) are costly engagements with differences as well, but less physically invasive since they do not have death as their object. Violence – be it physically or psychologically enacted and experienced – may also be more hidden and concealed in the course of our everyday life, in domestic affairs, in educational and institutional settings, legitimized and enforced by the law and so forth. History clearly shows that there seems to be no global remedy that protects or cures the potential of violent conflicts.

Western countries like the US are known for their notorious inner-societal problem of and controversies around gun violence where thousands of people are killed every year. Here, the techno-moral of weaponry plays an ambivalent role: Made for waging war they are also meant to contribute to peace and protect and deter from war. The gun violence debate in the US reflects this notoriously controversial issue. For many, guns are seen as a necessary means to keep violent acts under better control. For the gun lobby and its promoters, guns perform and symbolize the necessary power of protecting and safeguarding everyday life from violent eruptions that may lead to the emergence of conflicting interests and adverse behaviour in the first place. Carrying guns in everyday life became part of a 'war machine' culture and confirms the 'schizophrenic taste for the weapon' (Deleuze & Guattari, 1988: 444) that accompanies and affects the American way of 'life' (and death).[5]

Thus, weapons such as pistols or guns are not only designed for military use, but are profound, more or less mundane techno-moral objects of everyday conflict and destruction. The use of weaponry carries the violent dealing with differences, understood as oppositions, the enactment of the 'either-or' to its extremes. Whenever weapons are part of a conflict, the production of deadly victims is – willingly or not – part of the solution. In the moment you pull the trigger your aim is to enforce a fast ending to a situation of conflict. Weapons speed up oppositional strife-action. Once you pull the trigger, the split second unleashes the ruthlessness of violence overshadowing everything else, the past, present and future of the situation. In the moment of pulling the trigger, time is in rage, sheer force exercised, nothing but a regime of affective relations (Deleuze & Guattari,

Figure 11.3 Schoko kid M (from the series 2sweet2kill).
Source: ©YLS Yvonne Lee Schultz.

170   *M. Schillmeier and Y. L. Schultz*

1988: 441; Weil 1965).[6] There is no lived struggle. No time for hesitation. No time for choices. No time for communication. No time for thinking. No time for possible contrasts to the violent act. No time for lived dissent. No time for lived consent. No time for caring about differences. Full speed and standing-still go hand in hand. Clearly, the *victimology of weaponry* names a social disaster. In what follows, we will propose a possibility of how the techno-moral *victimology of weaponry* can be redesigned and become a playful and non-violent source of engaging with differences.

2Sweet2Kill

PPK

The PPK ('Polizeipistole Kriminal' or 'Polizeipistole kurz') is a classic actor within the weaponry of war. It was developed by the German weapon manufacturer Carl Walther primarily for the use in departments for criminal and customs investigation. The PPK was considered ideal as a concealed handgun. For its compact and handy design as well as its reliable technology the PPK became a widespread pistol before, during and after World War II. In the 1970s most of the German police forces stopped using the PKK since the calibre of the gun was considered too small. At the same time the PPK/S (S = Sport) model with a bigger calibre was designed especially for the US gun market. Even today, the PPK appears to be a classical weapon for gun lovers and gun enthusiasts. A random view in the World Wide Web (WWW) confirms that the PPK is praised as a 'timeless weapon', deemed to be 'very sexy' and a truly 'nice weapon'.[7] The PPK is 'a beauty of a pistol', 'enjoyable', 'awesome' and 'feels great to conceal' (ibid.). It is an '[e]xcellent carry weapon. Light, but with a nasty sting', '[n]ice fit and finish, safe, and reliable'. The PKK is 'man's best friend' (ibid.) and appears to be a great present for the man's wife as well (ibid.). For many Americans (and some others) the PPK assembles a most effective sports tool and weapon that confirms a rather strange taste for the ambiguous. The PPK resembles an object of desire, which is well designed and praised for its reliability. It is a great weapon to shoot with, which, due to its design, partially assembles the everyday man as the hidden 'policemen', protected by the law, for whom the PPK is always ready-to-hand to 'perform' its secret service. Everyday (working) men turn not only into good sportsmen with a stylish piece of sports equipment, but also into latent warriors for the 'good' – if needed. You never know, seems to be the message of the culture of wearing guns. So better wear a weapon and be prepared than being exposed unarmed to the risk of violence. With the PPK everyone – man or woman – may become James Bond, a potential hero well equipped to better protect and save the word from evil.

The PPK comes very close to the idea of enacting a perfectly ambiguous object. As a weapon of violence and war, it is meant to protect from war and conflict. It is praised for its safe usage; the PPK is a 'safe killer'. It is also seen as an object of desire as well as a piece of dangerous equipment to have fun

2Sweet2Kill   171

with. It fits so well in one's hand that it almost disappears as a weapon and becomes a mere tool, a Heideggerian 'Zeug' (Heidegger, 1996): 'ready-to-hand' and easy to conceal its presence. But clearly, as Heidegger notes, what is ready-to-hand is not merely the tool itself, but (one's) world which, in the case of carrying a weapon in everyday life, is a risky and latently violent one.

Re-composing the PPK

With this in mind, Lee Schultz's idea was to re-materialize the pistol and re-contextualize the PPK in a way that it keeps its ambiguous character, but, at the same time it becomes a novel 'percept', a work of art. As a work of art it is meant both to resemble the weapon/tool assemblage and its ambiguous worlds and to lose its technological mode of existence. As a result, the original PPK weapon was turned into a series of high quality and most beautiful porcelain and sweet chocolate pistols. The novel percepts are 1:1 replicas of the original PPK. It was done so accurately that even the weapon manufacturer Carl Walther licensed the replicas. In a second step the PPK porcelain pistols were restaged in situations and places in which weaponry doesn't seem to belong, e.g. at a well-set table setting for tea time, at a party dinner table and so forth.

The porcelain pistols were partly coloured and hand-daubed by Lee Schultz, perfected with the help of a master painter from a China world-renowned German manufacturer of china, KPM (Königliche Porzellan Manufaktur, Berlin). KPM also produced a small series of the luxurious porcelain pistols. Reflecting Lee Schultz's ideas the KPM catalogue says:

> Amidst the idyllic tableware the striking surprise: a fragile Porcelain Pistol attracts attention, lying as naturally on the table, as if it belongs to the table-setting ever since (...). As a part of the tableware, the Porcelain Pistol symbolizes the fragility of life within the everyday routine, luxury and happiness. The piece unites beauty and death in an irritating way: 'Et in arcadia ego' – Even in Arcadia I exist, death says.

Whether happy strewn flowers, a classic golden rim or the even more traditional blue onion pattern, the PPKs blend harmonically into the perfect table setting. The beauty of the material is seductive, almost naturally the fragile weapon lies next to coffee and cake, asking to be picked up. The PPK's pleasant coolness and surprisingly comfortable grip increase the qualms of the user – the pistol fits just a bit too well. The comfort level is almost alarming, leaving the user in a quandary between the pleasure of luxury, the fascination of a well-designed weapon and its inherent potential for violence and death. Even though it may be a mere facade, this tension is illustrated in a spectrum of beauty creating a skewed perception of an idyllic setting and homely cosiness, which nevertheless is infected by the uncanny lures of violence and conflict.

These novel PPKs also made their way in and through the web. Someone posted his/her thoughts when s/he saw the PPKs and table settings:

172   *M. Schillmeier and Y. L. Schultz*

'Don't they creep you out just a little, it speaks of complete irony to me. I have thoughts of a sad lady planning to shoot herself over tea.' Comments add: 'a lone tea set, so prim so proper, and an equally pretty weapon of destruction. I don't know what it says about me, but I sort of like the guns'.[8]

Or at www.watch84.com/ someone said:

> Awesome right? I didn't know if it's the idea of elegant violence, or the power of pistol being reduced to something as fragile as porcelain but my attraction to the piece remains the same. They're decorated with classic tableware themes which send an odd mental image into my mind's eye. The image of my grandmother blowing smoke across the top of the barrel like she's just lit someone up (...). The photos are brilliantly sinister.

It is the beauty of being brilliantly sinister that attracts the human eye. The novel percepts make us hesitate of the possibilities of our being and reflect upon the openness of the situations and their ambiguous gestures. Affected by the artificial staging of the PKKs the viewer are drawn into the ambiguous, which links the joy of life with the possible destruction of it. Moreover, the possibility of mutilation and killing is not portrayed as a rare event. Quite on the contrary, what makes the staged scene so dramatic and frightening are the potentially uncanny and potentially violent stories emerging from the everyday. The deadly pistols become the disturbing accomplice of more or less civilized routines that celebrate the joyful coming together that is adorned with a bit of luxury and style. It seems that we never know enough about the routine staging and presentations of our everyday life.

With the interstices of the porcelain PKKs the normalcy show of everyday life along supposedly peaceful interaction is disrupted, questioned and altered. A violent intruder politicizes the idyllic, innocent, secure and protected cosmos of civilized engagement, of traditional zones of interaction etc. But are the PKKs really intruders? Do they appear as violent? Or is violence already part of the civilized playground so beautifully staged? Does the porcelain PKK makes us aware of the ubiquity of violence in the conduct of everyday life? It seems, that the PPK pistols delightfully adapted themselves to the civilized routines. They seem to be part and parcel of a 'feud/al' scenery; as if there are always pistols involved. Our gaze is left with the ambiguous, which makes us think, reflect, question, feel irritated, scared, attracted and deterred at the same time. The materiality chosen by Lee Schultz enhances the ambiguous. Porcelain is a radiant material. Its smooth surface reflects light in clear lines of flight, its colour suggests inviolacy and purity. As the white gold, porcelain is valuable as it is fragile. It is precisely this materiality and its presence in everyday life which initiate a percept that draws attention to the precariousness of everyday life and makes us be affected, hesitate, think, talk and write about it. Clearly, then the porcelain weapons will not help us to decide what they 'are' – at least not along violent means to sort out the conflict. Rather, transfigured, it is the beauty of the

Figure 11.4 Schoko kid L (from the series 2sweet2kill).
Source: ©YLS Yvonne Lee Schultz.

artful staging of matters of violence that questions *and* protects the scene from becoming instrumentalized by the auspices of the technologies of adverse opposition, conflict and war. The porcelain PKKs are unusable for the desire of oppositional strife and its hideously costly operations. Quite on the contrary, the Walther PPKs – praised for their robustness and reliable technology – turn into fragile pieces of art. But nevertheless, the fragility of the materiality draws attention to the peculiarity of weapons as well: Being objects designed to harm and mutilate others, all weapons need hyper cautious handling to not inflict unintended (self-)harm and killings, which – as it is well known – cannot be fully ensured. Quite on the contrary, the risk of fatal accidents increases significantly with weapons kept in the home (cf. Kellermann et al., 1998).[9]

Becoming chocolate

Lee Schultz kept on thinking about violence and her pistol-art when she observed kids playing in a park, some of them were still wearing nappies but were already armed with water pump-guns, shooting at each other. They know the cool postures of violence. Aggression was clearly part of their communication and interaction. Again, the question arose of how the seduction of a power tool like the gun can be irritated or even be broken up by art? Could the parental behaviour be affected by this artwork? Could she highlight the aggression in our society,

174   *M. Schillmeier and Y. L. Schultz*

especially in children's behaviour, and bring the problem to our minds, make it public by setting up another artful/artificial staging? How to create a percept so paradoxical as to seduce us into thinking?

The aim was to change the pistol's material into something completely contrary to the normal and expected. Clearly, though, the material needed to be different than porcelain to become 'suitable' for children. The selection of the material seemed obvious. What seduces children more than chocolate, the artist speculated. In effect, the Walther PKKs turned into chocolate pistols, 1 to 1 replicas of James Bond's most loved weapon, licensed by Walther. Again, the pistol's material has changed into something significantly contrasting to its normal material configuration.

The artist made chocolate guns for all different tastes: white, dark, mint, chili and golden leave. Once the guns were ready to be artfully staged, the idea was to distribute them between kids. The artist gave the handcrafted pieces of art to kids, watched and documented what happened. The experiment led to 'Schoko-Kids', a series of photographs and a four-minute video, filmed by four cameramen simultaneously.[10] The resulting footage documents children mid-bite or mid-'shot', chocolate-smeared smiles on their face. The first reactions of the parents were surprising: They weren't sure why the chocolate guns needed to look so serious and asked if they couldn't be designed in a more funny and colourful way. One nanny shouted to her kid biting into the chocolate barrel of the gun: 'Don't you shoot yourself, shoot the others!' The kids' eyes beamed when they saw the chocolate pistols, but at the same time there was clear hesitation in the kids' play: The kids could not easily decide whether to eat the chocolate first or shoot somebody down. It was irritating to watch that the pistol made many kids perfectly performing their spontaneously invented play. They declared themselves special agents, navy seals, and immediately took on typical postures of gun fighters, displaying and re-enacting one perfect pose after the other and always with the finger placed on the trigger. Their smiles while enjoying the different tastes of the chocolates were strangely opposed to their war-like gestures. One boy just ate up most of the PKK and surprisingly even the ultimate melted leftovers served him playing the dangerous guy.

Another boy seemed to be contemplating the impact such a deadly weapon could have. At the age of three he already put his finger precisely on the trigger. But nevertheless, he was disappointed, because he didn't like the taste of dark chocolate. Meanwhile his sister loved the bittersweet taste and avidly enjoyed her favourite chocolate. Others, whilst 'killing' the best friend over and over again, wouldn't stop nibbling as well. Even a half-eaten chocolate pistol wasn't stopping them from shooting at each other, always looking for random victims. Still, some kids liked the taste of chocolate more than using it as a shooting-toy. The kids were confronted with a seemingly ambiguous toy, which could either be a treat – and disappear bite by bite – or could be used as a perfect tool of power which melts in their hands.

At the playground there was fun and laughter going together with playing a killing game. Enjoyment and death were simultaneously present. The kids also talked with a double sense. 'Take this. (Chocolate).' Or: 'Open your mouth, (eat the chocolate) you have to die'. 'Headshot! and I'll get a chocolate allergy', another shouts. 'Hands up!' turns into 'Show me your smeary fingers!' Another boy cries out loud and call for his mother: 'Mama, look, he destroyed my gun by biting in it!' Another boy shouts 'Russian Roulette! I kill myself with Nutella!'. Or: 'Take this you bastard! – I bite your gun, dude'.

Their smiles performed a strange contrast to their warrior-like gestures. The chocolate gun action unfolded the tightrope walk between seriousness and play, deadly power and sweet seduction. The artificial staging enacted a strange mix of pleasures and the odd performance of killing, suffering and mutilation. Clearly, though, the sugar- and bitter-sweet PKKs were fun. Watching the kids one had to realize that the longer they were in the hands of the children the more harmless they got. It was precisely the chocolate, which translated the ambiguous game into a play with a happy ending. Peace was brought about by eating the gun or by melting away in the hands of the kids. The average life span of a chocolate gun was about ten minutes. After which the PKK was not recognizable as such since it was nibbled from all sides.

Being 100 per cent chocolate clearly testified that these guns were 2sweet2kill. Still, to stage the chocolate pistol within the everyday territory of kids' interaction was not meant to glorify, belittle or kitschify weapons. Rather, it was thought to draw attention to the often-veiled presence of violence and the strange attraction to and uncomfortable curiosity for the use of weaponry. The public

Figure 11.5 Schoko kids_2 boys.
Source: ©YLS Yvonne Lee Schultz.

Figure 11.6 Schoko kid S.
Source: ©YLS Yvonne Lee Schultz.

reaction to the exhibition of the chocolate PKKs and kids was even more controversially discussed than the porcelain pistol installation. Newspapers and TV programmes reported on the Berlin shock-artist and discussed whether her bizarre work is too provocative, too unsettling still to be art! Parents articulated their anger and gallery owners made clear that the artist went too far by engaging innocent children who didn't know what there were doing. Discussions on the web whether the artist is glorifying and trivializing weapons or whether she should be sued for child molestation. The artist got hate mails and was denunciated as the 'disgrace of the nation', as a ruthless populist artist who merely desires to be known throughout the country by producing scandals. At the same time, others articulated that they love her work to death, saw a clever idea artfully performed that unmistakably revealed the presence and 'normalcy' of violence as well as the dangers of being at the mercy of violence. Kindergartens and schools discussed the issue of violence. Lee Schultz's work also inspired new events: A Berlin ATTAC activist called for robbing a bank with chocolate pistols, which was brought to court as the 'chocolate-process trial'. Someone else asked for 500 chocolate pistols to be armed against the police force on 1 May.

Contributory action and speculative research

Lee Schultz, the artist, is a master of what can be called semblance techniques in the way her subtly crafted artefacts 'break-an-relate to make felt an effect' (Massumi, 2005: 37). The art pistols remain ready-to-hand since they are 1:1 replicas of the original Walther PKK. The perceptual resemblance of the art pistols is also a betrayal, a radical one. It betrays technologies of war and violence with an artful contrast that takes the artist's pacifism to its extremes and enacts the possibilities of 'civil conflictuality' (Stiegler, 2015: 175), contrasting and challenging the logic of oppositional strive, war and violence. The PKKs are bereft of their technical functionality, but remain their symbolic power of shooting agents. Metal turns into porcelain and the robustness and reliability is translated into fragile beauty. Metal turns into chocolate and its *physis* is to melt away in the hands of its user or to be nibbled away. These novel percepts are put into action in the unexpected spaces of everyday life in order to unleash disruptive but playful and affective scenarios by which hesitation, doubt, questionability, insecurities, uncertainties and controversies occur which may or may not be limited to the spaces of artful enactment. In Tarde's words, we may say that PKK art is a 'type special' (Tarde, 2000 [1899]) of political engagement that introduces an *inventive repetition*, which affects a *contrasting gesture* that questions, disrupts and alters the logic of oppositional strife. Through Schultz's art, the PPK turns into a social event, it *adds* a problem (gun violence) by problematizing it in the way it *singularizes* percepts and thereby resists the problem as taken for granted. Art gives the contrast its singular character that problematizes the common and normal/ized.

Lee Schultz's art-mediated publics bring 'into disclosure an ingredient that both belong to the territory and connects with an outside against which this territory protects itself' (Stengers, 2008: 42). In the case of Schokokids and 2sweet-2kill it is the relationship between conflict and violence, which becomes an issue in the way her gun-art interferes with supposedly gun-free spaces where violence isn't supposed to govern interaction. Schultz Lee's work on violence and weaponry is not primarily crafted to be on display at traditional expositing spaces of art. Moreover, rather than being at the mere disposal for the public gaze, her work is meant to assemble 'publics' (Dewey, 2012 [1927]; Marres, 2005) that draw attention to a publically shared problem. Her work experiments with the affects of the participants and observers at the same time. It triggers off unforeseen reactions and has the capability to make us think and to jolt new events.

Mediated by works of art these publics give importance to a specific matter of concern (Latour, 2005) for which no immediate answers and fixed solutions are available or can be easily expected (Marres, 2005; Schillmeier, 2015). The collaboration between social sciences and art *experiments with a speculative research agenda* that articulates a playful and non-violent form of intervention and disruption of the fragile normalcy show of the every-day by enunciating challenging contrast to the lures of the 'either-or' – in thought and practice. It is precisely through art and its work of reassembling materialities from which we

178 *M. Schillmeier and Y. L. Schultz*

can learn how the encounter between the human and nonhuman *preserves and creates* social realities. Through art, 'percepts' and 'affects' emerge that gain existence on their own and contribute to the enrichment of social relations. Clearly, art is capable of assembling a much more varied set of enunciations than social sciences traditionally do. For social sciences on the other hand it offers the possibility to engage in speculative research that unfolds *contributory action* that links the academic and non-academic to create publics for issues that remain unsolved and problematic. Speculative social research that engages with the worlds of art can be understood as a novel research practice that aims at the composition of possible futures of a common world that unfolds productive contrasts to the economies of violence and war.

Notes

1 Tarde (2000[1899]) adds:

> Yet how often does the invention that it calls for fail to respond! How often does war cut down genius, instead of raising it up! How many talents are rendered worthless by the polemics of the press, parliamentary debates, or even the foolish fencings of congresses and associations!

2 See www.yvonneleeschultz.com
3 See e.g. 'averagejoamerican', who posted a comment to the YouTube video:

> Have one and love it. Carry it all the time. Put a Wolf 18# spring in it and it shoots flawlessly. Put Rosewood grips on it too. Does have some snap to it. Sweet carry gun. BTW, wicked accurate … just feels so comfortable in your hand. Everyone want to shoot it when I am at the range.

4 See e.g. www.youtube.com/watch?v=B9hmFIhCjQM
5 The 'war machine' unfolds war-like situations without necessarily states being at war. Moreover, the war machine 'institutes an entire economy of violence, (…), a way of making violence durable, even unlimited.' See Deleuze & Guattari (1988: 437).
6 As Deleuze & Guattari (1988: 436) note: '[T]he weapon invents speed, or the discovery of speed invents the weapon (the projective character of the weapon is the result).'
7 See www.youtube.com/watch?v=B9hmFIhCjQM
8 See http-//greenlaundry.net/blog/2008/06/06/tea-time-death
9 Kellermann et al. (1998: 263) argue that '[g]uns kept in homes are more likely to be involved in a fatal or nonfatal accidental shooting, criminal assault, or suicide attempt than to be used to injure or kill in self-defence'.
10 See the video at https://vimeo.com/9312897

References

Debaise, D. (2013). A philosophy of interstices: Thinking subjects and societies from Whitehead's philosophy. *Subjectivity*, 6(1), 79–100.
Deleuze, G., & Guattari, F. (1988). *A thousand plateaus. Capitalism and schizophrenia.* London: The Athlone Press.
Deleuze, G., & F. Guattari (1994). *What is philosophy?* London: Verso.
Dewey, J. (1980 [1934]. *Art as experience.* New York, NY: Perigee.
Dewey, J. (2012 [1927]). *The public and its problems: An essay in political inquiry.* The Penn State University Press.

Heidegger, M. (1971a). *Poetry, language, thought*. (A. Hofstadter, Trans.). New York, NY: Harper & Row.

Heidegger, M. (1971b). … Poetically man dwells…. In M. Heidegger (Ed.), *Poetry, language, thought* (pp. 211–229). (A. Hofstadter, Trans.). New York, NY: Harper & Row.

Heidegger, M. (1996). *Being and time*. Albany: SUNY.

James, W. (2003 [1912]. *Essays in radical empiricism*. New York, NY: Dover.

Kellermann, A. L., Somes, G., Rivara, F. P., Lee, R. K., & Banton, J. G. (1998). Injuries and deaths due to firearms in the home. Journal *of Trauma, 45*, 263–267.

Latour, B. (2005). *Re-assembling the social. An introduction to actor-network theory*. Oxford: Oxford University Press.

Marres, N. S. (2005) *No issue no public: Democratic deficits after the displacement of politics*. Amsterdam: University of Amsterdam.

Massumi, B. (2011). *Semblance and event. Activist philosophy and the occurrent arts*. Cambridge, MA.: MIT Press.

Mitchell, A. J. (2010). *Heidegger among the sculptors. Body, space, and the art of dwelling*. Stanford, CA.: Stanford University Press.

Mitchell, A. J. (2015). *The fourfold. Reading the late Heidegger*. Evanston, Il.: Northwestern University Press.

Schillmeier, M. (2014). *Eventful bodies. The cosmopolitics of illness*. Farnham: Ashgate.

Schillmeier, M. (2015). Caring about social complexity in nanomedicine. *Nanomedicine, 10*(20), 3181–3193.

Schillmeier, M. (2016). Design and the art of care: Engaging the more than human and less than inhuman. In: C. H. Bates, R. Imrie, & K. Kullmann (Eds), *Care and design: Bodies, buildings, cities*. Oxford: Wiley-Blackwell.

Stengers, I. (2005). The cosmopolitical proposal. In B. Latour, & P. Weibel (Eds), *Making things public. Atmospheres of democracy* (pp. 994–1003). Cambridge, Massachusetts, London: MIT Press.

Stengers, I. (2008). Experimenting with refrains: Subjectivity and the challenge of escaping modern dualism. *Subjectivity, 22*, 38–59.

Stiegler, B. (2015). *States of shock. Stupidity and knowledge in the 21st Century*. Cambridge: Polity Press.

Tarde, G. (2000[1899]. *Social laws: An outline of sociology*. Batoche Books.

Tarde, G. (2012). *Monadology and sociology*. Melbourne: re.press.

Weil, S. (1965). The Illiad, or the poem of force. *Chicago Review, 18*(2), 5–30.

Part IV
Speculative implications

Introduction

Speculative implications

Martin Savransky, Alex Wilkie, and Marsha Rosengarten

Speculation and its ripples

After developing propositions to reclaim speculation against the modern histories with which it has been associated; after asking ourselves the question of when, where, and how, a diverse range of practices might become lured by the (im)possibles that speculation seeks to affirm; after experimenting with situated tools and techniques that may succeed and fail here and there in cracking open the (im)possible, and cultivating a different kind of future; after all of this, what? What difference might the speculative make, not just to how we think about and practise social and cultural research, but to how we learn to relate to the many others that compose the presents and futures in which we live, for which we think, do and feel?

Addressed to the kind of gesture we have been calling 'speculative', such questions are doubly important. For as many of the chapters in this collection have thus far shown, unlike critical forms of social and cultural thought and research, speculative differences are not achieved by revealing, to those they seek to transform, something that might finally awaken them from their slumber. If the difference this collection makes is that of a 'shock', that of an experience of finding one's dreams being shattered by a mode of thought that is unconcerned with how those dreams matter and only seeks to denounce as illusions the hopes and fears that animate the thinking doing and feeling of others, then it would be necessary to declare it a failure. To ask what difference might speculative research make, then, demands that we simultaneously entertain a similar, but irreducible question – how may those differences be expressed?

In his *Modes of Thought*, Whitehead (1968) recognised that of the various ways of expressing thought, language may well be the most important. The reason for this is that language deals with those elements of experience that are most easily abstracted from the complexity of the concrete situations in which they happen, and in doing so, it makes them available for conscious entertainment, for retention, recollection, and communication. The importance of language in relation to thought is thus not to be underestimated, for '[h]uman civilization is an outgrowth of language, and language is the product of advancing civilization' (ibid.: 35). But to extract from this the conclusion that thought

184 *M. Savransky* et al.

and language are one and the same; or that the difference that thought makes is only to find expression in language, as a matter of abstractions that can and should 'correct' both previous modes of expression as well as the experiences therein expressed; now that is quite another matter. Indeed, it is a step too far.

For thought is the outcome not just of language, but of a coordination of concurrent activities that are at once cognitive, emotional, and physical. This is why, rather than associate it with a 'new enlightenment' effected by a critical language with which to judge and denounce how others experience the edges of the present, for Whitehead the difference that a thought can make is that of 'a tremendous form of excitement.'. 'Like a stone thrown into a pond' he suggested, thought 'disturbs the whole surface of our being' (ibid.: 36). This disturbing effect, however, is never to be confused with an action that speculative thought may singlehandedly exert upon the surfaces it affects. Rather, 'we should conceive the ripples as effective in the creation of the plunge of the stone into the water. The ripples release the thought, and the thought augments and distorts the ripples' (ibid.: 36).

Folding, refolding, unfolding futures

This image of the differences that thinking and knowing can make situates speculative research at a considerable remove from the transcendental position required by the shock of critique. Instead, it enables an *immanent* understanding of the effects that speculative lures, techniques, and propositions can have, effects that rather than *impact on* the situations to which they are addressed, are rather *enfolded* in them as they simultaneously *refold* the shape of the patterns that compose them, and allow alternative, (im)possible futures to *unfold.* It is for this reason that we have organised this section under the sign of speculative *implications.* An 'im-pli-cation', whose etymological debt to the french word *pli* –which is to say, 'fold'– should not go unnoticed, describes precisely a process of involving, the enfolding of a novel proposition within a situation –with all its com-pli-cations – such that an alternative course, a different explication, might become available.

As Gilles Deleuze (2006: 9) argued:

> [f]olding-unfolding no longer simply means tension-release, contraction-dilation, but enveloping-developing, involution-evolution. The organism is defined by its ability to fold its own parts and to unfold them, not to infinity, but to a degree of development assigned to each species. Thus, an organism is enveloped by organisms, one within another (interlocking of germinal matter), like Russian dolls.

To ask what difference speculative thought and research might make, then, is to consider how they may become ethically, politically and aesthetically *implicated* in hopes, dreams, and fears that, while situated, need not be arbitrarily limited to the specific issues that the situation makes present. It is a matter, rather, of

Introduction: speculative implications 185

following the manners and processes by which, once enveloped in specific situations, speculative research may enable them to unfold onto possible futures that might not have been available without its rippling distortions.

Exploring different modalities of speculative implications and explications, of folding and unfolding, is precisely what the chapters composing this section address in different ways. What might, after all, be the implications of cultivating a speculative sensibility to the world? If it is not simply to be associated with the threat of 'death' or poor w/health, as in the Parisian banner mentioned in the introduction to the first part of the book, then how might the speculative become implicated in how we *live?* The chapters in this part explore the implications of some of the themes and issues posed by speculative research as they connect with broader, pressing questions of politics, ethics, and aesthetics. By returning to some of the philosophical sources that provide inspiration for the development of more practical and empirical forms of speculative research, they provide a series of meditations on the relation between speculation and the art of life: that is, the political, ethical, and aesthetic task to live, to live well, to live better: arguably a key aim of social and cultural research.

Concerned with the ethico-political implications of the speculative in relation to heterogeneous others, Vikki Bell develops a sustained engagement with Stengers' concept of 'cosmopolitics', to ask what kinds of 'others' may reconnect our engagements with the sense of wonder and excitement that the speculative *implies.* Of particular concern to Bell here is, to be sure, the ways in which such ethical and political questions concerning speculation themselves become enfolded in, and therefore may enable us to unfold differently, questions of aesthetics. Constructing a much needed connection with the recent work of political theorist William Connolly, Bell asks whether these others that can complicate our politics-as-usual by implicating speculation in a cosmopolitics may also be 'products of the literary imagination', thus forcing us to relate differently to 'the possibilities of fictionality', that is, to 'the possibilities that accepting fictions as part of the speculative endeavour might yield'.

If Bell's meditation on the ethical and political possibilities of fictionality unfolds an appreciation of the importance of aesthetics in how speculative research may be implicated, Michael Thomas's chapter refolds the aesthetic to situate it at the centre of his understanding of the relations between speculation and culture. Focusing on Whitehead's notion of 'aesthetic experience', Thomas's chapter works to 'unpack two key ideals to signal the connection between thought and reality: speculation and civilization'. In so doing, he poses a crucial, if demanding, question concerning this interplay between between ripples that release thoughts, and thoughts that transform the patterns of future ripples. The question, that is, of how the speculative might become implicated in our modes of living: what might it mean to 'live speculatively'?

If, once released by the ripples, the task of speculative propositions might indeed be to *augment and transform* them, then it is paramount that we pay close attention to what this process of 'augmentation' might entail, beyond all-too-easy metaphors. This is precisely the central concern of Didier Debaise's

186   M. Savransky et al.

chapter. Indeed, by providing a careful reading of Whitehead's later texts, he proposes that the very *function* of speculative propositions is nothing other than 'the intensification of an event's importance to its ultimate level'. As the relationship between the stone and the pond suggests, however, we should not assume that 'importance' is a form of value that human researchers may simply *project* upon a future to which thoughts are proposed. Indeed, to say that something matters, that a possible future may be important, is to suggest that 'there is value beyond ourselves' (Savransky, 2016). For this reason, Debaise proposes that in order to understand the function of speculative propositions, we need to develop 'a concept of nature where each existence would be defined as a centre of evaluation of what matters, a perspective on and of the universe'. Thus, if the sense of importance belongs to all events of existence, the aim of speculation, Debaise argues, is to become implicated in events in such a way that it can 'dramatize or intensify them, by the invention of possible worlds, to maximal levels'.

As such, the chapters in this part offer important and wide-ranging insights on what is at stake in cultivating speculative adventures in thought and research, adventures that, in cracking open the (im)possible, may just enable the rippling present to unfold onto a different future for a possible world.

References

Deleuze, G. (2006). *The fold: Leibniz and the Baroque.* London: Continuum.
Savransky, M. (2016). *The adventure of relevance: An ethics of social inquiry.* Basingstoke and New York, NY: Palgrave Macmillan.
Whitehead, A. N. (1968). *Modes of thought.* New York, NY: Free Press.

12 On Isabelle Stengers' 'cosmopolitics'

A speculative adventure

Vikki Bell

> [C]osmopolitics is, of course, a speculative concept, and its effects will first of all affect the way in which we understand ourselves and understand others in contrast to ourselves.
>
> (Stengers, 2011b: 356)

If abstractions work to "vectorize" experience, then it seems that the notion of 'cosmopolitics' is one that Isabelle Stengers offers to lure us into an adventure of thought in which we entertain the proposition that "what we perceive may be transformed if the way we pay attention changes" (2008a: 5). Steeped in the Whiteheadian position that perception is "the most primitive form of judgment" (1978: 162), her arguments attempt to open up scenes of perception and to invite intrigue about how perceptions arise. In her sights is any power that seeks to impose its Truth, to disqualify others, to "bully" (2005: 1000) the world into its frame. Where that Truth succeeds, it disqualifies the relevance of multiple potential contributions and disqualifies those that speak a different idiom, or that do not speak at all, preventing the emergence of a newly perceived situation. By contrast to such attempts, "[c]osmopolitics makes present, helps resonate, the unknown affecting our questions" (2011b: 355). In order to explore her provocations, this chapter will consider four key aspects of Stengers' argument: presences, propositions, the argument against symmetry and the importance of wonder.

Presences

By obliging that their presences be felt, these unknowns – these other worlds and other struggles – contest a simplification that is also a judgment. To cut away complexity is to engage in the distribution of value. Praising Donna Haraway's book *When Species Meet*, Stengers has written:

> When writing about Cayenne [Haraway's dog] and about what she has learned with her, Haraway is exposing herself to her colleagues' derision, and knowingly so, but she is making present, vivid and mattering, the

188   *V. Bell*

imbroglio, perplexity and messiness of a worldly world, a world where we, our ideas and power relations, are not alone, were never alone, will never be alone. As she recalls with joy and wonder, human genomes can be found in only about 10% of the cells that live in what we call our body, the rest of the cells being filled with the genomes of bacteria, fungi, protists, and such.

(2011a: 371)

For Stengers, Haraway's attention to this "imbroglio" is able to complicate our understanding, connecting it with many struggles "against what simplifies away our worlds in terms of idealist judgments about what would ultimately matter and what does not" (2011a: 371).

Among the first things to insist upon in relation to discussions of speculation, therefore, is the necessity that it be accompanied by a concern for multiplicity, where multiplicity becomes the prompt and the justification that prevents the "mere" forever accompanying the practice. In order to be something more than "mere speculation", from which nothing follows, speculation involves an opening toward other presences heretofore ignored, un-consulted or otherwise rendered irrelevant to the scene in hand. It is not the ruminative practice that takes place in contemplative comfort, but that which follows an interruption and a consequent re-orientation. For Isabelle Stengers, that re-orientation results when self-assurance falters (2005: 996). When actors are faced with an indeterminacy concerning how to proceed following an intervention, be that a shout, a murmur or a newly imposed constraint (we will return to this idea), they are forced to consider how to "sign" that event, how to *inherit* from it. For this reason – that there is a hesitation that will not be resolved through the presentation of argument – the question of the cosmopolitical is precisely "speculative" (2011b: 356).

In Stengers' "The Cosmopolitical Proposal", the re- or even dis-orientating scene is described as one that calls upon the participants within it to consider their habits and ways of "busying" themselves in the light of a newly felt presence. It is not that these "others" have in fact newly emerged, but that their relevance is newly recognized, and in such a way that the recognition reverberates. She writes of the ways of speaking heard in laboratories where experiments are performed on animals, ways of speaking that, she suggests, do the work of protecting the human workers. These "grand tales about the advancement of knowledge, rationality defined against sentimentality, and the necessities of method" (2005: 997) mask the habitual evasion that has become the laboratory's ethos. The legitimacy of the experimentation is not a decision that is usually taken "in the presence of" those that will potentially be the victims of that decision. What would happen if they were? Might these self-protective modes of continuing be challenged (or, to put it somewhat differently, newly constrained)? Might the shadows cast by those that "do not have, cannot have or do not want to have a political voice" (2004: 996) send a chill which insists upon a problem? Such a chill amounts to a sense of exposure, registered in and as the disoriented moment. It is not that the existence of others is a complication of our lives,

Stengers writes, but the existence of others retains the potential to "force ... us to recognize that complication" (2011b: 351).

The example of the scientist at the animal experimentation laboratory clarifies, better perhaps than her evocation of Cromwell's cry "by the bowels of Christ, I beseech you, bethink you may be mistaken!" or indeed her citing of Bartleby's "idiotic" stance ("I prefer not to"), the sense of disquiet that differentiates Stengers' call for (speculative) thought from a liberal democratic model of debate. To be exposed, to be obliged to hesitate and to attempt to decide "in the presence of" those that may turn out to be the victims of that decision, is to put at risk the ethos of one's way of being. It is to allow the truths by which one lives to be suspended. Furthermore, that this approach concerns a response to presences that are not necessarily human, which are present but are un- or under-articulated, is clear in this example. It is for this wider multiplicity, the multiplicity by which a common world is invented, that Stengers employs the term "cosmos".

Such hesitation and such wondering require the faculty of the imagination, but it is not a fanciful process. Prompted by the real world, concerned and engaged with it without being straightforwardly answered there, the questions that arise in the hesitation are not necessarily accompanied by representatives or translators who will explain the contributions or objections of these "others". Indeed, it is foolhardy to set out to require the multiplicity to debate proposals or to express its various objections. Yet Stengers suggests that all that constitutes the *oikos*, the habitat or "environment", *may* somehow make propositions and may even *demand* that perceptions and habits change. Without being able to articulate that change, and without allowing the transcendence of the present arrangements of things, Stengers suggests the cosmos might be able to effect a change in the ethos allowing "[t]he common world" the freedom to "emerge" (2005: 999) from and in its multiplicity. How can the propositions of the *oikos* be made?

Propositions

Clearly, this freedom to emerge cannot be understood within those models of politics based on notions of speech and representation, which rely upon the agonistic articulation of disagreement. The cosmopolitical question forces an interruption or at least a *ritando* that conveys an expansion beyond such models. Into this widening, it asks:

> by which artifacts, which procedures, can we slow down political ecology, bestow efficacy on the murmurings of the idiot, the "there is something more important" which is so easy to forget because it cannot be "taken into account" because the idiot neither objects nor proposes anything that "counts". The question is "etho-ecological".
>
> (Stengers, 2004: 1001)[1]

Different aspects of the world will require different apparatuses, artifices or scenes within which to appear and make contributions. The "slowing" mentioned above is required in order to wonder about these other protagonists. Our first questions need to be about how to effect their appearance. Under what conditions will they appear? What do they require in order to contribute to the gathering and its decisions? In this sense cosmopolitics has regard for the *mode of presence* of different types of protagonists and becomes a technical issue (rather than one driven by a desire to achieve the "re-enchantment of the world"). Stengers advocates an "ecology of practices" (2011b: 367) as an endeavour that would allow for the "coexistence of disparate technical practices corresponding to distinct forms of reciprocal capture, characterized by different logical constraints and different syntaxes" (2011b: 359).

Stengers emphasizes the need for artifice, like the apparatus that scientific experimentation uses in order to persuade and convince those gathered about them of the significance of a proposition. Thus Galileo's experimental apparatuses of inclined planes for rolling balls had the capacity to produce an event, in Deleuze's (1993) sense. Such artifices become reliable witnesses that testify to the persuasiveness of the proposition, compelling those gathered to take note, if they are interested enough to do so. And it follows that where the artifice is able to repeatedly "prove" a proposition or show a correlation, or simply the relevance of its enquiry, it confers a power on the experimenter to speak in the name of that proposition, and to challenge those who maintain otherwise. But by the same token, the artifice is also described by Stengers in terms of its potential to become a place to complicate and to welcome, even incite, doubts and objections (2010: 27) in a gathering that becomes potentially a transformational event. Yet what must one do to sense the propositions that might emerge within the 'art of the event'?

New relations in new environments may require a new disposition, and a new vulnerability, since what one has accepted in prior contexts may be newly challenged. If the artifice of a scientific experiment, to continue with her example, must cut away certain factors from its scene, then as soon as its propositions leave their originary or "native environment" they may well leave behind their relevance and/or reliability. To accept this, is to attend to this new environment and those for whom it is "a matter of an active concern" (2012). In the weave of new relations, one remains at the 'meso' level, thinking with and through the milieu. Stengers notes that one is obliged to stay and think "with the surroundings" since no theory gives one the power to disentangle something from its particular surroundings, that is, to pass beyond the particular appearances that emerge in a specific situation (on "mesopolitics", see Stengers, 2008c).

Elsewhere, Stengers takes inspiration from eighteenth-century chemistry. She writes of the art of chemistry:

> chemical "actants" are defined as "active" without their activity being able to be attributed to them; it depends on circumstances and it is up to the chemists' art to create the type of circumstances in which they become capable of producing what the chemist wants: art of catalysis, activation, moderation.

(2005: 1000)

On Isabelle Stengers' 'cosmopolitics' 191

The "etho-ecological art of the manipulative chemist", is one where manipulation is understood as a positive quality, drawing out the "propensity of things" (the term Stengers adopts from François Jullien [1999]).

When Stengers celebrates manipulation as a kind of speculative art, if you will, she does so to applaud the ability to gather, to be open to new combinations and to prepare the stage for new emergences. She envisages multiple "actants" gathered together with no compulsion to "represent" or "argue" their interests since, in contrast to reigning models of democracy, the "world order is ... not an argument" (2005: 1001). This she likens, in another extended metaphor, to what she understands of the process in a palaver, where the participants gather to share – without having to *own* – their opinions. That is, they are each recognized as knowing something about the world order, but are called together precisely because none has sufficient knowledge of how it relates to the issue at hand. Thus, in their gathering no one challenges or refutes another, but collectively and "in the presence of world order" something emerges that is understood to be consonant with it (2005: 1001). Stengers evokes the de-personalization strategies of feminist practice ("the personal is political") and the summoning of the goddess at gatherings of contemporary neo-pagan witches (2010: 27) as resonating with this practice. This is not a struggle wherein one actant or group of actants attempts to persuade or convince others. The scene is one in which there is a gathering without victors or hierarchical imposition of an order. So, not an "application" of a vision of "world order", but rather the order "plays a role":

> comparable to the acid solution (the "menstrue") that dissolves and enables the chemical actants to enter into proximity, or to the fire that activates them. In short, it can be characterized in terms of efficacy: it compels everyone to produce, to "artefactualize" themselves, *in a mode that gives the issue around which they are all gathered the power to activate thinking*, a thinking that belongs to no one, in which no one is right.
>
> (2005: 1001, emphasis added)

The notion of cosmopolitics, it seems, is not necessarily about "us" asking *more* things to engage, therefore – although this does also seem to often be the case in her examples – but about new modes of attention, allowing new stagings to rearrange multiple relevancies whose practices may engage in very different ways with the issue in new arrangements of consultation. At such gatherings, Stengers insists we must de-throne the fact–value distinction from which it has been assumed that procedure must flow from the presentation of a matter "factually" before "value-laden" opinions are invited. Instead, for Stengers, this is about the creation of a political ecology in which all for whom or for which the issue or situation is a matter of active concern, are able to participate.

Stengers' "cosmopolitics" envisages what she admits is a kind of utopia in which the issue at stake has the ability to attract participants who will force the consideration of the world via "other questions" (2005: 998) that may transform the situation. This, she notes, is "what Greenpeace understood when it contrasted

192 *V. Bell*

'stakeholders' with what it called 'shareholders'" (2005: 999); even if that term had unfortunate connotations, it meant to expand the issue to include those for whom an issue *mattered*. The aim is to oblige any decision – or presumably any way of "carrying on" – to face up to its repercussions, meaning especially the challenges and difficulties it entails for others, be they other actors (human others and other-than-humans), other struggles or other worlds.

"Elaborating and experimenting with artifices", involves working out from the milieu at the "meso" level (see 2010: 27). This is a level that Stengers notes is most under threat within contemporary neo-liberal capitalism, yet she does not understand this political ecology as subversive. Rather, her envisaged political ecology is composed with multiple participants and potentialities, and hence as political in a minoritarian key. The guiding hope here is that such gatherings might be places to discuss *objections* (Stengers & Whatmore, 2015) that potentially "trigger", "catalyze" or "convoke". Stengers uses all three terms to suggest an event that transforms each protagonist's relations not with a newly emergent Other, but with his or her "*own* knowledge, hopes, fears and memories" (2005: 1002). Collectively, moreover, the hope is that the gathering might be able "to generate what each one would have been unable to produce separately" (2005: 1002). In other words, it produces a change in the *oikos* as the presence of other modes of existence returns participants to an altered configuration of their (same) present.

Against symmetry

As we have seen from the above arguments, Stengers' cosmopolitics is decidedly not about attempting to think *from* the place of the other. She comments: "I try not to think in the place of others ... [since] I look to a future where they will take *their* place" (2010). We get a sense of the stance Stengers wants to argue against with her disdain for the development of what she terms "symmetrical anthropology". This relates also to her phase "the curse of tolerance", a notion she uses to expose a "pride barely hidden" whenever we "believe" the alternative epistemologies of Others, a stance she characterizes thus: "We are 'adults,' we are capable of confronting a world stripped of its guarantees and enchantments" (2011b: 303), so that the West tolerates other beliefs of others elsewhere, but maintains they are illusory. She critiques Georges Devereux's "ethnopsychiatry" on this count, for ultimately resting on a proposition that the therapist–researcher can maintain a position in which she can not only remain a psychoanalyst even if from the Indian patient's point of view she is a healer, but also that her analytic practice can understand what a healer means to the Indian: "She can understand the other, but the other cannot understand her" (2011b: 323). This "poison/curse" operates through a process whereby the "'others' who ethnopsychiatry makes exist as humans are themselves at the service of [its] science" (2011b: 323). Symmetrical anthropology seems to think the task is that "we" do more symmetricizing in order to allow or foster a cosmopolitical view. But this display or stance risks becoming merely a requirement for the

On Isabelle Stengers' 'cosmopolitics' 193

constitution of the science of anthropology. Indeed, the task of cosmopolitics risks failure wherever we convince ourselves of a solution that we imagine will improve and change us (e.g. into good cosmopolitans) while setting a requirement that others become like us (imagined in that new version). What is forgotten in the imposition of such solutions is their own artifices, so failing to allow new gatherings to generate new thought.

Wonder

> This pragmatism, which I take from William James, from his more speculative dimensions (meaning the concern for consequences, in terms of invention, of speculation on consequences), this is what pragmatism, in its common usage (which is an insult), passes over in silence. We don't know how these things can matter. But we can learn to examine situations from the point of view of their possibilities, from that which they communicate with and that which they poison. *Pragmatism is the care of the possible.*
>
> (Stengers, 2010)

Rather than imposing "cosmopolitics" as a solution, Stengers offers her speculative notion in order to propose attending differently in order to allow different perceptions and thus different possibilities. As such, she wishes that it be understood as both pragmatic, insofar as it is concerned with what is possible, and as a tale that is full of wonder. Indeed, Stengers suggests that cosmopolitics requires the creation of *obstacles that allow wonder*. Such obstacles presumably promote a requisite interruption, the slowing down Stengers insists is needed in order that we wonder about conditions that may arrive from elsewhere, the instigators of which she suggests we will not know before they put "us" at risk. Of course she states that these obstacles are not solutions in themselves and are without guarantees, since we cannot assume that we ourselves are capable of the requisite understanding or sharing that these other protagonists might require before exchange becomes possible. (Nor do we even know that they would want it to enter exchange.) Yet despite this problem, "our" problem as Stengers calls it, it seems that an obstacle or artifice that provokes wonder in this sense may aid those who may wish to bring her cosmopolitical proposal to fruition.

In this respect Stengers has an ally in the recent work of William Connolly. In his recent *The Fragility of Things* (2013) Connolly writes of the fragility of the human estate as "entangled by a thousand threads and resonances to a cosmos of multiple force fields, most of which are not first and foremost predisposed to our welfare.... The issue of how to respond to [this world] is unsettled" (2013: 172). He notes that one mode of response has been the rejection of this entanglement, those "bellicose political movements of denial and deferral" of which he cites several, from the virulent attacks on scientists of climate change, to creationists, new atheists and evangelical defenders of the neo-liberal machine. This multiplication of Nietzsche's figure of *ressentiment*, understood

194   *V. Bell*

as a response to uncertainty and the refusal to articulate it, may be an "over-doing" of beliefs newly challenged (2013: 173). In the face of such denial and *ressentiment*, Connolly sounds something like a call for more wonder about our entangled situation, influenced in part, like Stengers, by Whitehead's process philosophy. We engage life, he argues "from the middle of things", and in this "world of becoming" his hope is that the multiple struggles that are taking and will take place at multiple sites, will develop an enhanced sensitivity, attuning to what he terms the "noise" (2013: 13, 192). For Connolly wants to argue that creativity, including political creativity, arises from dissonances within the entangled world. "Uncanny drafts of creative energy" drawn from "this or that incipience" may fan new directions. Amongst other things, he lists endeavours such as films, music and spiritual exercises as enabling and encouraging the energy of critical movements:

> They sometimes encourage new thoughts to surge forward as if from nowhere and to become infused into critical action. Who will be the musicians whose performative experiments do for our day what, say, the Weavers, Joan Baez and Bob Marley did for several constituencies during another time? Who will be the film directors? The bloggers?
>
> (2013: 192)

Thus while Connolly wishes to retain an important role for active humans who engage in "strategic role experimentation" and maintain pressure on the numerous institutions in which they are located (2013: 192), he also includes much more, including creative productions such as theatre, music and – it seems especially – film that seem to act as something like "objects of wonder".

In an 'interlude' to his theoretical argument, Connolly discusses Lars von Trier's film *Melancholia* (2011). Here, Connolly presents an argument against "exclusive humanism", arguing that more attention is needed to the ways:

> other dimensions of being are infused into us and help us to constitute what we are, extending the radius of care from the human estate narrowly defined to encompass a large variety of entities and processes with which it is entangled.
>
> (2013: 47)

In its dramatic telling of the end of the earth as a strange emergent entity, another previously unknown planet – Melancholia – approaches and eventually collides with it, Connolly argues the film "peels away issues of responsibility and existential revenge", i.e. the modes of blaming and desire for revenge that human experiences of suffering tend to promote among ourselves. Instead the film is able to gradually "allow the experience of *attachment to the world* to soak into our pores" (2013: 46). Faced with its end, the importance of ourselves and human relations cannot be all that matters on earth (or to us); we love and wish to protect the Earth.[2]

On Isabelle Stengers' 'cosmopolitics' 195

Yet Connolly's concern is not the demonstration of entanglement and unacknowledged dependencies; his concern remains to a large extent as it has been in his earlier works, where Foucault has taken a guiding role, with the *ethical* dimensions of this extended "radius of care". He employs his reading of the film to emphasize the different temporalities our ethical attitudes can cultivate. Certainly, if we immerse ourselves in daily routines, we neglect to take the planetary perspective into account. Yet Claire's character in *Melancholia* indicates that the obverse – a total immersion in the future – is also problematic since it can lead one to "neglect daily duties". To substitute "long term" relations over the short cannot be the solution.

Nor, despite his thorough critique of "exclusive humanism" and species provincialism, is Connolly drawn to post-humanism or anti-humanism insofar as these "too readily" give the impression of "not exuding care for humanity at all" and neglecting therefore the *ethical connections* to "that which is unlike us or a strange part of us, or more encompassing than us" (2013: 50). Maybe he too is worried about promoting a form of attachment that subsumes all subjectivity within objectivity, that like Justine in the film, can no longer see discrete entities at all, and so embraces and surrenders in the path of the oncoming planet.[3] Indeed, there is even precisely a sense of melancholy here for the theoretical humanities, which are being asked to risk the surrender of their focus; a hesitation that glances back because it senses an unknown opening up before it.[4]

Concluding remarks

The whole weight of Stengers' intervention is to promote such a hesitation, to advise that its interruption is crucial to a process of re-orienting our attentions. But it is right that, since the question of which approach the humanities and social sciences should adopt is at stake, these scholars speak their concerns. Moreover, it is consistent with the perspective explored here that one ponders also the risk that one is on the cusp of surrendering to someone else's definition of the problem. Yet this just *is* the conundrum of attempting to engage a speculative political ecology, where we seek to imagine ourselves entangled with entities and energies that do not necessarily speak to our concerns with them, and where "we" have no privileged part in the ecology, in the *oikos*. Our arts, artifices and manipulations are re-imagined. Here, although we are not necessarily in a new place, we are in new relations, and in a new mode of attentiveness. "Our" questions can still be asked, but with an attentiveness now to how they may curtail, sometimes brutally, the possibilities for other modes of appearance and for their renderings of the problem. Knowing when these limitations on what emerges are acceptable and when they are not becomes a task that, still, I would want to name "ethical", but that in the senses explored here, is also practical, technical and speculative.

196   *V. Bell*

Notes

1 Ecology must always be etho-ecology, since no thing appears without the relevance of the surroundings of its appearance remaining relevant: "there can be no relevant ecology without a correlate ethology, and … there is no ethology independent of a particular ecology" (Stengers, 2013: 187).
2 Here there is a resonance with the arguments of Paul Gilroy's *Between Camps*, where he used a contemporary reflection on Fanon and Adorno to call for a "planetary humanism"; we are, after all, just the third stone from the sun (2000: 327).
3 In the film, Justine lies naked bathed in the glow of the planet Melancholia as it approaches to destroy the earth. The overture to Wagner's *Tristan and Isolde* plays; its theme famously that of *liebestod*, or love/death. See the reading of Melancholia as romantic art by Curtis White (2012):

> *Liebestod* is Wagner's version of the romantic project to resolve or harmonize the opposition of the subjective and objective…. For Wagner this question becomes "how does the subjectivity of love resolve its opposition to the denial of love that is grim nature, social convention, and, ultimately, the explicitness of death (the finite)?" For Schelling this was *the* question of philosophy. He writes, "… the whole of theoretical philosophy has this problem only to solve, namely how the restriction becomes ideal…." Put in Wagnerian terms, the fundamental question of philosophy is how death (restriction) becomes love (the ideal).

4 See also my "Declining Performativity, or Ecologies of Concern: Elaborations on a Concept" (2012).

References

Bell, V. (2012). 'Declining performativity, or ecologies of concern: Elaborations on a concept'. *Theory, Culture & Society*, *29*(2), 107–123.

Connolly, W. (2013). *The fragility of things: Self-organizing processes, neoliberal fantasies and democratic activism.* Durham, NC: Duke University Press.

Deleuze, G. (1993). *The fold: Leibniz and the Baroque.* London: The Athlone Press.

Gilroy, P. (2000). *Between camps: Nations, cultures and the allure of race.* London: Penguin.

Jullien, F. (1999). *The propensity of things: Toward a history of efficacy in china.* New York, NY: Zone Books.

Stengers, I. (2005). The cosmopolitical proposal. In B. Latour & P. Weibel (Eds), *Making things public: Atmospheres of democracy* (pp. 994–1003). Cambridge, MA; London: MIT Press.

Stengers, I. (2008a). A constructivist reading of process and reality lecture. Available at: t3h.hfk-bremen.de/…/Stengers%20-%20Constructivist%20Reading.pdf.

Stengers, I. (2008b). A constructivist reading of process and reality. *Theory, Culture & Society*, *25*(4), 91–110.

Stengers, I. (2008c). History through the middle: Between macro and mesopolitics. Interview by B. Massumi, and E. Manning. www.senselab.ca/inflexions/volume_3/node_i3/PDF/Stengers_en_mesopolitique.pdf.

Stengers, I. (2010). The care of the possible. Interview by E. Bordeleau. (K. Ladd, Trans.). SCAPEGOAT: Architecture | Landscape | Political Economy, Issue 01 'Service' 2010, 12–17, 27.

Stengers, I. (2011a). Wondering about materialism. In L. Bryant, N. Srnicek, & G. Harman (Eds), *The speculative turn: Continental materialism and realism* (pp. 368–380). Prahran: re.press.

Stengers, I. (2011b). *Cosmopolitics II.* Minneapolis: University of Minnesota Press.

Stengers, I. (2012). Cosmopolitics: Learning to Think with Sciences, Peoples and Natures. Lecture at St Mary's University, Halifax, Canada. www.youtube.com/watch?v=1I0ipr61SI8, March 2012.

Stengers, I. (2013). Introductory notes on an ecology of practices. *Cultural Studies Review*, *11*(1), 183–196.

Stengers, I., & Whatmore, S. (2015). Seminar at Nottingham Contemporary.

White, C. (2012). Crazy wisdom: Von Trier's 'Melancholia' http://bigother.com/2012/02/24/crazy-wisdom-von-triers-melancholia/

Whitehead, A. N. (1978 [1929]). *Process and reality: An essay in cosmology.* Gifford Lectures of 1927–1928 (corrected ed.). (D. Griffin, & D. Sherburne, Eds). New York, NY: The Free Press.

13 Aesthetic experience, speculative thought and civilized life

Michael L. Thomas

Aesthetic Experience, in relation to works of art or nature, refers to forms of experience in which objects are judged in terms of their value. The subjective nature of value, and the inability to clearly define what separates the beautiful from the ugly, has led to the rejection of aesthetic categories as a solid basis for understanding anything at all. This is why the common phrase that there is an "aesthetic difference" between two judgments of an object is often interpreted to be a superficial one. The basis for this judgment lies in the fact that there is a tendency to prefer the rational over the sensual as the former gives us a firmer ground for justifying our position than the latter. Yet, sensual judgments and cues make a significant difference. For example, consulting firms frequently advise job candidates that how they are perceived by their potential employers plays as much a role on an interview as their particular skills and talents. One is encouraged to enhance their self-presentation through proper gestures, appropriate dress, and other persuasive features that may separate them from other applicants. Examples such as this demonstrate that while the rationalized, objective features of reality provide a sense of having a concrete basis for decisions and evaluation, they are not always the most certain or the most significant feature in perception and decision making. The sensual features of things draw our attention to them in ways that, while not clearly captured by rational principles, give them priority in experience.

In many cases, this sensual draw is the crucial criterion in evaluative judgment. The notion of "looking the part" for a job extends beyond manners of dress and self-presentation to the race, gender, and class of job candidates, which also play a role in choosing the "best fit." In many cases, discrimination based on these feature is not the result of deliberation, but rather on internalized prejudices that reflect themselves in judgments of "qualification". The dominant role of the sensual in these cases shows why it is necessary to take the aesthetic seriously in social theory. The problems that are usually labelled as social (as opposed to the political, economic, structural, etc.) refer to vague areas of experience that are seemingly impossible to address directly.

Drawing on his own theory of experience as feeling, Alfred North Whitehead develops two notions for articulating this aesthetic dimension of experience in theory and practice: Speculation and Civilization. Speculation is a process of

Aesthetic experience   199

developing novel concepts that enrich felt experience. In Whitehead's usage, speculation strives to produce concepts that resolve analytic dichotomies into distinctions, producing new relations in previous gaps in analysis that are felt as new aspects of an intensified encounter with reality. It also involves the development of general notions that orient how experience is valued. Civilization is a prime example of such a notion. The presentation of Civilization in *Adventures of Ideas* serves as a "lure" for evaluating our societies and ourselves in aesthetic terms. Civilization serves as a regulating ideal for evaluating modes of thought and practice based on their capacity to generate novelty. In this way, the connection between Aesthetic Experience, Speculation, and Civilization connects the notion of speculative thought with speculative forms of life In this chapter, I examine how the these notions establish a mode of thinking that orients individuals to attend to the relationality of experience and its qualitative enrichment. The aim of Whitehead's speculative philosophy is to align our forms of thinking with the active relational process at work in the order of the actual world. Embracing the aesthetic dimension of experience means orienting one's self to experience the richness of this process and, from this orientation, enhance the potential for novel forms of thought and living together.

Aesthetic experience

> The metaphysical doctrine, here expounded, finds the foundations of the world in the aesthetic experience, rather than – as with Kant – in the cognitive and conceptive experience.… The actual world is the outcome of the aesthetic order, and the aesthetic order is derived from the immanence of God.
>
> (Whitehead, 1996 [1926]: 104–105)

This passage from *Religion in the Making* reflects Whitehead's chief speculative proposition: the actual world owes its order and actuality to an ongoing process of aesthetic experience. The actual world is an ongoing process of novel moments of experience synthesizing the conditions of the past into a novel form. Within this process, actuality is the product of definiteness brought about by inclusion and exclusion of potential relations into a final unity. The unity is an aesthetic object insofar as the process of inclusion and exclusion is ultimately a process of valuation. Whitehead's discussion of Creativity in *Adventures of Ideas* (1966 [1933]: 179) argues that the initial situation (the primary phase of experience) is the "actual world" of the occasion. As felt, it serves as the ground of potentiality in need of actualization. The details discerned in experience function as passive objects derived from the feeling of the whole. The process of experiencing "actualizes" the potentiality of the world by creating a moment of experience that contributes to moments to come. This interplay serves as both the "form of unity of the Universe" and the unity of experience that ties together thought and life in Whitehead's system. The actual world owes its reality to the aesthetic process of giving form to felt content and actualizing that content into the world, contributing its value to the future.

200   *M. L. Thomas*

This process replicates itself in individual experience through the synthesis of sensual and conceptual abstractions into a perspective with respect to their importance. The locus of this organization is a contrast between vague sensation and clear immediate perception in each encounter with reality. For Whitehead, "The experience starts as that smelly feeling, and is developed by mentality into the feeling of that smell" (1967 [1933]: 246). Experience is a process organizing feelings through distinct categories of thought and normalized perception. This process synthesizes the world into a portrait that we view as our perspective.[1] This portrait is organized by foregrounding and backgrounding elements of the experience based on the interests of the subject having it.[2] The elements of the foreground are emphasized as important for experience, either for habitual purposes or the emergence of an issue in need of resolution, while other elements, which are negligible, are reduced to a background and eliminated from feeling. Perspectives are, thus, the product of aesthetic experience and the point of departure for aesthetic production. Like works of art, they initiate a process of sensual and conceptual activity that generates a sense of novelty, which alters our experience of the world around us.

Within this process, concepts play a problematic role. They reduce the effort of composing perspectives by organizing a familiar framework for encountering the world. This process is necessary since it is nearly impossible, and highly problematic, to sense every potential relationship in a moment of experience. Yet, this preselection reduces our attention to novel elements of experience and the possibilities they afford. Initially, emphasis on what is clearly and distinctly present fixes attention to a preselected range of elements in experience, limiting its intensity (the combination of its range and the varieties of entities included). Individuals, thus, have a consistent mode of viewing the world, but one that lacks variety and dulls perception.[3] Consequentially, this mode of experience reduces the ability to view novel possibilities. Concepts owe their clarity to having been identified in previously established relationships or by a familiar mode of seeing. While they were actual when originally identified, they are merely potential in the subsequent moments. Thus, by organizing our perspective in terms of these concepts, we run the risk of reducing our perspective to the familiar. Unless something shakes us from our habitual perceptive mode, the uniform orientation of our perspective reduces our capacity to sense subtle differences that would enrich experience or bring alternatives to light.

This function of concepts also plays a positive role in experience. Whitehead's notion that propositions are "lures for feeling" underscores how the concepts we entertain draw our attention to particular aspects of reality. Concepts and past experiences function as an index for present experience, bringing certain elements to relevance and reducing others to the background. Whitehead proposes his notion of speculative philosophy for this reason. The aim of speculation is to generate concepts that enrich experience by sensitizing individuals to more aspects of their environment. In this way, thought appears as an aesthetic process. It concretizes aspects of material reality in a form that reflects the individual's subjective experience producing an objective, value-laden perspective.

Speculative thought

Speculative thought is a trajectory of thinking that uses concepts to intensify experience and enrich our philosophical and theoretical analysis. Whitehead's speculative philosophy aims to avoid the "fallacy of misplaced concreteness", "neglecting the degree of abstraction involved when an actual entity is considered merely in so far as it exemplifies certain categories of thought" (Whitehead, 1985 [1929]: 52). In the same way that experience loses its liveliness through habitual modes of perception, intellectual inquiry can be stifled by the ease with which concepts can be used to stand in for elements of experience. In response to this risk, Whitehead's speculative philosophy aims to produce forms of thought that are consistent with the solidity and activity of the actual world.

Whitehead's speculative philosophy is consistent with the notion of speculation deployed by the pragmatists. As Savransky notes earlier in this volume, James's notion of thought indicates that Thoughts are felt. Thus, no account of thought that seeks to take experience seriously can presuppose a thinker as an "observer" in retreat from the flux of reality but must conceive of thinking as an element in the fact of experience. Thinking is always thinking with and in the midst of experience, being taken by an intellectual experience such that "the thought is itself the thinker, and psychology needs not look beyond". (James, 1957 [1890]: 401, in Savransky, this volume). Whitehead draws on James's statement in *Process and Reality*, noting that he "conceives the thought as a constituent operation in the creation of the occasional thinker" (1985 [1929]): 151). In contrast with the focus on experimentalism in the case of the pragmatists, Whitehead aims to present the world in a consistent and creative tension that promotes novel modes of thought. Maintaining this tension sustains aesthetic experience in the interest of producing creativity.

This aim of Whitehead's thought is already present in *The Concept of Nature* (2004 [1920]), where he attempts to rescue the experience of nature from an instance of the fallacy of misplaced concreteness, here termed the "bifurcation of nature". The bifurcation of nature occurs due to a conceptual distinction between "nature apprehended in awareness" and "nature which is the cause of awareness" (Whitehead, 2004 [1920]: 31), i.e. the aspects of nature which can be described in terms of their causal force (waves of light, DNA, subatomic particles), and secondary aspects of nature (colour, sound), which can be explained through these causes. This distinction between causal nature and nature as it is apprehended develops into a division between the experience of nature and nature itself. To counter this tendency, Whitehead argues that:

> For natural philosophy everything perceived is in nature. We may not pick and choose. For us the red glow of the sunset should be as much part of nature as are the molecules and electric waves by which men of science would explain the phenomenon. It is for natural philosophy to analyse how these various elements of nature are connected ... I conceive myself as adopting our immediate instinctive attitude towards perceptual knowledge

202   *M. L. Thomas*

which is only abandoned under the influence of theory. We are instinctively willing to believe that by due attention, more can be found in nature than that which is observed at first sight. But we will not be content with less.

(2004 [1920]: 29)

The justification for this common sense view of experience provides the impetus for an unfolding of the intimate relationship between the development of thought and the evolution of life. The response to the bifurcation is, initially, a consistent application of Whitehead's principle that thought about the actual world must be consistent with qualitative experience. By making this move, he reunifies scientific and ordinary observations of nature through a link between thought and perception. The argument that the sensation of redness and the elements of their transmission are on an equal plane, for example, reflects the lack of analytic division in our encounters with colour. It is not that colour or its constitutive elements have priority in explanation; each is mutually present to be perceived. Making this connection restores the sociality of nature, its intense relationality.

His second contention, that "by due attention, more can be found in nature than that which is observed at first sight", integrates his understanding of the aesthetic dimension of experience with the task of scientific inquiry. Scientific insight, obtained through extensive controlled observation, is a form of "due attention", which has its source in human perception in general. It should help us to "see" more in nature than what was experienced previously due to the sharpness of its instruments and strength of its framework. Thus, thought and perceptual experience become modes of sharpening our senses to discern more elements than have been previously experienced. The connection between thought and sense transfers the knowledge of natural relations to a *feeling* of sociality in nature. This sense of sociality becomes the ground for the pursuit of creativity through thought.

Whitehead's contention that we are "instinctively" willing to believe that there is more to be seen makes the enrichment of experience an element of the development of the human species. The connection between thought and perception tied together in Whitehead's notion of experience establishes intellectual inquiry as an innate drive towards discovery. The discernment of nature is an emotional, perhaps biological affair. This connection is made explicit later in *The Concept of Nature*, where Whitehead links the refinement of perception with the evolution of *life*:

Evolution in the complexity of life means an increase in the types of objects directly sensed. Delicacy of sense-apprehension means perceptions of objects as distinct entities which are mere subtle ideas to cruder sensibilities. The phrasing of music is a mere abstract subtlety to the unmusical; it is a direct sense-apprehension to the initiated.

Whitehead, 2004 [1920]: 163

The notion of "evolution in the complexity of life", takes on a dual sense that mirrors the connection between perception and life I have just raised. Whitehead refers, on the one hand, to the heightened ability to perceive the "indefinite number of objects which exist in nature" (162). Theoretical and philosophical insight are necessary to deepen the perception of reality by drawing attention to the distinct, yet unperceived, objects at work in its structure. Making these objects present for experience brings our perception of nature further in line with its own inherent complexity. On the other hand, this transition from "subtlety" to direct apprehension is part and parcel of the evolution of human beings. Whitehead's musical analogy shows how the perception of distinct entities underlying our experience of reality generates a greater *appreciation* of processes and elements involved in experience. We move from perceiving the world as Novices to a delicate understanding of the richness at work in the structure of nature and ourselves.[4] From this perspective, life evolves through the development of a richer web of connections between entities. This unification of the advance in complexity of knowledge and perception is central for Whitehead, as it establishes a trajectory for speculative philosophy: the production of creativity by provoking novel relations in experience.

The production of creativity of thought requires that thought proceed in the mode of aesthetic experience. The fallacy of misplaced concreteness presupposes a subject–object relationship captured in terms of a "knower", the individual having the experience, and an object to be "known", the elements of experience that have to be determined (Whitehead, 1967 [1933]: 175). In this relationship, the knowledge produced reigns over both subjective experience and the inherent qualities of the object, generating a conceptual view of it that has to mediate the two sides. For Whitehead, on the contrary, "the basis of experience is emotional" (176). The clear, distinct perceptions that form the foundation of scientific and philosophical knowledge are secondary to the feeling that leads the subject to pay attention to some object in the first place. To capture this emotional aspect, Whitehead argues that a moment of experience is best characterized as a process of "provocation" in which entities form relations by inducing a response from others. Initially, there is an immediate felt sense of experience characterized by "complexity, vagueness, and compulsive intensity" (ibid.). This vague experience is clarified into the mode of sense perception, "the triumph of abstraction in animal experience" (Whitehead, 1968 [1938]: 73), in which the actual world is organized into a recognizable order. This notion of experience aligns knowledge with aesthetic experience. Aesthetic encounters in nature and the museum owe their significance to the intense experience of feeling that destabilizes thought and reorients both perception and conceptual understanding. The subject and object form a relationship in which each are transformed through the rich texture of feeling that ties them together. Whitehead's presentation of experience as an aesthetic encounter makes the thinker an integral part of the world's transition, and her capacity for involvement depends on the degree to which thought is able to follow the processes at work in its structure. In this way thought should aim to intensify the sense of relatedness with others in experience and through it, participate actively in the creative process of the actual world.

204 *M. L. Thomas*

Speculative philosophy is creative to the extent that it uses abstractions to generate a "leap of the imagination" in order to see "what it does to thought, what it obliges one to do, what it renders important, and what it makes remain silent" (Stengers, 2014: 22). For Whitehead, theories use concepts (mental abstractions) to guide us to appreciate new aspects of experience. In his view, "the primary function of theories is as a lure for feeling, thereby providing immediacy of enjoyment and purpose" (Whitehead, 1985 [1929]: 184). For Whitehead, theories use concepts (mental abstractions) to guide us to appreciate new aspects of experience. In his view, "the primary function of theories is as a lure for feeling, thereby providing immediacy of enjoyment and purpose" (Whitehead, 1985 [1929]: 184).

Speculative philosophy takes advantage of this feature of abstractions by reconceptualizing concepts as tools for being affected and changing experience, generating systems that point beyond themselves, and encouraging further discovery. In Whitehead's system, it also leads to the production of evaluative ideals, such as Civilization, that orient the evaluation of reality for the production of creativity.

Civilized life

The notion of Civilization does not denote a particular "modernized" form of social organization, but a mode of thinking that reflects Whitehead's desire to centre thought and life on the production of creativity.[5] Whitehead's definition of civilization as involving "truth, beauty, adventure, art, and peace" (Whitehead, 1966 [1933]: 274) generates a mode of aesthetic evaluation of thought and life based on the capacity for individuals and communities to evolve through the production of intense experience. The first three aspects of Civilization: Truth, Beauty, and Art, establish the grounds for attending to the constructed nature of knowledge and its relation with, or resonance with the structure of reality. Through this ideal individuals and societies can be viewed as aesthetic objects.

Whitehead's proposition that: "in its broadest sense, art is civilization. For civilization is nothing other than the unrelenting aim at the major perfections of harmony" (1966 [1933]: 271) is a lure towards a qualitative evaluation of the form and contents of individual understanding and social structures. Art, as the "purposeful adaptation of Appearance to Reality" (1966 [1933]: 267), involves the use of representation (Truth) to invoke a harmony of contrasts that amplify the feeling of the whole in the individual (Beauty). The production of Truth is consistent with the presentation of speculative thought above. It refers to the construction of perspectives that represent reality in such a way that new contrasts become present. The notion of contrast here is essential to delineate what separates greater from lesser forms of truth. As Whitehead's notion of aesthetic experience indicates, the order of the world has an inherent beauty that is felt more or less clearly depending on our sensitivity to its provocations. It is not enough to present the world as harmonized. This configuration constitutes a "minor form of beauty" which may strike us as pretty, but lacks an interplay that

Aesthetic experience 205

provokes deep engagement (Whitehead, 1967 [1933]: 252). The "major form of beauty" produces intense contrasts such that "the parts contribute to the massive feeling of the whole and the whole contributes to the intensity of feeling of the parts" (ibid.). The variety must produce a harmony that generates new provocations for feeling that expand social relations, harmoniously evolving the complexity of life.

Art is the production of intense contrast though the awareness of a wider scope of experience and the deep levels of interaction that ground it. Theories are artistic insofar as they present the world in a way that alters the intensity of experience. Whitehead's critique of the fallacy of misplaced concreteness is, in essence, a critique of poor aesthetic practices. Such theories, through their specificity, may complete our portrait of the world, but fail to provoke a sense of relatedness. Speculative philosophy aims to provoke this sense by suspending the urge to act as knowers and opening ourselves to provocation. Speculative constructions like "hesitation" are essential as ways of creating a space for the inclusion of new entities in our understanding of reality and grasping the dual composition of knowledge and empirical relations.[6] Such contrasts, in their positive and negative aspects, continue to lure us towards new forms of social life.

The notions of Adventure and Peace shift the discussion to two additional modes of slowing down to evaluate the conditions of Civilization and the mentality required for its advancement. Adventure refers to the open-endedness of any attempt to construct civilization in the many fields that constitute society. We see this already in the notion of Art, which promotes a form of construction whose effects cannot be decided in advance. On the other hand, it also implies the necessity of experimentation to maintain the vividness of ideals.[7] Whitehead's examples of "great art" are described as great precisely because they continue to generate new meanings and interpretations of reality beyond the context that they immediately reference. The complexity of great works of art resides in the balance between the composition of the whole and the details of its parts, which maintain a certain tension between actuality and possibility. For Whitehead, "[Art] must create, so that in the experience of the beholder there appear Individuals as it were immortal by their appeal to the deep recesses of feeling" (1966 [1933]: 282).

The notion of Peace completes the portrait of Civilization insofar as it serves as a disposition and capacity for resilience in the face of the risks of Adventure, and a consideration of the presence of good and evil in any social configuration. This notion is the closest Whitehead comes to giving to a characterization of a speculative "way of life", but it is not presented as something that can be composed in advance. It "comes as a gift" and is "beyond control and purpose" (1966 [1933]: 285). It is generated through a particular feeling of the whole beyond the concerns of the individual self.[8] Like Adventure, Peace points beyond a superficial harmony characterized only by positivity. This naïve idealism is associated with "Youth" is an optimism isolated to the personal, meaning that it lacks a wide enough vision to see discord that lies beyond personal interest. Because civilizations are always incomplete and always

206   *M. L. Thomas*

include sites of discord, there is an element of Tragedy in any given instantiation. A failure to engage with the tragedy of civilization, its imperfections and exclusions, runs counter to the ability to extend ideas beyond the limitation of the few to the experience of the whole.

In the conclusion to his discussion of Adventure, Whitehead makes the claim that:

> [C]ivilization in its aim at fineness of feeling should so arrange its social relations, and the relations of its members to their natural environment, as to evoke into the experiences of its members Appearances dominated by the harmonies of forcefully enduring things.
>
> (1966 [1933]: 282)

We see in this quotation that the experience of the members of the community is arranged with reference to the lived relations with the environment and one another. The harmony aimed at through the production of thought and the organization of life forms the ground in which occasions of experience draw their inheritance. From this perspective, the goal of speculative theory to change the examination of the social is essential as it generates forms of intervention that have the capacity to find sites of social order that can be recomposed to enrich the experience of its members. A key problem is that the points of discord that inhibit the civilized impulse remain present, stunting the capacity for individuals to have a wider perception of the whole due to the seeming necessity to attend to the needs of the self. Whitehead does not offer a solution to this problem beyond gestures towards the feelings of positive and rich experience that should be produced, but this is precisely the point at which the constructive aspect of social theory should begin. Whitehead provokes us to explore how social norms and institutions contribute to the enrichment of individual experience by tying their own progress with the progress of others, both in power and marginalized.

Conclusion

The shift towards speculative thought and civilized life are emerging in current theoretical models that draw on the work of Alfred North Whitehead. Bruno Latour's (2008) understanding of "matters of concern" builds on Whitehead's idea of lures for feeling to examine how the deployment of theoretical concepts can reanimate a world that has become static in current modes of thought. Isabelle Stengers' "cosmopolitics" (2005) draws from the history of scientific practices as forms of discovery to develop a form of political action involving an "ecology of practices" that can be deployed for propositions to "emerge within the art of the event".[9] These proposals tend to centre on the necessity of including non-humans into felt experience as a way of developing inclusive forms of individual consciousness and political deliberation.

My position is that Whitehead's aesthetics of social life may be equally useful for developing modes of combating prejudice and structural discrimination.

Aesthetic experience 207

In the example in the introduction, prejudice persists due to a devaluation of lives of members of certain groups, which are reinforced by social inequality and, often times, "social facts". Speculation as a mode of thought combats this devaluation by rejecting the circular relationship between discriminatory facts and social practices. The characteristics gathered in the notion of Civilization provide a ground for the normative evaluation of practices based whether they produce, facilitate or, inhibit richer forms of sociality. At the heart of Speculation and Civilization is an insistence on the aesthetic quality of experience: that who and what we are is intimately tied with whether our contexts produce intensely social or anti-social forms of experience. The "black lives matter" movement in the US is one example how to combat the justification of social inequality through categories of bifurcated experience. Although debates continue over relationships between law enforcement and the African-American community, this movement has shifted the argument to the different ways in which the experience of fear in the police, for example, gains more weight than the fear produced by persistent harassment and fear of false arrest. Addressing this and other issues begins with a shift from the investigation of facts to the experiences that produce them in the pursuit of civilized life

Notes

1 The use of perspective in this sense ties it to the notion of what is seen, felt, touched, and tasted in experience. However, it has the additional element of the rational framework that identifies and organizes these elements. Thus, perspective is both a rational and a sensible object. Like a work of art, it combines ideas and feelings in a way that captures or alters our experience of the world around us.
2 Whitehead presents these two processes of "reduction to a background" and "raising to a foreground" as a means of dealing with the disharmony of the world, his term for our encounters with destruction and contradictions in reality. It is also the "habitual state of human experience, a vast undiscriminated, or dimly discriminated background, of low intensity, and a clear foreground" (1967 [1933]). This notion of intensity is important as it grounds experience on the richness of connections that enter into our conscious consideration. Its presence in ordinary experience gives us the first indication that the subjective valuation of experience is the byproduct of the presence of objective value intensity. In Jones (1998), this notion of value is essential to understanding Whitehead's metaphysics.
3 Dewey also marks this as a particular form of perception, "recognition", which he contrasts with genuine experience:

> Recognition is perception arrested before it has a chance to develop freely. In recognition there is a beginning of an act of perception. But this beginning is not allowed to serve the development of a full perception of the thing recognized. It is arrested at the point where it will serve some other purpose, as we recognize a man on the street in order to greet or to avoid him, not so as to see him for the sake of seeing what is there.
>
> (2005: 50)

4 The capacity to perceive this richness is what, for Whitehead, separates human beings from other organic living entities. He expresses this in a brief thought example following his musical analogy:

208　*M. L. Thomas*

For example, if we could imagine some lowly type of organic being thinking and aware of our thoughts, it would wonder at the abstract subtleties in which we indulge as we think of stones and bricks and drops of water and plants. It only knows of vague undifferentiated feelings in nature. It would consider us as given over to the play of excessively abstract intellects. But then if it could think, it would anticipate; and if it anticipated, it would soon perceive for itself.

(Whitehead, 1985 [1929]: 163)

5　The notion of civilization is very baffling. We all know what it means. It suggests a certain ideal for life on this earth, and this ideal concerns both the individualized human being and also societies of men. A man can be civilized, and a whole society can be civilized; although the senses are somewhat different in the two cases.

(Whitehead, 1966 [1933]: 273)

6　In other words, the knowledge-practices of the social sciences are always already involved in the shaping of the worlds they address, and in inducing processes of unification of its many disparate inhabitants. The question, thus, is rather one which concerns the modes of unification that scientific propositions entail – not whether knowledge circulates or not, but the question how it does so, in which manner, with what consequences, and in the name of what.

(Savransky, 2014: 13)

7　Thus in every civilization at its culmination we should find a large measure of realization of a certain type of perfection. This type will be complex and admit of variation of detail, this way or that. This culmination can maintain itself at its height so long as fresh experimentation within the type is possible. But then these minor variations are exhausted, one of two things must happen. Perhaps the society in question lacks imaginative force. Staleness then sets in. Repetition produces a gradual lowering of vivid appreciation. Convention dominates. A learned orthodoxy suppresses adventure.

(Whitehead, 1966 [1933]: 277)

8　Thus, Peace is the removal of inhibition and not its introduction. It results in a wider sweep of conscious interest. It enlarges the field of attention. Thus Peace is self-control at its widest – at the width where the "self" has been lost, and interest has been transferred to coordinations wider than personality. Here the real motive interests of the spirit are meant, and not the superficial play of discursive ideas.

(1966 [1933], 285)

9　See Vikki Bell in this volume.

References

Bryant, L. Srnicek, N., & Harman, G. (2001). Towards a speculative philosophy. In L. Bryant, N. Srnicek, & G. Harman (Eds), *The speculative turn: Continental materialism and realism* (pp. 1–18). Melbourne: Re.press.

Dewey, J. (2005). *Art as experience.* New York, NY: Perigree Trade.

Jones, J. (1998). *Intensity: An essay in Whiteheadian ontology,* Nashville: Vanderbilt University Press.

Latour, B. (2008). *What is the style of matters of concern.* Amsterdam: Van Gorcum.

Marx, K. (1992). *Capital: Volume 1: A critique of political economy.* (Ben Fowkes, Trans.). New York, NY: Penguin.

Savransky, M. (2014). In praise of hesitation: "Global" knowledge as a cosmopolitical adventure. In W. Keim, E. Çelik, C. Ersche, & V. Wöhrer (Eds.), *Global knowledge production in the social sciences* (pp. 237–250. Farnham: Ashgate.

Stengers, I. (2005). The cosmopolitical proposal. In Bruno Latour, & Peter Weibel (Eds.), *Making things public: Atmospheres of democracy* (pp. 994–1003). Cambridge: MIT Press.

Stengers, I. (2014). Thinking with Whitehead: The free and wild creation of concepts. Cambridge: Harvard.

Whitehead, A. N. (2004 [1920]). *The Concept of Nature.* New York: Prometheus Books.

Whitehead, A. N. (1996 [1926]). *Religion in the making.* New York, NY: Fordham UP.

Whitehead, A. N. (1985 [1929]). *Process and reality* (David Ray Griffin, & Donald W. Sherburne, Eds). New York: Free Press.

Whitehead, A. N. (1967 [1933]). *Adventures of ideas.* New York, NY: Free Press.

Whitehead, A. N. (1938). *Modes of thought.* New York, NY: Free Press.

14 The lure of the possible

On the function of speculative propositions[1]

Didier Debaise

Speculative philosophy finds itself, today, at the centre of a renewed interest. How it can be defined and its requirements understood have become the subject of intense debate. Strangely, the question of the function of speculative philosophy, of the effects that it has on experience, has remained less than clear. I would like to offer a possible definition of this function: *the intensification of an experience to its maximal point*. In order to outline this function, I will draw upon on two elements that come from Whitehead's last great work, *Modes of Thought*. When he gave the lectures on which this book is based, Whitehead was already well known for his work on logic and mathematics (notably in *Principia Mathematica*), on the philosophy of science (*The Concept of Nature* and *Science and the Modern World*), but most of all for his greatest enterprise, the construction of a cosmology (*Process and Reality*) that would come to captivate philosophers as diverse as J. Dewey (Dewey, 1937), M. Merleau-Ponty (Merleau-Ponty, 1995), J. Wahl (Wahl, 2005, 2010) and even G. Deleuze (Deleuze, 1992, 1994). From logic to cosmology, passing through the history of ideas and the philosophy of science, what was left to explore? To what new problems could this series of lectures that makes up *Modes Of Thought* respond? One of the questions that is stressed throughout this book, which expresses a new requirement absent or latent in previous works, is knowing what gives us a *sense of importance*. It is this question that I want to place at the centre of the speculative enterprise, for it seems to me to have found a new relevance today. It is a question which unfolds in Whitehead's lectures and gains its consistency through an intersection with a series of other questions: does this sense of importance refer to a particular faculty, a faculty of feeling, imagining or reasoning which projects its own interests and values onto the things of the world? Or, should importance be situated at the heart of existence itself, as if things are important by themselves, independently of the intentions of those who affirm such importance? Does importance vary from one era to another, undergoing historical fluctuations, which make us reject as outdated what another era believed to be crucial? In a nutshell: does this sense of importance refer to a human faculty or to a dimension that goes beyond the realm of the exclusively anthropological?

Before offering a definition, I will start with two contrasts that readily come to mind regarding importance. First of all, importance differs from matters-of-fact.

On the function of speculative propositions   211

Whitehead places both at the heart of all experience: "There are two contrasted ideas which seem inevitably to underlie all width of experience, one of them is the notion of importance, the sense of importance, the presupposition of importance. The other is the notion of matter-of-fact" (Whitehead, 1938: 5). Importance concerns the value of a thing, whereas facts designate brute existence. Such a notion of brute existence is a pure abstraction that comes from an act of simplification carried out by the intellect. What would a factual existence that is essentially, absolutely, without importance be like? Even if we found an example of such a fact, would we not make the possibility of such a fact a matter of importance? Would it not confirm or deny the importance of the hypothesis that is being tested? But we could say the same of the concept of importance. What would importance in itself *be*, independently of any situation, of any factual existence? Would it not immediately lose all value if it did not refer, in one way or another, to those beings that support it or make it important? The contrast between importance and matters-of-fact is not an opposition, it is the highlighting of distinct qualities of experience. Consequently: "There is no escape from sheer matter-of-fact. It is the basis of importance; and importance is important because of the inescapable character of matter-of-fact" (Whitehead, 1938: 5).

As a result, the notion of importance can be differentiated from another notion with which it is regularly confused: interest. When we say that something is interesting or of interest, are we not, ultimately, saying that it is important? In this sense, does it not have the same value as when we say it matters, that it has importance? Likewise, does the importance that we attribute to a thing not refer simply to the interest that we have in it? However, there is a clear and fundamental difference between these two notions: importance expresses the manner in which an event crystallizes what is at stake beyond its immediate existence *hic et nunc*. We say of a discovery or an invention that they are important when we wish to highlight the fact they have genuinely changed a situation in the world in which they take place. Whitehead is willing to take up this commonplace view and affirm that the importance of a historical event, for example, is proportional to the transformations that it produces in the course of history, beyond its own reality. Ultimately, if we extend this view then we are led to assert that importance is the expression of a "unity of the Universe" (Whitehead, 1938: 11). From the moment that a historical event has taken place, all the preceding events seem to converge, retrospectively; the historical event makes them adjust to a new era that has importance precisely because it is essentially a question of the course of the world in which the event is situated but which exceeds it. The notion of interest is not so broad, it relates to the particularity of an event, to its individuality. If we link what is conveyed by these two contrasts (importance and matters-of-fact/importance and interest), we arrive at the idea that *importance is this unity of the universe, always situated in an actual event.*

Whitehead provides a more technical definition: importance "is that aspect of feeling whereby a perspective is imposed upon the universe of things felt" (Whitehead, 1938: 15). This definition is somewhat obscure, and Whitehead limits himself to announcing it with looking to justify or develop it, as if the

212 *D. Debaise*

definition were self-evident and no other explanation was necessary. It is true that the terms used, notably those of feelings and perspectives, have been the subject of numerous analyses in other works. Whitehead dedicates a complete chapter to perspectives in *Modes of Thought*. Nevertheless, the speed with which this definition of importance is formulated is certainly not justified by the fact that its components have been dealt with elsewhere. I will take this definition as it is given in this passage, without overloading it with such interpretations. We find that the term "feeling" appears twice, giving the impression of a circular definition which starts with "feeling", with an aspect of "feeling", and ends up with feeling as a perspective on the world felt. However, this insistence on placing feeling at the heart of the definition has a direct and radical effect. Feeling takes the place of that which, when it comes to importance, is usually ascribed either to consciousness or intentionality. We can, therefore, infer that the importance of an event is not related to the consciousness that we may have of it, to the intentions that we project on to it, to the effects that we may foresee, or imagine we can deduce. Whitehead reiterates this point several times, leaving no doubt as to the reason why he gives such a place to feelings: "we put aside, and we direct attention, and we perform necessary functions without bestowing the emphasis of conscious attention" (Whitehead, 1938: 15); or again, "a feeling does not in itself involve consciousness"(Whitehead, 1978: 256). This does not mean that consciousness has no role in relation to importance, but it is neither its origin nor its basis. A sense of the importance of events, a manner of experiencing and feeling what matters (what is important), is prior to any consciousness. This sense of importance indicates a wider dimension than that expressed by consciousness; it can be found in the activity of living: "the sense of importance [...] is embedded in the very being of animal experience" (Whitehead, 1938: 12).

Propositional lures

However, this placing of importance within feelings, at a level prior to consciousness, leaves a critical question unanswered: how to intensify this sense of importance? If importance is uniquely "that aspect of feeling whereby a perspective is imposed upon the universe of things felt", then where does its increase and its gradation come from? How can events that were previously insignificant grow in importance or, similarly, lose importance after either a longer or shorter period of time? If, as Whitehead's suggests, there is a cosmological element to this definition, in that it concerns all feelings, then how can we explain the variations, intensifications, reductions or even the ranking of importance? This question of changes in importance is central to the task of defining the function of speculative thought. For, if importance is given once and for all, instantly, for each event, then speculative thought will have no purpose, except to state that there is importance, but now importance has become so widespread that it has lost all relevance. In this chapter, I am suggesting that the unique function of speculative philosophy is to make experience *matter*, to make it important, to intensify it to its maximum. It is, therefore, the increase in the

On the function of speculative propositions 213

importance of an experience that is of interest. Unfortunately, the definition of importance that Whitehead has given, in so far as it seeks to give a central role to feelings, does not help us at this point. It needs to be completed.

In *Process and Reality*, Whitehead dedicates an entire chapter to "propositions". The question of propositions, what characterizes them, what they require and their effects is one of the constants of the work of Whitehead at least from the time of *Principia Mathematica*. My aim is neither to trace the history of the concept of "proposition" in Whitehead's work, nor to establish any links between it and other philosophical positions that were in existence when Whitehead was writing. Nor will I compare Whitehead's "propositions" to other philosophical approaches, such as logic, epistemology or semiotics, which also try to grant propositions a fundamental status. My aim is more precise: to understand how there can be an intensification of experience. For, when he deals with "propositions" in *Process and Reality*, Whitehead presents certain elements that have the sense of such an intensification, as I will demonstrate shortly. A proposition is not a description of matters-of-fact, nor is it a representation, or a judgment, it is a *"lure for feeling"* (Whitehead, 1978: 184; see also, Stengers, 2011). The making of a proposition is, essentially, the luring of a multiplicity of feelings.

We should consider the term" lure" for a moment. Whitehead uses this in quite a particular sense, removing all negative connotations. In Whitehead's vocabulary, it certainly does not carry the idea of either an artifice that is designed to fool someone or an illusion that masks reality. For Whitehead, the term is resolutely neutral: a lure incites a change which can be either positive or negative, according to the circumstances; it entices someone, producing a diversion, modifying the course of an event by giving it a new direction. The situation is different for those who read Whitehead's texts in French, where the term "lure" carries the sense of a misleading appearance, of a bait designed to fool someone, of hidden motives. Thus, when Whitehead says of propositions that they are "lures for feeling", there is no criticism, no denunciation, intended by his use of this phrase. In this sense, it is imperative not to confuse propositions with judgments. Their functions complement each other but they are not identical. Thus, Whitehead is particularly virulent in his numerous attacks on those theories that try to make propositions particular instances of judgments. For example: "Unfortunately theories, under their name of 'propositions', have been handed over to logicians, who have countenanced the doctrine that their one function is to be judged as to their truth or falsehood" (Whitehead, 1978: 184). This attack on logic is only a pretext. The problem is much broader and relies upon an illegitimate belief according to which the primary function of a proposition is to be the vehicle for a judgment. This is not to deny completely this aspect of propositions, but to limit its relevance: "The doctrine here laid down is that [...] 'judgment' is a very rare component, and so is 'consciousness' " (Whitehead, 1978: 184).

In order to make this difference as telling as possible, Whitehead starkly summarizes, almost to the point of caricature, any conflation of propositions with judgments as being not only illegitimate, but also almost comical:

214   *D. Debaise*

The existence of imaginative literature should have warned logicians that their narrow doctrine is absurd. It is difficult to believe that all logicians as they read Hamlet's speech, "To be, or not to be: ..." commence by judging whether the initial proposition be true or false, and keep up the task of judgment throughout the whole thirtyfive lines. Surely, at some point in the reading, judgment is eclipsed by aesthetic delight.

(Whitehead, 1978: 184–185)

Although Hamlet's soliloquy is a purely theoretical series of statements, it has a function that clearly goes beyond its exclusively verbal expression: the capture of a multiplicity of feelings. When judgment is taken as operating in an overly narrow dimension, it loses the imaginative leap implied in the proposition. The feelings that are implied in the soliloquy might well be of different orders: aesthetic, moral, axiological and, in certain cases, even logical. But they run through the 35 verses of the judgment. These verses cannot be judged individually or through a series of judgments that would somehow reveal the true meaning of these feelings. Taken as a proposition, the soliloquy produces a clear and dramatic intensification of the feelings that they lure. These feeling aim at "value as elements in feeling" (Whitehead, 1978: 185). In this sense, it would be absurd to ask if the propositions uttered during Hamlet's soliloquy are true or false, as they have a completely different function: increasing the importance of the experience which is embodied in the feelings, and to which these feelings are attached.

Alternative worlds

The function of propositions is to produce an intensification of feelings. But a question still remains: how do they manage to do this? What exactly do propositions put into perspective that enables them to induce such an intensification of these feelings? To be precise, what is captured in these propositions, when they act as lures, so that these feelings now acquire a dimension that was previously unknown to them? Let us take a new example: The Battle of Waterloo.

This battle resulted in the defeat of Napoleon, and in a constitution of our actual world grounded upon that defeat. But the abstract notions, expressing the possibilities of another course of history which would have followed upon his victory, are relevant to the facts which actually happened. We may not think it of practical importance that imaginative historians should dwell upon such hypothetical alternatives. But we confess their relevance in thinking about them at all, even to the extent of dismissing them.

(Whitehead, 1978: 185)

Using the example of a battle to explicate a theory of propositions is not without certain dangers. Because it accentuates the idea of an irruption, of an event as a rupture that leads to a new epoch, this might seem to situate the concept of propositions in a predominantly anthropological framework. This example of a battle

On the function of speculative propositions   215

is both pertinent and risky. However, the way in which Whitehead presents this example, the elements that he musters, the terms that he uses, allow us to pinpoint the speculative dimensions of propositions that are required for the argument that I am making.

Propositions link actual feelings (subjects) and possible worlds (predicates). When he mentions the Battle of Waterloo, Whitehead introduces something very specific that forms one of the ongoing concerns of his theory of propositions and that is the central point of the question of intensification, according to the role that I want to give it in the framework of speculative propositions. He raises the idea that another "course of history was possible". This is neither a slogan nor a simple assertion that could be added to any interpretation of historical events – that things could have been otherwise. This insistence on another course resonates at the heart of an event. The question of another course of action, for either the event or for history, is an urgent one which is posed in each act which makes up the battle, at all its levels of its existence; in both the daunting possibility of defeat and the hesitations of the soldiers at the very moment that they take occur. Running through these hesitations, a multiplicity of possible worlds is attached to each act as it plays out: the French armies come out victorious; they are defeated; the coalition crumbles and a new equilibrium comes to light; the battle continues and carries on without any victory making sense. Without doubt, Whitehead only knew of Renouvier through the praise that William James had given him.[2] Nevertheless, the emphasis that Whitehead gives to envisaging other courses of history, taking account of events as they could have been, is not so different from a genre established by Renouvier in his book *Uchronie* (Renouvier, 1988). What is the function of these uchronies?[3] Are they not just abstract exercises, whose aim is to relativize events and remind us that history is not totally determined in the moment that it is made? Uchronies are much more substantial than this; they are not simply pedagogical or heuristic tools. They are the condition of what I have called the rise in importance, of intensification.

This point is key to the function of speculative thought, so there is a need to be more precise. If the outcome of the battle had always been written, if it followed a routine course which had been established once and for all, if it only actualized historical overdeterminations, then all the value of the event would dissipate, and with it our heritage. This would make the battle only one event in a linear sequence; it would miss out precisely what makes *this* occasion *that* historical moment where the creation of our actual world was played out. These possibilities dramatize, and thereby intensify, the defeat. However, it is important not to exaggerate the status of these possible worlds. They would only be pure, general, abstractions if their existence were not always local, situated in concrete events: the hesitation in *this* action; the worry felt at *that* moment; the bifurcations which come to be in *this* lack of action. Thus, of all the deeds, of all the actors, of all the actions, it is necessary to state that they are "a hybrid between pure potentialities and actualities" (Whitehead, 1978: 185–186). In this sense, speculative propositions require a milieu that gives them their consistency. They do not make decisions for the world; they articulate events differently. In order

216 *D. Debaise*

that the idea of another course of history can acquire any consistency, it must lure, or capture, the real worries, the effective feelings, which partially pre-exist them. These feelings are the feelings of the battle which develop in the memories of the participants, in literary works, in books written by historians as they depict its unfolding. This group of physical, aesthetic and imaginative feelings form the milieu of new propositions that persevere with regard to the battle. When the "imaginative historian", as described in Whitehead's example, meditates on these other courses of history, life is given to the possibilities that are attached to that historical occasion. The propositions that the historian develops, and to which he is closely tied, will gain in importance as they bring together the hesitations that accompanied this singular historical event. The importance of propositions is, therefore, related to the relevance of the articulations, beyond human intentions, that they produce. At this point, it is certainly legitimate to ask who judges this relevance. Where might we find the criteria which would allow us to say that one proposition is more relevant than another, and according to what perspective would we be able to evaluate the extent of the articulations which they entail? If, in reality, a plurality of possible worlds is formed in the course of the battle, if these possible worlds come to be confirmed or refuted by the histories that tell us of this battle, how can we establish any differences between them? Should we take them all as equal, as having the same level of existence, the same force and intensity? In the passage that I have cited, Whitehead gives us a way of responding: "This battle resulted in the defeat of Napoleon, and in a constitution of our actual world grounded upon that defeat" (Whitehead, 1978: 185). It is not in the battle itself that its importance can be found. This would be a rather uninspiring finding. Intensification carries all the hesitations that run through the battle, all the possibilities that animate it and which come to destabilize its grandeur. Ultimately, the relevance of a proposition is related to the constitution of our actual world. We cannot go beyond this. This "other course of history", these alternative worlds that are dramatized by the "imaginative historian" who develops such uchronies – these have no other function than making sense of our actual world, what it inherits, the fragility of the history from which our world is derived, the possibilities which continue to have a latent presence. These past conditionals, these "could have been", are focused on the constitution of our actual world, a world-in-the-making, with its hesitations, its latent bifurcations, its tendencies, which says nothing definitive beyond itself.

It is now possible to return to my initial definition of the function of speculative philosophy: the intensification of an experience to its maximal point. Importance is given. It belongs to all existence in so far as importance embodies a particular perspective on the universe that is expressed in each of the elements of the cosmological dimensions that it inherits. The ways of feeling, of connecting, of grasping, and the importance that these assume, are constitutive of nature itself. There are not primary qualities on one side and secondary qualities on the other. Rather, there are the specific articulations of each existent that are the affirmations of what matters here and now. But even if importance is

On the function of speculative propositions 217

everywhere, it is nevertheless up to speculative philosophy to intensify it, to give importance to all the dimensions that it requires. In a word, to establish its value. Even if this question has been posed in terms of a historical event, it is clearly not limited to the realm of history and its legacies, as it concerns our contemporary experience and the possibilities that animate it. The duty of speculative philosophy is to devise some tools that allow to increase all aspects of experience (physical, biological, technical or social) to their maximal importance. This is why speculative philosophy is inherently a moral and political activity whose maxim could be: "our action is moral if we have thereby safeguarded the importance of experience so far as it depends on that concrete instance in the world's history" (Whitehead, 1938: 20).

Notes

1 Translated by Michael Halewood.
2 James mainly praises Renouvier with regard to his position on "phenomenism". See the letters between James and Renouvier, published by Perry (Perry, Renouvier, & James, 1929), and, more generally, Jean Wahl's book *The Pluralist Philosophies of England and America* (Wahl, 1925).
3 Although the term "uchronie" is related to that of "utopia", it also has a significant difference. Uchronie involves the rewriting of history based on a change in a past event.

References

Deleuze, G. (1992). *The fold: Leibniz and the Baroque*. Minnesota: University of Minnesota Press.

Deleuze, G. (1994). *Difference and repetition*. New York, NY: Columbia University Press.

Dewey, J. (1937). Whitehead's philosophy. *Philosophical Review, 46*(2), 170–177.

Merleau-Ponty, M. (1995). *La nature: notes, cours du Collège de France*. Paris: Seuil.

Perry, R.-B., Renouvier, C., & James, W. (1929). Correspondance de Charles renouvier et de William James. *Revue de Métaphysique et de Morale, 36*(1), 1–35.

Renouvier, C. (1988). *Uchronie. Esquisse historique apocryphe du développement de la civilisation européenne tel qu'il n'a pas été, tel qu'il aurait pu être*. Paris: Fayard.

Stengers, I. (2011). *Thinking with Whitehead. A free and wild creation of concepts*. Cambridge, MA: Harvard University Press.

Wahl, J. (1925). *The pluralist philosophies of England and America*. London: The Open Court Company.

Wahl, J. (2005). *Les philosophies pluralistes d'Angleterre et d'Amérique*. Paris: Empêcheurs de penser en rond.

Wahl, J. (2010). *Vers le concret. Etudes d'histoire de la philosophie contemporaine, William James, Whitehead, Gabriel Marcel*. Paris: J. Vrin.

Whitehead, A. N. (1978 [1929]). *Process and reality: An essay in cosmology*. Gifford Lectures of 1927–1928 (corrected ed.). (D. Griffin, & D. Sherburne, Eds). New York, NY: The Free Press.

Whitehead, A. N. (1938). *Modes of thought*. Cambridge: Cambridge University Press.

Afterword
Thinking with outrageous propositions

Monica Greco

'It is always better to produce an interesting disease than a mediocre painting' (1988: 540): with this proposition, as with so many others from the lectures he delivered to patients at his Marienhöhe clinic in Baden-Baden between 1916 and 1919, Georg Groddeck rejoiced in provocation. In 1918 he had no qualms in naming the sanatorium's new house magazine *Satanarium*, in explicit homage to Hell as the only place where, it seemed to him, a man could scream his agony 'unimpeded, without shame or reserve' (1992: 15). Nor should we imagine that in invoking Hell he had in mind the metaphorical 'hell' of WWI – which some of his patients would have experienced first-hand – rather than a more literal Hell with the full complement of damning moral connotations. The hellish agonies that the *Satanarium* was to vent were first and foremost those of ordinary patients, whom Groddeck encouraged to experiment with regarding their illness as expiation for their criminal desires. They, the patients, might disagree with this or other similar pronouncements. But they must make an effort not to disagree. As he put it:

> You must make an effort to believe, you must silence all doubts in yourselves. It makes no sense to refute what I say through reasonable arguments. It is easy to find this or that false, but that is not the point of the exercise. You have come here to be helped. What I deliver is a remedy, a medication.
>
> (1987: 95)

In his medical version of a re-evaluation of all values, Groddeck thus staged a joyous obliviousness to the modern settlement, the one whereby disease and illness have become equally divorced from questions of aesthetic appreciation as from the metaphysics of evil and sin. His provocations playfully unhinged and reshuffled the customary relations between these conceptual frames, and in so doing they worked their healing magic. By all accounts, he was much loved and highly sought-after as a doctor, known for his 'astonishing success with patients suffering from chronic symptoms long since abandoned as non-curable by others' (M.C., 1951: 6).

The essays in this volume have addressed, in different ways, the question of how we might cultivate a speculative sensibility in our engagements with the

Afterword: thinking with outrageous propositions   219

empirical, and thereby also foster 'deep empiricism' (Stenner, 2008) in cultural and social research. Following Stengers, this sensibility has been described as defined by a concern with 'resisting a future that presents itself as probable or plausible', through practices designed to actively explore the 'unrealised potential of the present' and to summon latent (im)possibilities in the becoming of the world (Savransky, Wilkie and Rosengarten, this volume). In this concluding contribution I propose to think both with and through the 'maverick' Georg Groddeck in order to address a double challenge involved in this speculative task. On the one hand, this is the challenge of taking the (im)possible seriously. Often this will entail developing a mode of paying attention that might allow us to feel the latent (im)possibilities in propositions, in modes or life and practice, that have 'fared badly, thrown into the dustheap, neglected' (Whitehead, 1978: 259). To the extent that such propositions have already been dismissed, surpassed or denounced – whether retrospectively or preemptively – the speculative venture will thus demand that we associate with entities that may be epistemically weak and, for that reason, marginal. There is therefore an element of thinking 'against the grain' involved in a speculative ethos of research: not in the sense of thinking polemically or oppositionally, but in the sense of thinking against the inertia of thought, resisting the mental habits that unconsciously structure our judgment and channel our interest, which may include habits of reasonableness and critique. In this process of thinking against the grain we strive to ignore the multiple sedimented strata of all that might tempt us to be dismissive in the interest of caution – whether to preserve a sense of our own plausibility, safeguard a reputation, or build a career. We might then find ourselves in the penumbrae of liminal disciplinary locations, or drawn to the quagmires of 'liminal hotspots' (Greco & Stenner, 2017) – the wicked problems that can accrue from the solutions to mainstream ones, chronic symptoms of a way of life that have long-since been abandoned as incurable (or inevitable) by others. In reaching towards the improbable to activate new possibilities, the propositions we entertain may well involve a degree of inconvenience and may well appear objectionable, if taken at face value, on a variety of immediately reasonable grounds. If we do take this risk, it is in order to allow ourselves to stay with the improbable and the inconvenient, to prolong it into far-reaching implications that could only be obtained in conjunction with the imagination of a different world, so as to summon the possibility of such a world.

If this, on the one hand, is the challenge involved in speculative research, taking the risk of such an adventure, on the other hand, cannot mean throwing all caution to the wind. A different set of risks concerns the probability that this adventure may itself fare badly in a variety of ways, such that, as we craft propositions to summon the (im)possible, we must also strive to *take care of the possible* (Stengers, 2010). There are many aspects to this challenge but here – and with reference to the practice of cultural and social research – I want to attend specifically to the aspect that relates to thinking with 'outrageous' propositions. Propositions that may have been tolerable by virtue of being neglected can acquire an outrageous character when we propose to take them seriously. And

220   *M. Greco*

the challenge associated with this outrageous character concerns the extent to which it may hinder the proposition from becoming *interesting*, and thus detract from its capacity to lure, to bridge the way into novelty.

Indeed let me suggest that the speculative adventure may have about it something inherently *outrageous*: this word gifts us with an ambivalence that leads to the heart of the double challenge I have sought to describe so far. From the Latin *ultra*, in terms of its pure etymology it refers to 'what goes beyond', in any sense. Current meanings listed in the Oxford English Dictionary include 'wildly improbable' as well as 'very bold and unusual'. But historical usage also links *outrageous* explicitly to acts of violent excess, injury and affront, meanings further consolidated in the English language by the folk etymology of *out* + *rage*. An outrageous proposition, in this sense, would be one that provokes the outpouring of extreme anger, indignation and shock, with the probable effect of entrenching existing lines of difference and polemical contradiction, rather than opening them to new possibilities of relation. These meanings convey the sense in which, as we seek to articulate 'what goes beyond' the pivotal actualities of the present, as we seek to unhinge and reshuffle the registers through which we make sense of experience, there is a genuine potential for this operation to become destructive, and we should be mindful of this potential. One aspect of this problem is linked to what authors working on the dynamics of transition in political anthropology have addressed through the concept of the 'trickster', a marginal figure able to exploit the uncertainty and indeterminacy of liminal situations to 'institute a lasting reversal of roles and values' with the sole aim, however, of placing themselves at the centre and maximising their own power (Szakolczai, 2009: 155; see also Horvath, 1998, 2007; Horvath & Thomassen, 2008). In a different context, and in relation to the efficacy of her own interpretations, Isabelle Stengers has addressed this negative potential through what she calls the 'Leibnizian constraint': the idea that the statement of what one believes to be true should 'bear the responsibility not to hinder becoming: not to collide with established sentiments, so as to try to open them to what their established identity led them to refuse, combat, misunderstand' (2000: 15). In both cases we are warned about the dangers of following outrageous propositions – propositions whose lure is to offer a springboard for the imagination of different possible futures – at the expense of a *commonsense*, in what might become an unwitting pursuit of 'ignoble curiosities of the understanding' (Whitehead, 1962: 154).

The relevance of Groddeck to this problematic, as a case to think with, is multi-layered. On one level, we may describe his own practice as an instance of speculative experimentation with (im)possibilities, mobilising an array of lures for feeling, like other practices of healing have done since time immemorial and indeed continue to do. What appears distinctive about his practice, at least among those operating in the horizon of the modern settlement, is that from an initial position of established authority – he trained and later collaborated with Ernst Schweninger, the private physician of Otto von Bismarck, and members of the Emperor's family were among his own patients – Groddeck put outrageous propositions into play *as such*, that is, he took deliberate care to maintain their

Afterword: thinking with outrageous propositions 221

speculative character. Groddeck not only did not attempt to systematise and stabilise his lures into theoretical claims, but actively resisted doing so, in the same way as he actively refused to qualify himself as a scientist, at a time and in a context that would have been particularly conducive to him doing precisely that. Instead, he introduced himself as a 'wild analyst' before the Psychoanalytic Association at the Hague in 1920, prompting remarks that he had, in this and other ways, 'endangered the carefully earned esteem of psychoanalysts with his carefree behaviour' (Storfer, in Tytell, 1980: 93). In *The Ego and the Id*, where Freud credited Groddeck for inspiring him to use the term *Id* (the Latin equivalent of the German *Es*, which was Groddeck's preferred form), Freud attributed Groddeck's self-distancing from the 'rigours of pure science' to personal motives, and described it as a form of vanity (1984: 362). While there may be some truth in this characterisation, it fails to capture the sense in which Groddeck's gesture of refusal expressed a form of coherence with the obligations inherent in his practice first and foremost as a healer. While Freud was busy developing concepts – such as countertransference – designed to safeguard the objectivity of his method, Groddeck happily conceded that '[a] certain harmony of feeling on the animal level between doctor and patient is the fundamental basis of medical treatment, which is, in essence a *reciprocal* activity', adding that:

> [t]he term 'animal' is meant to indicate that this important factor in treatment has, to begin with, nothing to do with the knowledge and skill of the physician, but arises from the contact of two human worlds and from their *mutual human sympathy and antipathy*.
>
> (Groddeck, 1949: 46, my emphases)

This, for Groddeck, was the basis for insisting on the importance of physical contact in healing, and of massage as a form of psychotherapy in the treatment of organic disease. Both 'psychotherapy' and 'organic disease' are here to be taken literally (he wrote of them as such) and yet, to some extent, they are misnomers, in so far as he also never tired of pointing out their character as abstractions from the *Es*, the 'Universal Whole' that merely expresses itself in everything we are and do, including our concepts (1951: 72 and ff.). The possibility of healing, then, did not depend for Groddeck on the application of an objectively 'true' theory, a theory whose truth would be predicated on an operation of separation and distinction of the subject of knowledge from its object. It depended exactly on the opposite, that is, on the recognition of a fundamental continuity (not separation) that obtains between human beings and indeed the whole world at the level of experience, such that they can come to 'resonate' in sympathy, and thus act as lures for each other.[1] We might regard this fundamental continuity in experience – between doctor and patient, in this case – as the foundation of a *commonsense*, a shared form of thought and discourse that would reflect the multiplicity and indeterminacy, and thus the hesitations and the speculative tendency, that arise from the 'radically untidy' character of actual

222   *M. Greco*

experience itself (Whitehead, 1962: 157). We can see therefore that, while being biomedically trained, Groddeck had very good reasons for refusing to subject his propositions as a physician to the 'rigours of pure science' in so far as doing so would precisely have produced *rigidity*, compromising their capacity to communicate at the level of this *commonsense* in the most responsive and suggestive way possible.

In his practice, then, Groddeck put outrageous propositions into play, explicitly subordinating their truth-value to the value of their interest, of their capacity to effect a change of perspective in those whom he lured into resonating with them. He did this by making a home for such propositions at Marienhöhe, a medical clinic, where they formed, as he put it, part of his treatment. Alongside physical therapy mainly based on massage and diet, this treatment routinely included asking patients questions about the intention and purpose of their illness, regardless of the type of condition they suffered from, be it a broken limb, heart disease, or a tumour:

> it is my custom to ask a patient who has slipped and broken his arm: 'What was your idea in breaking your arm?' whereas if anyone is reported to have had recourse to morphia to get to sleep the night before, I ask him, 'How was it that the idea of morphine became so important yesterday that you had to make yourself sleepless in order to have an excuse for taking it?' So far I have never failed to get a useful reply to such questions and there is nothing extraordinary about that, for if we take the trouble to make the search we can always find both an inward and an outward cause for any event in life. In medicine the external cause has received so much attention – it is in some ways, of course, much the simpler to deal with or at least to name – that there can be no great harm if a few doctors here and there seem to exaggerate the importance of the neglected inward cause, and maintain as I do that man creates his own illnesses for definite purposes ...
>
> (1951: 81)

We are prompted to wonder about the system of relations that made the efficacy of this question – about the purpose illness served, and what a patient might want to obtain through their illness – so very different in the context of Marienhöhe from virtually any other context since then. It is significant, for example, that the question was asked *as part of the treatment*, and not as a condition of admittance into treatment. One hundred years later, however, we are so far from being able to feel the proposition expressed in Groddeck's question, that it seems superfluous to dwell on the details of such relations. Instead, we hear it muffled by the historicisation of the figure of Groddeck, through which any lure or challenge it might pose becomes qualified and tamed by the fact that, *as we know*, he was a maverick. His propositions might be excused and indulged, in the same movement by which we might be excused for not taking them seriously.

What might it mean, then, and moving now to a different plane of analysis, to take the (im)possibilities latent in Groddeck's propositions seriously, today?

Afterword: thinking with outrageous propositions 223

I have chosen this example because, as well as expressing so well the features of a speculative ethos and the risks it entails, it also resonates strongly and directly with a number of polemics that define the political context of contemporary healthcare, particularly in relation to the growing number of so-called contested illnesses and 'medically unexplained symptoms' (Greco, 2012). As a category of illness these are epistemically marginal and yet empirically prevalent; for the purpose of challenging our habits of thought they represent, I contend, an exemplary case of much broader relevance. It is in this context that Groddeck's propositions, if we take them seriously and at face value, sound distinctly *outrageous* in the negative sense of this term. They sound outrageous, that is, not in the sense that they might provoke curiosity and perhaps amusement, stimulating an effort of comprehension, a personal 'flight after the unattainable' (Whitehead, 1958: 65) that might effect a new perspective. They sound outrageous, rather, in the sense that they are likely to provoke outrage and polemical entrenchment – the familiar 'How *dare* you suggest that I have brought this on myself, that it is my fault! How *dare* you suggest that my illness is all in the mind, that it isn't real!'. Groddeck himself – in his lectures, delivered in the last two years of WWI – pointed to the conditions under which the type of questions he routinely asked of his patients would soon become outrageous in this way. He claimed that the medical profession had been irrevocably compromised by the Great War, in so far as doctors had been called upon to perform functions of policing (1988: 515). From then on, asking a patient 'What do you want to obtain with your illness?' would be associated with questioning the authenticity of the illness, and implicitly accusing the person of lying. For Groddeck, this had been a question to be asked of *every* patient and *every* type of illness. By contrast, within the modern settlement that strictly bifurcates 'external causes' from 'internal' ones (to use Groddeck's terminology), questions about the intentionality of illness, coupled with the attribution of a forensic function to any objective evidence of disease, are only asked as part of a process of *differentiating between* more or less authentic, more or less legitimate 'illnesses'. The potential *interest* of the question in relation to the possibility of effecting a change of perspective becomes unintelligible, pre-empted by the possibility of judgment, disqualification, and exclusion, while the question as such becomes for the ill person something to be actively avoided and resisted at all cost.

Notwithstanding the specific local genealogies of this predicament, it is one that now obtains generally, and ever more so, in so far as medicine is moving increasingly in the direction that Groddeck resisted. Rheumatologist Nortin Hadler (1996) captured the essence of this situation when he described it as a iatrogenic vortex whereby *if you have to prove you are ill, you can't get well*. Research by sociologists and anthropologists has amply illustrated how people with contested illnesses or 'unexplained symptoms', in their struggle to obtain legitimacy and to become a credible patient in the absence of a biomarker for their condition, become caught in a pragmatic paradox. On the one hand they will adopt rigidly biomedical idioms of explanation in their interactions with medical gatekeepers, 'resonating' with the constraints of those settings, as well

224 *M. Greco*

as in wider public forums (although, importantly, they might use other, richer idioms elsewhere, as in conversations with family or friends). At the same time, these strategies will tend to make them conspicuous in a psycho-behavioural rather than biomedical sense, as deliberately 'performing' – and therefore faking – their illness.[2] Conversely, in the presence of a biomedically recognised disease, as in the 'lifestyle diseases' that are now leading causes of death worldwide, the biomarker acts de facto as a guarantor of 'external' causality – the necessary and sufficient condition for access to the system, at least ideally – such that it appears superfluous and inappropriate to ask questions about intentionality and purpose in any therapeutically competent sense. This does not mean, however, that such questions are not asked in relation to these diseases, on the contrary: they proliferate in non-medical, political and public discourse, in the context of angry polemics where they are typically mobilised to apportion blame to (categories of) individuals. In both cases, we can fully appreciate how the proposition that 'man creates his own illnesses for definite purposes' might be one that anyone who is wary of stigmatising the sick, or blaming the victim, would want to steer clear of – hence the tendency for social scientists to align with mobilised patients in denouncing the outrageousness of anything that might suggest it. In simply rejecting the proposition as outrageous, however, they collude in reinforcing the bifurcated logic that renders it so, and they allow it to proliferate in conditions of enunciation that are not conducive to exploring it or qualifying in any constructive sense.

Groddeck's questions to his patients were challenging and outrageous already in his own time, but primarily from the perspective of a *commonsense* already informed by a bifurcated understanding of nature, which has consolidated more widely since then. It is only in the context of this bifurcation that an illness that is real in a biophysical sense must, in essence, be considered devoid of any spiritual, existential, moral or aesthetic value, and that any illusion to the contrary pertains to a subjective judgment that has no place in orienting a medical practice that claims its authority on the basis of scientific facts. We can now appreciate how, in the context of Marienhöhe, Groddeck did not so much shock his patients as *surprise* them, by authorising them – in the space he protected from the 'rigours of pure science' – to follow his lead in exploring and trusting a more primordial, 'animal' *commonsense*. This *commonsense* might be described as the sense that would experience illness as a totality of relations involving every other aspect of life, a sense made not of clear demarcations but of hesitant intuitions and wonderings about all these relations. Groddeck's outrageousness was to propose that such *commonsense* should be at the core of a therapeutic venture, rather than being admitted at best as an afterthought or an accessory. In pursuing this aim, Groddeck maintained, it was specifically important to avoid fostering '[t]he absurd superstitions about medical matters which one finds in all social classes, [and which] have become in their half-knowledge a general danger' (1949: 49). He also made it clear that such 'superstitions' typically had their origin in 'the mistakes of the expert' – among which he counted medical diagnostic practices – adding that such mistakes 'continue long after they have been

Afterword: thinking with outrageous propositions 225

recognised as such by experts; they are tough, inert masses and difficult to get rid off *[sic]*' (1977: 242).

Moving now towards a conclusion, what can we learn from thinking with Groddeck about the value and risks, more generally, of engaging with outrageous propositions in speculative research? The possibility of taking Groddeck seriously depends, as Foucault taught us (1969), on removing the filters that would prevent us from relating to his propositions as equal to our own, that is, as deserving of the same serious consideration. In Groddeck's case, this is the filter of historicisation that would have us regard and 'forgive' him as a maverick. Other filters are possible in relation to other propositions that similarly 'go beyond' what our habits of thought would allow us to take seriously. Once we remove such filters, the world appears full of outrageous propositions pointing to wondrous possibilities. One conclusion to be drawn here, therefore, concerns simply the importance of learning to recognise outrageous propositions that are good for the purpose of thinking with them, in relation to our problems.

Groddeck's propositions draw our attention precisely because, taken at face value, they are simultaneously so similar and yet so different from propositions that are ubiquitous, and that tend to cause outrage, today. We have learned to distrust the contemporary propositions, for good reasons; but Groddeck offers the opportunity of reading similar statements in the context of an entirely different system of relations, where they point to a completely different set of conclusions and surprising consequences. Taking the (im)possibilities latent in his propositions seriously thus means appreciating this contrast, which produces a hesitation where previously there might have been a knee-jerk reaction of dismissal. My particular example has illustrated how social scientists can often be outraged *by proxy*, and dismiss outrageous propositions in the name of siding with the underdog, against power; but in such hasty dismissals, as we have seen, they can reinforce the system of relations that has rendered a proposition offensive and injurious in the first place. Learning to hesitate would then mean that we gain a deeper insight into the contextual, situated impulse behind the need for such a dismissal; that we become aware of some of its potential unintended consequences; and that we become capable of entertaining the thought that, in a different system of relations, a given proposition might become interesting rather than offensive.

What we also learn from this example is that, while it is useful to think with outrageous propositions in order to reactivate latent (im)possibilities, we must take very great care in how we re-propose them. In this respect Groddeck is interesting specifically because of the explicit care he took in relation to the efficacy of his thought. He situated his statements in such a way that they could 'go beyond' and thus provoke surprise, but not outrage. While it is impossible to turn his strategy into a general prescription, it points to the importance, once again, of evaluating what doing this might mean in the context of relations within which we hope to intervene.

226 *M. Greco*

Notes

1 Groddeck's language in describing experience comes remarkably close that of White-head and William James. Indeed, when read alongside their work it ceases to seem so outlandish and becomes an exemplary instance of what Stenner (2011) calls their 'deep empiricism'. Consider for example this statement, from an essay entitled *The Part as Whole*:

> I assume … that the assertion 'I live' only expresses a small and superficial part of the total experience, 'I am lived by the It'. Every human happening depends on the It, yet no human thought or invention can ever lead us to the heart of its mystery, since none of us however learned, wise, lucky, or imaginative, can ever hope to jump out of his skin and view man's nature as a whole. At the same time, it is possible by close and careful observation of human behaviour – our own and other people's – to discover something about the It's modes of expression.
>
> (1951: 73)

2 See e.g. Dumit, 2000, 2006; Werner & Malterud, 2003; Bech-Risør, 2009; Barker, 2011. See Greco and Stenner (2017) for a discussion of this iatrogenic vortex as an illustration in the broader context of a theorisation of the dynamics of 'liminal hotspots'.

References

Barker, K. (2011). Listening to lyrica: Contested illnesses and pharmaceutical determinism. *Social Science and Medicine, 73*, 833–842.

Bech-Risør, M. (2009). Illness explanations among patients with medically unexplained symptoms: Different idioms for different contexts. *Health, 13*(5), 505–521.

Dumit, J. (2000). When explanations rest: 'Good enough' brain science and the new sociomedical disorders. In M. Lock, A. Young, & A. Cambrosio (Eds), *Living and working with the new medical technologies* (pp. 209–232). Cambridge: Cambridge University Press.

Dumit, J. (2006). Illnesses you have to fight to get: Facts as forces in uncertain, emergent illnesses. *Social Science and Medicine, 62*, 577–590.

Foucault, M. (1969). *The archaeology of knowledge*. London and New York: Routledge.

Freud, S. (1984). *On metapsychology: The theory of psychoanalysis*. London: Penguin Books.

Greco, M. (2012). The classification and nomenclature of 'medically unexplained symptoms': Conflict, performativity and critique. *Social Science and Medicine, 75*, 2362–2369.

Greco, M., & Stenner, P. (2017). Liminality and affectivity: Introducing liminal hotspots. Forthcoming in *Theory & Psychology*.

Groddeck, G. (1949). *Exploring the unconscious*. London: Vision Press.

Groddeck, G. (1951). *The world of man*. London: Vision Press.

Groddeck, G. (1977). *The meaning of illness – Selected psycho-analytic writings*. London: The Hogarth Press.

Groddeck, G. (1987). *Vorträge I*. Basel and Frankfurt-am-Main: Stroemfeld/Roter Stern.

Groddeck, G. (1988). *Vorträge II*. Basel and Frankfurt-am-Main: Stroemfeld/Roter Stern.

Groddeck, G. (1992). *Satanarium*. Basel and Frankfurt-am-Main: Stroemfeld/Roter Stern.

Horvath, A. (1998). Tricking into the position of the outcast: A case study in the emergence and effects of communist power. *Political Psychology, 19*(3), 331–347.

Afterword: thinking with outrageous propositions 227

Horvath, A. (2007). The trickster motive in Renaissance political thought. *Philosophia*, *52*(1–2), 95–111.

Horvath, A., & Thomassen, B. (2008). Mimetic errors in liminal schismogenesis: On the political anthropology of the trickster. *International Political Anthropology*, *1*(1), 3–24.

M.C. (1951). Georg Walther Groddeck, 1866–1934. Biographical introduction to Groddeck, G. *The World of Man*. London: Vision Press.

Stengers, I. (2000). *The invention of modern science*. Minneapolis and London: University of Minnesota Press.

Stengers, I. (2010). The care of the possible. *SCAPEGOAT: Architecture | Landscape | Political Economy*, Issue 01, 12–17, 27.

Stenner, P. (2008). A. N. Whitehead and subjectivity. *Subjectivity*, *22*, 90–109.

Stenner, P. (2011). James and Whitehead: Assemblage and systematization of a deeply empiricist mosaic philosophy. *European Journal of Pragmatism and American Philosophy*, *3*(1), 101–130.

Szakolczai, A. (2009). Liminality and experience: Structuring transitory situations and transformative events. *International Political Anthropology*, *2*(1), 141–172.

Tytell, P. (1980). Un précurseur des fictions théoriques. *L'Arc*, 78, 92–103.

Werner, A., & Malterud, K. (2003). It is hard work behaving as a credible patient: Encounters between women with chronic pain and their doctors. *Social Science and Medicine*, *57*, 1409–1419.

Whitehead, A. N. (1958). *The function of reason*. Boston: Beacon Press.

Whitehead, A. N. (1962). *The aims of education*. London: Ernest Benn Limited.

Whitehead, A. N. (1978). *Process and reality*. New York: The Free Press.

Index

Page numbers in **bold** denote figures.

2Sweet2Kill 165, **169**, 170, **173**, 176–7

Abrams, M. 121
abstract 53, 120–1, 155, 214; abstract 53;
    conceptual basis 102; exercises 215;
    future 12; imagination 54; principles 29;
    reflection 39; speculation 37; subtleties
    202, 207n4; thought 10
abstractions 22, 52–3, 102, 121, 184, 187,
    200–1, 203, 221; mental 204; pure 211,
    215; universal 109n2
accidental 101; shooting 178n9
accidents, fatal 173
actuality/actualities 92, 199, 205, 215; of
    healthcare provision 93; particular 12,
    54; present 7, 220; stubbornness of 32
Adam, B. 24
Adkins, L. 13, 114, 126, 133, 141, 143n3
aesthetic 9, 13, 214; appreciation 218;
    delight 33; encounters 203; ethico-
    aesthetic event 114; evaluation 204;
    feelings 216; order 199; practices 205;
    process 200; qualities 155; rejection of
    198; task 185; value 224
aesthetic experience 185, 200–1, 203–4;
    dimension of 198–9, 202; quality of 207
aesthetics 33, 136, 185; of social life 206
alternative 12, 67, 78; approaches and
    sensibilities 2, 117; art practices 136;
    conceptual personae 115;
    epistemologies of Others 192;
    expression 55; futures 8, 10, 32, 35;
    126–7, 184; to identification 155; mode
    of exchange 141; mode of relating to the
    archive 114; paths of thinking 40;
    patterns of contrast 31; questions 13;
    reality 130; sense of the speculative 7;

stances towards sociological data 123;
    style of exchange 131; understandings
    of the speculative 24; version of
    creativity 89; way of conceptualising 9;
    ways of living 133; worlds 214, 216
Amazon 132, 137, 143n6; patent for
    speculative shipping 141–2; shipping
    assemblage 115; speculative
    (anticipatory) shipping 114, 130–1, 133,
    135–6, 139, 143n3
Amoore, L. 6
Anthropocene 1
anthropologists 118–20, 162n2, 223
anti-intellectualism 27, 39
anti-speculative 78; philosophy 27
anticipate(d) 6–8, 33, 77, 133, 207n4;
    death 158; defamiliarizing of the
    everyday 118; goal 42; unanticipated
    interference 115
anticipation 1, 4, 143n3; of the future 2;
    practices of 7, 25
anticipatory 147; shipping 114, 132, 135,
    143n3
archived data 114, 117
Arendt, H. 10, 23, 40–4, 48–9, 49n3, 49n5,
    50n7, 50n8, 50n9, 50n11, 50n15
attractors 158–9
Atwood, M. 8
Auerbach, J.D. 76
Australian 70, 104–6; Government 2015
    Intergenerational Report 41, 49n4;
    Research Council 39, 128n10; settlers
    107

Baker, T. 3
Bao, P. 87, 89
Bazalgette, L. 122

Beck, U. 23
Bergson, H. 4, 7, 9
biomedical 73, 224; commercial invention and innovation 85; futures 93; HIV research field 80; idioms of explanation 223; training 222
brainstorm 85–6, 89, 91; events 90, 94; process 88
brainstorming 70, 87–90, 94; event 91–3
Britain 114, 118–21; post-war austerity 122
British 120; population wartime morale 119; Telecom Phone Book online 137
Brown, N. 24
Bryan, D. 9, 98, 108n1

Cairns, G. 76
capitalism 61, 102; analysing 60; commodity form 100; contemporary 59, 132, 192; disembedded structures 101; late 21, 88
Casey, E. 119–21
Center for Interdisciplinary Research (ZiF) 158, 162n2
civilization 27, 147, 163, 183, 185, 198–9, 204–7, 208n5, 208n7
civilized 72, 208n5; life 204, 206–7; routines 172
climate change 1, 67, 193
Coleman, R. 10, 114–15, 131
commodity/commodities 99, 101, 109n2, 143n6; exchange 103; value 100, 102
communication technologies 88, 136
competitive 101, 115, 163
conceptual 1, 218; abstractions 200; basis for calculating value 102; contrasts 10; creation 167; distinction 201; personae 115; product of speculative research 45; research 46; tools 2, 4–5; understanding 203
conceptualization of community 134; of creativity 88
conceptualize/conceptualize(d) 3, 9, 102, 167, 204
Connolly, B. 105
Connolly, W. 7, 10, 105, 185, 193–5
constraint 6, 14, 24; in design practices 90; on the event of the brainstorm 91; on imagination 55; newly imposed 188; of the project 139; on thinking 58; on thought 53, 62
constructivism 3; constructivist approach 113
contributory action 177–8

Correspondents 122, 124
cosmopolitical spaces 50n9
cosmopolitics 50n9, 78, 185, 187, 190–3, 206
creating idiotic speculators 146, 161
creative 26, 32, 87–8, 194; alternatives to explore 7; attention 31; capacity 142; dynamics of change 12; experimentation 5; fabulation 165; potential 99; practices 94; process 203; resistance 147; sensibility 6; solutions 108; speculative philosophy 204; tension 201; thinking 45–7, 49; thought 8, 10, 36
creative of the future 8, 10, 26, 36; alternative future 8, 32, 35, 126–7
creativity 32, 68, 87, 90–3, 94n3, 94n5, 130–1, 135, 142, 146, 199; emphasis in education 88; ontological 89; political 194; production of 201, 203–4; pursuit through thought 202
curtail(ed) 78; possibilities 195; speculation 45
curtailment 45; political 50n13

death 19, 125, 168–9, 171, 175–6, 178n8, 196n3; anticipated 158; causes of 224; pre-planned 155; threat of 185
Debaise, D. 9–10, 27, 165, 185–6
Deleuze, G. 7, 9–10, 49n5, 68, 115, 131, 142, 146, 165–6, 168–70, 178n5, 178n6, 184, 190, 210
Dever, M. 128n8
Deville, J. 10, 69–70, 105, 143n7
Dewey, J. 9, 23, 26–33, 35, 41, 167, 177, 207n3, 210
diary 120, 123; data 126; keeping 119, 124
Diprose, R. 10, 22–3, 50n7, 50n13
disaster 159, 161; environmental 1; experts 147, 161n2; generating 5; non-expert responses to 115; prevention 3; social 170
disease 218, 222, 224; cardiovascular 85; management technology 86, 90; objective evidence 223; organic 221; of philosophy 62
disembedded 107; structures 101
dispositifs 113
dissymmetry 77
Dunne, A. 9, 94n1, 133–4

ecological 7; futures 25
ecology 147, 196n1; political 164, 189, 191–2, 195; of practices 68, 190, 206

Index

education 3–4, 49, 86–8, 113; budget cuts 41; community 75; higher 23, 120; philosophy of 50n15
educational 168; institutions 49, 140
embedded 45, 101, 107, 212; fabric of experience 23, 42
emergency provision 115, 147, 161
empiricism 40–1, 56, 130–1, 135, 141–2; deep 10, 219, 226n1; radical 27, 30, 33, 166; rigid 54
engagements 2, 13, 48, 86, 113, 115, 131, 133, 135, 141, 166–8, 218; civilized 172; collective 49, 164; constraint upon 6; deep 205; ethnographic 85, 90, 92; interdisciplinary 94n1; interested 75; with issues of violence 165; political 177; with the possible 139; with potential futures 137; relational 77; situated 5, 10, 12; speculative 116; sustained 9, 185; user 88
environment 35, 47, 189–90, 200, 206; artificial and isolated 115; built 9, 94n5; changes in 31; infecting 36; for speculation 162; supportive for women 75
environmental 130; disasters 1; forecasting 3, 5–6; politics 161
Ericson, R. 3, 5
etho-ecological 189, 191
etho-ecology 196n1
ethnologists 72, 80
ethos 89, 188–9; speculative 219, 223
experimentation 2, 5, 10–12, 31, 33, 117, 205; animal 189; fresh 208n7; intellectual 29, 32; legitimacy of 188; scientific 190; speculative 30, 34–5, 114, 220; strategic role 194
extraterrestrial 93; implant 84, 90

Faste, H. 87, 89
Fem-PrEP 73–7, 80, 81n3
female 73–4; employment 122; research subjects 80; *see also* women
fold 42, 93, 184;
folding 185; empirical concreteness of social change 167; futures 184; time 4, 114; *see also* enfolded; refolding; unfolding
forecasting 3–4, 6, 23, 40, 98; model 132, 136
foreign 101; actors 102; relations 103
Friedman, K. 136, 138
future/futures 1, 3–4, 6, 8, 12–13, 22–3, 37, 40, 42, 61, 117, 130–1, 135, 138, 192;

after the now 123; alternative 10, 32, 35, 126–7; becoming of value 107; calculable 67; connection 104–5; contributing value to 199; creative of 26, 36; different 183, 186; disasters 147; entering 2, 5, 7; folding, refolding, unfolding 184; gap between past and future 43; healthcare technology 85, 93; hypothetical 94n4; immersion in 195; opening 46; patterns 185; perceptible 114; potentiality 133, 136–7; predictions 41; probability 70; resisting 219; speculation 103; thinking for 25; threat to 21; transition into 142; uncertain 98, 141
future possibilities 1, 4–5, 7, 13–14, 114, 127, 132–3, 178, 184–5, 220; closed down 143n3
futurity 2–3, 5, 7, 130; indeterminate 42

Garfinkel, H. 115, 145–7
genealogies 9, 223; of brainstorming 87
global 1, 7; capitalism 21; conflicts 169; consumer markets 85; economic crisis 5; health 12; healthcare delivery 87; living with HIV 81n2; microprocessor markets 93
globalisation 3
Goot, M. 119–20, 128n6
government 49, 113; Australian 39, 49n4; institutions 43, 106; neoliberal rationality 3; policies 41; regulation 45
governmental 3, 88
grooves 149; of thought 58

Hacking, I. 4, 25
Hagener 104–7
Halewood, M. 9–10, 23–4, 49n2, 58, 93, 94n3, 109n4, 146–8, 217n1
Haraway, D. 10, 52, 60–1, 142, 187–8
Harman, G. 9, 52
Harrison, R. 118, 127n3
Heidegger, M. 40, 49n5, 165–6, 171
Heider, F. 156
Herodotus 101
Highmore, B. 118, 121, 128n11
HIV 74, 76, 81n7; biomedical research field 80; infection 73, 81n2, 81n3; prevention 75, 78, 81
Hubble, N. 119–22
human excess 22, 24

illness 218, 222–3; faking 224
immanent 28, 131; modes of existence 115; understanding 184

Index 231

impossible/(im)possibles 29, 56, 151, 198, 200, 225; cracking open 186; creating 8; futures unfold 184; lured by 183; politics of 5; taken seriously 13, 219; unexpected eruptions of 7
infrastructures 6, 136; speculative 146
Ingham, G. 99, 102–4, 107–8, 109n3
innovation 3, 23, 39, 41–3, 45–8, 85, 87–8
innovative 23, 48, 70; thinking 44
inspiration 13, 23, 42–3, 45–8, 185, 190
Institute of Economic and Social Research 119
Intergenerational Report (Australian Government 2015) 41, 49n4
International Visual Sociology Association (IVSA) 138
Internet 136; based retailing 115; sourced photographs 86
intervention 2, 70, 80, 114, 117–18, 134, 146, 188, 195, 206; performative 137; playful and non-violent 177; sociological 167; speculative 135; uncoded 115; user-reliant 81; warranted 73
invention 2–3, 40, 53, 89, 117, 163, 178n1, 193, 211, 226n1; commercial biomedical 85; of new methods 127; of possible worlds 186; re-invention 11; technical 9
iPrEX trial 73, 75

Jahoda, M. 120–1
James, W. 9–10, 23, 26–30, 32–6, 41, 166–7, 193, 201, 215, 217n2, 226n1
Jeffery, T. 119, 128n6
judgements 6, 24n1, 33, 68

Kellermann, A.L. 173, 178n9
knowledge 1–2, 4, 28–30, 71, 85–7, 90, 135, 152, 158, 192, 203, 221; acquisition 42; advancement of 188; constructed nature 204; dual composition 205; half 224; human 34; insufficient 191; making 12, 31; of natural relations 202; objective 6; objects of 5; perceptual 201; production 40, 50n9, 88, 113; practices of the social sciences 208n6; pursuit of 43; reproducing 47; situated 60–1; specialist 46
Koenig, L. 74, 80, 81n4

language 2, 50n6, 55, 183–4, 226n1; English 220; ideality of 42; institution of

45; of sensation 166; shared 104; technical 36
Lapavitsas, C. 100–4, 107–8, 109n3
Lapoujade, D. 30
Latour, B. 1, 4, 77, 177, 206
Law, J. 13, 36, 86–7, 113, 131, 135, 142, 143n4
Leibnizian Constraint, the 13, 220
Levinas, E. 46, 48
Lezaun, J. 88, 146
limitations 22, 45, 79, 89, 91, 94, 145, 161, 195, 206
Lindsey, R. 121–2
lures 54, 67, 80, 98, 183, 213–14, 220–2; into adventure of thought 187, 199; computer 146; of the 'either-or' 177; experience 26; for feeling 33, 56, 70, 99, 103, 141, 200, 204, 206, 216; monetary 104–5; of peace 69; of pearl shells 106, 108; of possible futures 2, 5; propositional 212; to speculation 71, 78; speculative 12, 68, 184; towards new forms of social life 205; of violence and conflict 172
Lury, C. 13, 113, 131, 141

Mack, N. 74–5
Madge, C. 118–19, 127n3
mail art 114–15, 130–1, 136–8, 141–2, 143n5
Malinowski, B. 118, 120
manufacturer 171; drug 81n1; multinational semiconductor 85; of weapons 170
marginal 219–20; epistemically 223
marginalized 206; traditions 22
Marres, N.S. 177
Marx, K. 100–1, 109n3
Marxism 70
Marxist 100, 102, 109n2, 109n3
Mass-Observation 124, 126–7, 127n4, 127n5, 128n6, 128n9, 128n11; Archive (MOA) 114, 119, 121, 123; Limited 119, 122; project (MOP) 114, 117–18, 120–1, 127l, 127n2; materials 122–3
Meillassoux, Q. 9, 52
Menger, C. 99, 108
Merleau-Ponty, M. 10, 23, 40–6, 49n3, 49n5, 50n6, 210
Michael, M. 4, 9–10, 89, 92, 94n1, 98, 115, 131, 133, 141, 145
Ministry of Information 119
Mitchell, A.J. 165
Mol, A. 86–7

232 Index

monetary 98; exchange 102; forms 107; lures 104; objects 99, 103–7; origins 103, 106, 108; pre-monetary community 101; theory 100, 102; value 109n3
money 21, 70, 101, 104, 106–8, 108n1, 109n5; credit 109n3; emergence of 99–100, 102–3; make 24n1; role in contemporary life 98; as universal abstraction 109n2; valorisation through 132; waste of 39, 49n1; *see also* monetary, origins of money

Nancy, J.-L. 23, 41, 46
necessary evil 22–3
Nietzsche 40, 193
non-directedness 151–2
non-representational 13; dimensions of research methods 113
non-violent 116, 164, 170, 177

obscurantism 6, 79
observer 6, 28, 131, 177, 201
Observers 114, 118–20, 122, 124, 127n3; Mass-Observer 124, **125**; *see also* Correspondents
O'Connell, R. 122–3
oikos 189, 192, 195
oppositional strife 163–4, 168, 173, 177; strive 163, 177
origins of money 12, 69–70, 99–100, 107–8
Osborn, A.F. 87–9, 93
outrageous propositions 219–20, 222, 224–5

Papua New Guinea 70, 104, 106–7
Parisi, L. 26, 115, 147, 185
patterns 4, 7, 92; of contrast 31; emotional 54; of feelings 91; of future 185; of local exchange 106; of low contraception 76; pluralistic 58–9; of the present 67; refold 184; of thinking 14; traditional 171
philosophers 4, 7, 29, 39, 57, 59, 103, 145, 163, 166, 210
philosophy 11, 13, 26, 29, 43, 46, 50n8, 145–6, 196n3; anti-speculative 27; continental 9; disease of 62; of education 50n15; inventive 88; of life *tout court* 28; modern 39; natural 201; process 194; speculative 23, 40–1, 45, 53, 56–7, 99, 104, 134, 199–201, 203–5, 210, 212, 216–17; of science 9, 210; supposed anthropocentrism 49n5

Pignarre, P. 22, 5960
Plato 46–7, 79
Plummer, K. 121, 124
pluralism 23, 36, 41
pluralist 78; approach to inquiry 81; politics 68; research 69
pluralistic 37; pattern 58–9; universe 36
plurality 69, 78; of possible worlds 216; of the present 8
polemical: contradiction 220; entrenchment 223; thinking 219
political 1, 7, 12–13, 26, 43, 45, 48–9, 50n7, 50n9, 185, 198, 224; action 206; activity 217; agency 39, 41, 46; anthropology 220; context of healthcare 223; creativity 194; curtailment of agency 50n13; ecology 164, 189, 191–2, 195; economy 22; engagement 166, 177; futures 25; intent 67; movements 193; ontology 42, 44; practice 68; role of the speculative 23; voices 145, 188
politics 3–5, 29, 39, 41–2, 44–5, 68, 78, 163; as-usual 185; environmental 161; models of 189; of speculation 23; of war 164
Pollen, A. 119–20, 127n2
Porcelain Pistol 165, 171, 176
possibility 6, 22, 26, 32, 40, 44, 69, 71, 78–9, 80, 116, 133, 135, 158, 170, 205, 211, 219, 225; of alternative stances 123, 153; create 30; of defeat 215; effecting change of perspective 223; engage in speculative research 178; of engaging differences 163; envision 54; of futures 2, 58; of healing 221; imagining 55; of monetary exchange 102; of mutilation and killing 172; open to 42; of opening novel spaces 165; of recovery 93; speculative 68; trusting in 37; of understanding 127
possible, the 6–7, 11, 27, 113, 162; affirm 135; care of 193, 219; destruction 172; engagement with 139; exploring 13; freedom of 32; presence of different interests 76; trusting 31
possible futures 1, 5, 7, 13–14, 114, 126–7, 133, 178, 184–6, 220
potentiality 40, 43–4, 49, 54, 90, 114, 130–1, 133, 135–7, 142, 199
PPK 170–1; porcelain **167**, 171–2, 177; Walther 116, 165, 173
prediction 4, 40–1, 131, 136, 142; models 132; science of 44, 50n11
PrEP (pre-exposure prophylaxis) 73–4;

Index 233

licensing of 81n1; trials 75, 77, 81n4, 81n6
present 2–5, 7–8, 22, 25–6, 42, 46, 90–1, 93, 117–18, 123, 133, 142, 143n3, 164–5, 170, 175, 183–4, 186, 189, 200–2, 204; active 114; actualities 220; altered configuration of 192; concern to inquire 69; connect to 98; creativity 87; disrupted 43; ever-changing 124; extension of the 37, 147; formulas 28; fugitive 12; haunt the 108; impasse of the 1, 11; (im)possibilities latent 10, 13; inherited 21; making 187, 203; not present 115; opportunities 85; patterns 67; points of discord remain 206; under capitalism 100–1; unfinished 23, 30–2, 35, 130; unrealised potential 126–7, 219; worlds 40
presentation 191; of argument 188; of Civilization 199; of everyday life 172; of experience 203; individual 11; self-presentation 198; of speculative thought 204
processual 131, 134, 141; account of experience 35; character of experiences 28; demands 115; nature of reality 29; reality 13; world 37
propositions 9–11, 14, 31–2, 34, 37, 54, 57, 67–9, 77, 98, 187, 189–90, 192, 200, 204, 213–14, 216, 218, 223; developing 13, 183; devising 23–4; emerging 88, 206; imaginative 30; novel 22, 184; outrageous 219–20, 222, 224–5; of performative methodologies 135; pragmatic 26; scientific 208n6; speculative 12–13, 33, 35–6, 103, 185–6, 199, 215; theory of 94n4
provocation 73, 81, 135, 139, 187, 203–5, 218

rationalism 40–1, 54
rationalist 45; traditions 28
RCT (randomized control trial) 73–5, 78–81; research outcomes 76
recalcitrance 77–8, 80–1
recalcitrant 70, 77
reflexivity 57, 59–60
refolding: futures 184; time 114
represent(s) 3–4, 31, 34, 100, 133, 147, 153, 155–7, 159, 191, 223; data resource 121–2; reality 120, 204
representation 121, 189, 204, 213
representational idiom 114
representatives 189

research 12, 21, 41, 47, 70, 87, 113, 141, 186, 223; Australian Research Council 128n10; conceptual 46; corporate 86; cosmopolitical 166; design 89; diary 124; empirical 39, 115; evidence-based 79; governance of 23; humanities 48–9; innovation in 43; literacy 74; market 128n6; Mass-Observation 119–21; materials 93; outcomes 76; pluralist 69; practices 5, 114; projects 49n1, 147, 161; software robots 134; speculative 4, 7–11, 14, 40, 42, 44–5, 50n14, 117, 126–7, 164, 177, 183–5, 219, 225; subjects 73–5, 77–8, 80–1, 81n5, 85; techniques 13; ZiF 162n2; *see also* social research
researchers 45, 47, 49n1, 57, 69–70, 114, 122; Design 84–6; FEM-PEP 75; human 186; in human-computer interaction design 87; social 2, 6, 13, 53, 69, 141; survey 121; therapist 192
resistance 8, 34, 67, 77–8
ressentiment 193–4
retrocasting 98, 103–4
risk 2, 5, 10, 12–13, 21–2, 26–8, 33, 35–6, 53, 59, 62, 193, 201; aversion to 67; of fatal accidents 173; high-risk pregnancy 85; of HIV 74; inducing 74; internal 32; of loss 40; management 3–4; one's way of being 189; open to 49; running 200; surrender 195; taking 36, 60–1, 150, 219; of trusting 25, 30; of violence 170
Rose, N. 3, 88
Rosengarten, M. 4, 10, 69–70, 75–7, 79–80, 219
Russell, B. 34, 56

salvation of the world 22, 37
sandbox 115, 147, **148**, 149–53, 155–8, **159**, 161–2
Savage, M. 113, 121
Savransky, M. 1, 7–9, 22–3, 27, 39, 41, 50n10, 67, 77, 80, 126, 130, 141, 147–8, 186, 201, 208n6, 219
Schillmeier, M. 9–10, 116, 164, 166–7, 177
Schokokids 165, 174, 177
Science and Technology Studies (STS) 3, 130
scientific 2–3, 29, 41, 69, 77, 130; attitude 120; authority 75–6; engagement 166; ethic 28; evidence lacking 8; experimentation 190; facts 224; inquiry 202; knowledge 203; method 27, 40, 88,

234 *Index*

scientific *continued*
118; modern inquiry 71; practices 21,
206; propositions 208n6; social 52, 121,
135; speculation 61
scientists 56–7, 59, 75, 77, 81, 189, 221;
behavioural 87; biomedical 73; of
climate change 193; RCT 78; social 68,
76, 120, 224–5
sensibility/sensibilities 2, 5–7, 9, 45, 114,
127, 219; alternative 117; cruder 202;
speculative 8, 11 13, 78, 185, 218
Serres, M. 4, 7, 10, 71–3, 76–8, 80, 92
Sewell, W. 7, 126
sex-worker 74
SF (Science Fiction, Speculative Fiction,
Sci-Fi, Slipstream Fiction, etc.) 8
Shaviro, S. 52, 54, 88, 94n4
shells 70, 99; gold-lip pearl 105–6
situated 56, 70, 210–11, 225; abstractions
215; achievement 77; brainstorm event
90; constraints 76; data 85; engagements
5, 10, 12; knowledge 60–1; medico-
technological practices 86; practice 145;
process 107; production of multiple
ideas 93; relations 80; research practice
113; social theory 100; solution to a
problem 108; speculation 24, 62, 147;
tools and techniques 183
Skinner, B.F. 87
social research 52, 134, 177; Institute of
Economic and Social Research 119;
institution 121; scientific 135; social and
cultural 4, 6, 10–11, 13–14, 113, 140,
183, 185, 219; speculative 178;
techniques 114
socio-economic 101, 103
socio-political 41, 48
sociologists 57, 61, 72, 80, 99, 117–18,
120–4, 126–7, 162n2, 166–7; French
163; of money 102; research 223; of
risk 2
speculation 2, 6–11, 13, 21, 36, 43, 49n3,
49n5, 52–4, 67, 70, 75, 79, 81n7, 85, 91,
94n1, 98, 101, 130, 134, 148, 150,
155–6, 166, 186, 188, 198–9; abstract
37; aim 200; attempt to control 41;
attractor for 158; business 132, 137; on
consequences 193; constrained 94;
cosmopolitical 147, 185; creative
potential 99; creature of 68–9;
environment for 162; experimental 31,
33; financial 146; firmative 132–3,
135–6, 141–2; limitations 161; limited
93; logics of 115, 143n3; lure for 12, 71,

78; meaning of 39–40; micro-techniques
of 153; mode of 27, 30; as mode of
thought 207; notion of 201; object of
102; as ontology 42, 45; openness 58;
participate in 48; philosophical 55–6;
precondition of 152; process of 59, 92;
reclaiming 5, 22–3, 183; reduction to
expert practice 145; retroactive 100, 103;
scientific 61; senses of 131; situated 24,
60, 62; successful 56–7; under-
speculation 90; as a wager 25–6, 32
speculative 12–13, 21–3, 30, 35–6, 40, 45,
184–5, 199; audacity 27;
experimentation 32, 34, 220; lures 5, 68;
orientation 67, 69; philosophy 41, 53,
56–7, 99, 104, 134, 200–1, 203–5, 210,
212, 216–17; possibilities 7; practices
22–4, 90–1, 145–6, 148; pragmatics of
thought 25–6; properties 78;
propositions 33, 103, 186, 215; realism
9–10, 52; register 113; sensibility 8, 11,
218; shipping 130–3, 135–7, 139–42,
143n3, 143n6; techniques 114–15, 150;
thinking 39, 42, 44, 46, 48
speculative methods 85, 100, 130, 133,
135–7, 140–1, 143n9, 147; developing
131, 142; methodologies 134, 145
speculative research 2, 4, 7–14, 23, 39–47,
50n14, 69–70, 113–15, 117, 126–7, 164,
166, 183–5, 219, 225; contributory
action 177–8
speculative thought 6, 9, 12–13, 23, 31, 35,
113, 116, 141, 166–7, 184, 199, 201,
204, 206; function of 212, 215
speculators 145, 148, 152–3, 156, 158,
162; financial 146; idiotic 146, 161
speculatory 158, 162; attractors 158;
groove 149; practice 162
spéculer tue 21, 24n1
Stengers, I. 7, 9–10, 13, 22, 33–5, 39–41,
47–8, 49n5, 50n9, 50n14, 52, 56–61,
68–9, 71, 77–80, 90, 94n1, 103, 107,
109n4, 113, 115, 145–6, 164–5, 177,
185, 187–95, 196n1, 204, 206, 213,
219–20
Strathern, M. 4, 10, 104–5
structure/structures 47, 92, 101, 121, 152,
203–4, 219; analytical 100; create 155;
of governance 109n3; meaningful 85;
social 103
subjective 6–7, 57, 30, 39, 196n3;
experience 200, 203; judgment 224;
nature of value 198; valuation of
experience 207n2

subjectivity 107, 195, 196n3

Tarde, G. 10, 163, 166, 177, 178n1
Taylor, D.W. 87, 89
temporal 163, 165; atmospheres 128n11; dimension 123; distinction 75; paradox 40; patterns 4
temporality 1–2, 47, 40–1, 43, 45–6, 124, 126–7, 128n10
territorial insecurity 41
territorialise 87; deterritorialize 166
threats 2–3, 24n1, 41, 107, 120–1, 192; of death 185; to discipline 114; external 127; to the future 21; recurrent 22; to stability of Euro 107; threatens 1, 47
totalitarianism 41, 49, 50n11
traditional 178; expositing spaces of art 177; means of thinking 2; methods, limitations of 79; pattern 171; scientists and philosophers 59; speculation 61; zones of interaction 172
traditions 9, 23, 43, 133; Continental Philosophical 39; fiction writing 8; marginalised 22; philosophical 10, 130; pragmatism 33; preservation of 42; rationalist 28; social and cultural research 4; teaching 49
trans-subjective 23, 42
trial (randomised control) 69, 73–5, 81n3, 81n4, 81n6; chocolate-process 176; failed 74, 76, 80–1; outcomes 76–7; sandbox 147; successful 81n1; see also Fem-PrEP, iPrEX trial, PrEP, RCT
trialists 74–5, 80
Twitter 134

UNAIDS 81n6; Gap Report 81n2
Uncertain Commons 6, 131–3, 135, 141
uncertainty 3, 6, 23, 130–1, 133, 141–2, 194; exploit 5, 220
understanding 1, 26, 41, 68, 79–80, 90, 106, 121–2, 188, 193, 198, 207n2, 220; aesthetic dimension of experience 202; alternative 24; bypasses the productivity of the archive 128n8; changed 56; conceptual 203; of diaries 123–4; dualistic strategies of 163; empiricism 130, 135, 142; Haraway 61; Hawthorne effect 57; immanent 184; individual 204; innovative 23; Mass-Observation data 123, 127; matters of concern 206; money 98, 102; of nature 224; need for more 76; new ways of 42; oppositional

strife 164; pre-understanding 167; reality 205; relations between speculation and culture 185; trial aims 74; the world 103
unfinished 36; present 23, 26, 30–2, 35, 130
unfold 28, 119, 126, 150, 164–6, 168, 175, 178, 178n5, 184–6, 210
unfolding 73, 185, 202, 216; empirical concreteness of social change 167; eventuation of the brainstorm 90; futures 184
US Securities and Exchange Commission (SECC) 5

Valéry, P. 2
Van der Straten, A. 74
van Lente, H. 23
victimized 164
victimology of weaponry 170
victims 22, 168–9, 188–9; blaming 224; random 174
violence 103, 107, 164–6, 168–74, 176–8, 178n5
violent 48, 168, 170–3, 220; conflicts 169; less 164
virtual 93; catastrophes 115
virtualities 90–1, 93–4
VOICE 73, 76–7, 80, 81n3

wager 8, 23, 25–6, 30, 32, 35–7, 80, 130
Wang, H.-C. 88–9
war 8, 69, 106, 163, 165–6, 170, 173, 178n1; economies of 178; Great War (World War One) 218, 223; Korean 85; politics of 3, 164; post-war architectural design 9; post-war austerity Britain 122; Second World War 72, 119, 170; situations of 168; technologies of 177; war-like gestures 174; war machine 169, 178n5; weaponry of 170
weapon 169, 174, 176, 178n6; of destruction 172; manufacturer 170–1; porcelain 173; of violence and war 171
weaponry 164–5, 171, 176–7; techno-moral 169; victimology of 170
Weil, S. 168, 170
Whitehead, A.N. 4, 9–10, 12–13, 22, 25–8, 33–5, 37, 39–41, 43, 45, 47–8, 49n2, 49n5, 50n7, 52–9, 61–2, 67–8, 79–80, 88–91, 94n1, 94n2, 94n3, 94n4, 103, 106, 108, 109n4, 134, 145, 183–7, 194, 198–206, 207n2, 207n4, 208n5, 208n7, 210–17, 219–20, 222–3, 226n1

236   *Index*

Wilkie, A. 3–4, 9–10, 13, 69–70, 86, 89, 94n1, 115, 131, 134–5, 137–8, 141, 145, 147, 219
withdrawal 77
women 74–5, 122–3; enrol in trials 76; pregnant 81n5; young 73, 81n2
women's groups 74

Wynne, B. 3

ZiF *see* Center for Interdisciplinary Research
Zola, É. 21–2
zones 22; of interaction, traditional 172